Copyright © 1977 by
THE NATIONAL COUNCIL OF TEACHERS OF MATHEMATICS, INC.
1906 Association Drive, Reston, Virginia 22091

Library of Congress Cataloging in Publication Data:

Main entry under title:

An In-service handbook for mathematics education.

Bibliography: p.
1. Mathematics—Study and teaching. 2. Teachers—
In-service training. I. Osborne, Alan R. II. National
Council of Teachers of Mathematics.
QA11.I46   510′.7′1   77-7287
ISBN 0-87353-119-1

This material is based upon activities supported by the National
Science Foundation under grant no. SED75-20145.A.01. Any opinions, findings, and conclusions or recommendations expressed in this
publication are those of the author(s) and do not necessarily reflect
the views of the National Science Foundation.

Printed in the United States of America

An In-Service Handbook for Mathematics Education

Edited by

Alan Osborne

Advisory Committee

Edward Davis	**Alan Osborne**
Floyd Downs	**Thomas Rowan**
Alan Hoffer	**Richard Wilkes**

National Council of Teachers of Mathematics

Table of Contents

Preface

The In-Service Handbook is an extension of a project of NCTM's Commission on the Education of Teachers of Mathematics. The commission's responsibilities were limited to preservice education prior to 1973, when their charge was expanded by the Board of Directors of the National Council of Teachers of Mathematics to include in-service education.

The commission [1] sensed that teachers were dissatisfied with in-service education. At that time, federal support for in-service education was on the wane, and consequently the availability and the structure of in-service programs were changing. But the commission did not know the magnitude of the feeling of dissatisfaction or the precise nature of the changes in the availability and structure of in-service programs. They were loath to recommend to the Board of Directors actions and policy for NCTM in the interests of in-service education without a more precise understanding of the current status of in-service education.

Accordingly, in 1974 the commission conducted two projects to give them a better sense of the problems of in-service education. The first project was a survey of a sample of the teacher members of NCTM to determine their perceptions of in-service education. Considerable evidence of dissatisfaction was found, but strong hope and faith in the power of in-service education to solve the problems the teachers were facing were also expressed. It later became evident that NCTM members had a different sense of professionalism from, and were not representative of, mathematics teachers in general.

1. Commission on the Education of Teachers of Mathematics:

Ramona G. Choos, 1974–77
Helen Cunningham, 1972–75
LeRoy C. Dalton, 1972–75
Margaret A. Farrell, 1975–78
Virginia T. Gilbert, 1973–76
Ruth Greenwald, 1971–74
Viggo P. Hansen, 1972–74
A. Dean Hendrickson, 1975–78

Alan R. Hoffer, 1974–76; *chairman*, 1975–76
Alan R. Osborne, 1972–75; *chairman*, 1973–75
C. Alan Riedesel, 1974–77
James M. Sherrill, 1975–78; *chairman*, 1976–77
Max A. Sobel, 1974–77 (Board liaison)
Dorothy S. Strong, 1974–77
Irvin E. Vance, 1973–76

The second project grew from the survey. Teachers were requested to identify in-service programs they found helpful. The individuals responsible for these programs were requested to furnish descriptions of their programs in order to determine the critical variables in the designs of in-service programs. Enough different program designs were found to suggest that a document describing and analyzing these critical variables in the in-service process would be helpful and useful to mathematics educators.

The result of these two projects of the commission was a proposal *(a)* to conduct more broadly based surveys to determine perceptions about in-service education representative of all teachers rather than only members of the NCTM and *(b)* to produce a handbook for in-service educators identifying and describing critical variables in the in-service process that would cover the results of the surveys. The proposal was submitted to the National Science Foundation on behalf of the NCTM. The proposal was funded, and the NCTM In-Service Project was the result. The In-Service Handbook is one product of the NCTM In-Service Project.

The In-Service Handbook is organized around four purposes:

1. To examine the fundamental purposes and goals of in-service education
2. To report the perceptions of teachers and supervisors about the what-is and what-ought-to-be of in-service education
3. To discuss and analyze policies, processes, and procedures for in-service education in terms of the roles and responsibilities of individuals and institutions participating in the in-service effort
4. To consider the future of in-service education for mathematics teachers

Chapter 1 addresses the first purpose and asks the question, Why have an in-service education program? Then the benefits of an in-service program to teachers and to the schools are identified.

Chapters 2 and 3 report some of the results and interpretations of the surveys of teachers and mathematics supervisors. The emphasis is on the generalizations and conclusions evident in the survey data. (More detailed reporting of the statistical foundations supporting these generalizations and conclusions is on file in the ERIC system.)

The next six chapters explore policies, processes, and procedures for in-service education. Chapter 4 advocates a systemic process of relating in-service education to long-term curricular planning and to a thorough, comprehensive program of assessing needs. Chapter 5 focuses on means of implementing the plans once they are established and enunciates some mechanisms to encourage teacher participation. Problems of building and maintaining resources—a particularly difficult problem at this point

—are explored in chapter 6. Resources such as people and time are considered as well as the financial base of in-service education. Next, the roles and responsibilities of key individuals and institutions in the in-service process are examined in chapter 7. Chapter 8 is devoted to higher education; its role in in-service education may be changing, and the chapter explores some reasons for this and examines the unique contributions to in-service possible from institutions of higher education. Chapter 9 examines the touchy subject of evaluation and the aura of politics that surrounds it.

Finally, chapter 10 looks to the future of in-service education. The original intent was to formulate several recommendations and guidelines for in-service education that would be very specific in character. During the project, however, it became more and more apparent that in-service education is in a state of change. The changes are apparent in teachers' expectations, the financial base, who provides leadership, higher education's role, accountability, and in many other areas. Consequently, a set of eight general conclusions and recommendations are offered. These eight statements identify principles that should be understood and used to reorganize and revitalize the course of in-service education through the remainder of this century.

The planning of the In-Service Handbook began when the commission was preparing its proposal for the National Science Foundation. The content themes and overriding philosophy were developed and expanded further by the Advisory Committee for the NCTM In-Service Project during the summer of 1975. The Advisory Committee identified and invited a set of mathematics educators to assume responsibility for preparing each chapter of the handbook. These individuals all had extensive experience with in-service education.

The authors convened in September to refine and develop further the themes and positions of the handbook. The Advisory Committee was pleased when this group of experienced mathematics educators voiced such strong support for describing *processes* and *principles* of in-service education in the handbook. Each wanted the handbook to provide guidance to the in-service educator that would transcend shifts in the instructional needs of teachers, changes in the popularity of particular topics in mathematics or mathematics teaching, and fluctuations in the resource base supporting in-service education.

A result of the orientation to processes and principles in preparing the chapters has been to emphasize generality. Few specific examples of in-service programs are given in the body of the handbook because such examples would tend to have narrow applicability and would rapidly become outdated. However, the processes should be applicable to a specific in-service program. The NCTM In-Service Project did collect descriptions of many programs, abstracts of which are reported in Appendix 3 and reflect the processes and principles emphasized throughout the handbook.

In-service education is in a period of change and redirection. The changes taking place have led to some trauma and misunderstandings. They will lead to more in the future. Thus, the tried and true processes and policies may need modification to be effective. A brief examination of the history of in-service education in mathematics during the preceding twenty years will serve to explain much of the current situation in in-service education. It is the period in which the judgment and perceptions of the respondents to the surveys were generated; it is also the period when the preparers of this handbook were learning in in-service settings and were conducting in-service programs. Thus, the In-Service Handbook reflects the historical period of the immediate past.

Many of the problems uncovered by the NCTM In-Service Project stem from the dramatic attempt to revolutionize the content and teaching of school mathematics from 1957 to 1970. During this period, massive intervention by federal agencies in terms of supporting and sponsoring in-service programs was the pattern of the day. The programs were most typically designed and implemented through institutions of higher education. A societal ethos in support of the goals of scientific literacy for all and the identification and nurture of scientific talent made it easy to invest money in in-service education without facing the difficult problem of collecting information in defense of the investment. This thirteen-year period of broadly based support for in-service education has been followed by an era of little effort, attention, or resources being devoted to the continuing education of teachers.

The massive federal intervention into in-service education and subsequent withdrawal had four primary effects that, it is hypothesized, have had a major impact in determining the state of in-service education today. The four effects are a mixture of the positive and the negative.

1. The primary goal of the federal sponsorship of in-service education was to increase the base of mathematical knowledge that the typical teacher could use as a foundation for instruction. This goal has been accomplished. The gradual, but continued, increase in the mathematical requirements for teacher certification during the twenty years since 1957 in practically every state confirms this success.

The other side of the coin is that the in-service programs were often one-sided; they favored increasing teachers' mathematical knowledge over improving their knowledge and skills in teaching methodology. Although the in-service programs honored methodology as a goal, an examination of typical program offerings indicates that the set of mathematical experiences available to the participant was much richer than the set of methodological alternatives. An examination of the budget sheets for in-service programs reveals that resources were used primarily to accomplish disciplinary goals.

This is not to say that at the time, this was inappropriate. Textbooks with changes in content and terminology were developed for the classrooms, kindergarten through twelfth grade. Teachers needed better mathematical backgrounds to accommodate their instruction to the new materials. And the in-service programs did lead to the adoption and implementation of these new curricular materials.

One primary effect of respecting mathematical content almost to the exclusion of methodological content has been to make many teachers question the usefulness and benefit of in-service education. Their dissatisfaction revolves around in-service education's not being useful in treating the problems they encounter in the classroom. Content, knowledge about learning, and teaching methods have not been equally presented and meshed. An unfortunate side result for a small number of teachers is that they have begun to question the benefit of knowing and doing mathematics. The secondary effect is that in-service educators encounter problems of attracting participation by such teachers. Not all teachers have had this reaction. And there are other reasons for teachers being dissatisfied with in-service education; some teachers have participated in poorly designed and conducted programs irrespective of the goals of the programs. The teachers appear to want a better balance of content and methodological goals in in-service education. Many responses to the survey are determined by this desire.

2. Teachers' expectations concerning who provides and pays for in-service education changed as a result of the massive federal support of in-service education. Even though many teachers have had disappointing in-service experiences, more teachers prize in-service education than ever before. The percentage of teachers having master's degrees is significantly greater than in 1957. Teachers expect to continue their schooling. The precedent and continuation of the federal government's paying fees and stipends for in-service at institutions of higher education led teachers to expect that in-service education should be provided as their due and privilege and that teachers should not have to pay for it themselves.

3. Responsibility for in-service education shifted from the schools. Acquiring a second degree has been one of the primary means of in-service education, beginning around the turn of the century. The 1957 yearbook of the National Society for the Study of Education was devoted to in-service education and documents a trend in the schools, beginning in the 1930s, to build their own in-service programs using their own supervisory and coordinator personnel for general in-service instruction as well as

for specific instruction in subject-matter areas. That trend has stopped. Many schools have made the decision to do away with supervisory programs, others have cut back supervisory personnel, and others have replaced them with "generalists" having no expertise in mathematics or mathematics teaching. It is suggested that the rate of developing specialist supervisors did not keep pace with the influx of students resulting from the post-World War II baby boom and with the consequent expansion in the number of teachers. It is hypothesized that this lack of development and expansion of the staff responsible for in-service programs in the schools was due, in part, to the fact that in-service education was readily available elsewhere at no cost. The schools did not have to provide in-service education; their teachers could go to a federally supported program available at an institution of higher education.

A related effect is that many teachers chose to regard their in-service education as being planned for them institutionally. They merely had to "receive the package." They did not plan their programs according to their own needs and interests; they simply accepted an institution's program. This has produced some teachers who do not know what it means to seek out and identify their own weaknesses and then to help plan a program to overcome those weaknesses.

The effect of this diminution of responsibility by the schools for in-service education is twofold. First, many school systems have not established or maintained the capability to provide in-service education; they have neither the staff nor the fiscal base to support an in-service program in mathematics. Second, teachers who must seek in-service education outside of their school system often find that the in-service program is not coordinated with their school's curriculum or with their own instructional needs.

4. Colleges and universities expanded their course offerings and staff on other than sound principles of planning and fiscal management. The magnitude of federal support for in-service education during the 1960s made in-service programs a growth industry in higher education. The conditions on the support meant that in-service education could expand without the natural checks of supply and demand. Programs did not have to attract participants because of intrinsic worth; the students would come anyway, since they had the financial support and reward for participation. University personnel found it easy to design and continue in-service programs without asking fundamental questions about their usefulness to the teacher. Once a significant cadre of teachers was developed who had made significant progress in accomplishing the goal of increased mathematical competency, the federal support of in-service education was withdrawn, and many institutions found themselves in the mid-1970s in a crisis situa-

tion. Overstaffed, and with their programs not perceived as useful by teachers and with many teachers having acquired a postbaccalaureate degree, many mathematics and mathematics education departments were in poor shape to enter an era of apparent oversupply of teachers. Most institutions of higher education are, as a result, scrambling to find means of better serving the in-service needs of teachers by increasing cooperation with the schools and designing new mechanisms for in-service education.

In summary, four effects of the massive federal intervention into in-service education from 1957 to 1970 seriously affect the state of the art today in 1977. They are (1) teachers' dissatisfaction with the content of in-service programs, (2) teachers' expectation that in-service will be provided, (3) the school systems' lack of developed capability and resources for offering in-service education, and (4) institutions of higher education being overextended and hence willing to modify their efforts in in-service education. These four effects define the context within which teachers and supervisors responded to the surveys. They specify the nature of the experience and understanding that serves as the base for the creation of this handbook. As you read, weigh carefully the impact of the promise of in-service education that was realized during the 1960s. However, interpret the survey results and recommendations made within this handbook in terms of the problems that developed apace with the new traditions that emerged with the massive federal support of in-service education.

The picture painted above sounds negative. This is because the effects identified are related specifically to the problems of in-service education today. Nearly every mathematics educator could generate a longer list of positive results of the massive federal intervention into in-service education. And nearly every mathematics educator would like to see more support for in-service education from the federal government, particularly if it were controlled by what we have learned from the 1957–77 era.

A large number of people have responded willingly to requests for help and support from the NCTM In-Service Project. They have given freely of their time and wisdom because of their commitment to, and concern for, in-service education. The teachers and supervisors who completed long survey forms deserve particular recognition. Members of the National Council of Supervisors of Mathematics and of the Association of State Supervisors of Mathematics sent quantities of useful information. The broad base of cooperation made preparing this handbook much easier.

The unique and substantial contributions of many individuals to the NCTM In-Service Project and the handbook merit special comment:

  1. The Advisory Committee, for their overall guidance in all phases

of the project and their critical reading of manuscripts for the handbook

2. The Commission on the Education of Teachers of Mathematics, Glenadine Gibb, and Eugene Smith, for their constructive wisdom and guidance in the initial planning phases of the project (their sound suggestions made the proposal for the project attractive to the National Science Foundation)

3. Dwayne Channell and Arthur White, for helping design procedures of the survey and the computer processing of the survey data

4. Diana Sanders, for the efficient, accurate processing of several kinds of information

5. Charles Hucka and James Gates, for effective, responsive administration of the Reston end of the NCTM In-Service Project

6. Barbara Mackey, Charles Clements, and Robert Woolley for substantial help at various stages of production of the handbook

ALAN OSBORNE, *Director*
NCTM In-Service Project

CHAPTER 1

Why Have In-Service Education?

FLOYD DOWNS

The essential purpose of the public schools is to educate students to function in society. That skill can be taught only by teachers who are aware of the great and small changes within the immediate community and the wider world. Teacher training should be a continuing, never-ending process, closely related to the reality of the life of children and families. [Spillane and Levenson 1976, p. 439]

THE STUDY of mathematics comprises a significant portion of the school curriculum, at least in the expectation of the community if not always in practice. The schools have a responsibility to provide for each student all possible opportunities for maximal attainment of the mathematical skills and understandings necessary to academic, economic, and social growth. This obligates the schools to provide not only a rich and varied educational offering but also a staff well qualified to support the curriculum with sound, scientific, and humanistic instruction. In-service education is an important means to this end.

Maintaining and improving the competency of teachers is perhaps the most important factor in achieving better education in the schools. Education is a process of growth that builds on, and profits from, experience. Teachers of mathematics are not immune to this essential characteristic of educational growth. Thus, the significance of in-service education for maintaining and improving the competency of every mathematics teacher can hardly be overstated.

1

The purpose of this chapter is to review the rationale for investing substantial amounts of resources—in time, in dollars, and in human energy—in the in-service education of teachers of mathematics. The chapter begins by defining in-service education. Next, several conditions that justify an investment in the planning, implementation, and evaluation of a school-based in-service program are considered. After stating the goals of such a program, the chapter continues with a look at some of the consequences that lend further support to the expenditure of resources. The chapter concludes with some general observations.

In-Service Education Defined

In-service education is a generic term whose meaning tends to be altered from place to place, from time to time, and from situation to situation. On the one hand an in-service program can be planned to focus the attention of a large group of teachers on a specific topic or area of interest. On the other hand, an individual teacher who tailors personal, professional growth activities to his or her special needs on a day-to-day basis can be said to be engaged in in-service education. In this latter sense, the reading of professional journals is an in-service activity.

Morris Cogan, in the Seventy-fourth Yearbook of the National Society for the Study of Education (NSSE), provides a rather narrow, though commonly accepted, definition (1975, p. 220):

> In-service education of teachers is commonly understood to include the collegiate and school-based programs of professional study and work in which the teacher is involved after he has been certified and employed. . . . These include institutes, workshops, and after-school and summer activities.

To many thousands of mathematics teachers—for example, the members of the National Council of Teachers of Mathematics (NCTM) or any of its affiliated organizations—involvement in a professional organization's conferences and similar activities that are job related should be admitted as a significant element in any definition of in-service education. The excellent conferences for mathematics teachers sponsored by NCTM and its affiliates fall into this category. For other teachers, a more encompassing definition would be preferable. One teacher's response to the "Survey of In-Service Education" conducted in 1974 by the NCTM Commission on the Education of Teachers of Mathematics indicated this more encompassing orientation: "Inservice should be redefined in order that teachers can see themselves as professionals. Inservice should mean as little as a professional discussion in a teachers meeting to [as much as] a long term training program."

The intent of the Advisory Committee for this book is to include all of the aforementioned elements in its working definition of in-service education. The value of this book should not depend on any one interpretation. Accordingly, the committee chose not to restrict the authors or the reader by stating a concise, yet all inclusive, definition. In the chapters that follow, each reference to in-service education should be interpreted in light of the particular emphasis of each chapter. Most frequently, in-service education is used in the sense of staff development, in which the operating system—the school district—assumes responsibility for initiating, planning, implementing, and evaluating an in-service program. In no instance is there an intent by the authors to limit the term to a narrow interpretation of the various manifestations of in-service education.

Having said this, we should point out that in-service education should not be confused with *continuing* education. The latter term generally refers to adult education programs whose breadth of offerings ranges from basic education and leisure-time activities to personal-growth courses in economic, social, and cultural awareness. Although in some instances the distinction may be blurred and in some communities the two may occasionally overlap, we ordinarily intend that in-service education should refer to staff development activities.

The terms *teacher of mathematics* and *mathematics teacher,* as used interchangeably, should also be clarified. At the secondary, college, and university levels there is no ambiguity. But for many teachers in the elementary grades, the full meaning of these terms may be overlooked, thereby impairing the possible benefits of even the best mathematics in-service program. Most elementary school organizational practices and procedures dictate that each teacher is responsible for teaching the total curriculum. Consequently, almost every elementary school teacher is, in a very real sense, a teacher of mathematics. It is not realistic, however, to suppose that all elementary school teachers are fully adequate as mathematics teachers. This makes the role of in-service education—with emphasis on teaching mathematics in the elementary grades—strategically significant. School board members, administrators, and legislators who are concerned with improving the mathematical literacy and mathematical competency of youth will do well to take note of the deficiencies that exist in the abilities of elementary school teachers to deal adequately with the mathematics curriculum—deficiencies that can be corrected only through a well-planned and carefully implemented in-service program.

Preparing for the Complexities of Teaching

The enterprise of teaching and learning mathematics is so complex that preservice education alone cannot be expected to be sufficient for a lifetime of teaching. Even when supplemented by the traditional master's degree program leading to preferred certification and salary status, preservice education proves inadequate to prepare most teachers for the challenges of the classroom. Changing practices in preservice, such as the internships in public schools offered by some college and university programs, often at the graduate level, do provide some promise for better preparation of teachers entering the job market. But to expect any preservice program to prepare teachers for all future changes in school programs and teaching methodology is totally unrealistic.

On 15 March 1950, the middle of the twentieth century, the anthropologist Margaret Mead delivered the Inglis Lecture at Harvard University. Her published remarks provide a parable that describes the plight of the modern teacher and points to the compelling need to provide for continual professional growth of teachers in the schools (1964, pp. 33–34):

> Teachers who never heard a radio until they were grown up have to cope with children who have never known a world without television. Teachers who struggled in their childhood with a buttonhook find it difficult to describe a buttonhook to a child bred up among zippers. . . .
>
> Faced with this unwieldy circumstance that the modern teacher becomes not more but, in a sense, less fitted to teach the longer she teaches, we then, as a society, and particularly as those of our society professionally interested in education, have a problem to solve. How can we set up some pattern which will enable the teacher to grow through the years?

During the intervening decades since Mead delivered her lecture, the explosion of knowledge affecting mathematics teaching has inundated us almost to a point of insensitivity to the exigency of learning to cope. The extensive projects of revising the mathematics curriculum that occurred in the late 1950s and early 1960s have injected basic changes in the content of school mathematics that will inevitably survive the reactionary and regressive pressures of the 1970s. The growing impact of the educational philosophy of John Dewey as evinced through the research and teachings of Jean Piaget and a growing multitude of researchers investigating how children learn mathematics will be realized in school classrooms only to the degree that practicing teachers become knowledgeable about the results and implications of the research.

The technology of the classroom is also changing at an explosive rate. Although audiovisual equipment and materials have been common to many classrooms for several years, many mathematics teachers, notorious for their total reliance on chalk and the chalkboard, need to become more knowledgeable of ways to improve teaching through effective use of audiovisual techniques. The use of manipulative materials for investigative exercises in discovering mathematical ideas—especially in elementary school classrooms—has become a major activity of in-service workshops. Hand-held electronic calculators are fast becoming a classroom normality rather than an oddity. But learning how to use them effectively to increase arithmetic skills, the understanding of mathematics concepts, and problem-solving ability remains a gigantic task for research and for in-service education. Mathematics programs are suffering in many school districts because of the lack of staff adequately trained in the use of computers and minicomputers for educational purposes.

Add to this the cascade of new influences in the mathematics curriculum—new techniques for teaching problem solving, for using drill and practice, for relating evaluation to instruction, and of other evolving systems of instructional support. Add also a growing awareness of the importance of the affective domain in encouraging and improving the learning of mathematics.

Finally, consider the impact of the environment of the student external to the student's school environment on the process of education in the schools: changes in economic conditions, in family unity, in societal mores, in the role of religion, in the direction of race relations, in the role of women, and in affirmative action practices. Such external forces affect not only the content of the mathematics curriculum but also the way students act and the choices they make. A responsive and responsible faculty needs the opportunity and the resources to appraise such factors that affect their teaching practices.

Can there be any wonder that in recent years there has been a "clearly discernible shift in attention from pre-service to in-service teacher education on the part of the mathematical community and the funding agencies," as reported in the NACOME report, *Overview and Analysis of School Mathematics Grades K–12?* Yet as this is being written, there are other discernible trends that would categorize in-service education programs as purely a fringe benefit for teachers. In light of the number of conditions that make in-service education an essential part of improving education as a whole, such restrictive trends seem far too shortsighted.

Goals of an In-Service Education Program for Mathematics Teachers

The ultimate beneficiaries of in-service education for teachers must always be the students in the schools. All goals of an in-service program are directed toward this end.

The goals of an in-service program for mathematics teachers are essentially the goals of an in-service program for all teachers. And although improved student learning is the final aim, meeting the needs of teachers becomes the initial aim. Thus, the first four goals are oriented toward the teacher.

1. *To provide teachers the opportunity, the time, the means, and the materials for improving their professional competencies.* As professional educators, teachers have a sense of the importance of continued study, but under the pressures of teaching and of personal or family responsibilities, they often relegate concern for in-service education to a lesser priority. Historically, the burden for in-service education was shouldered mainly by individual teachers through enrollment in college- or university-based programs. Gradually, some school systems recognized the advantages of providing a school-based program complete with incentives to encourage acceptance and participation by the teachers. For an in-service program to accomplish its goals, there must be a balance of commitment and of responsibility between the teachers and the operating system.

2. *To assist teachers in applying to themselves new insights into the learning process.* Frequently our attempts to prescribe the characteristics of a good mathematics teacher are not borne out by educational research and we then take solace in the belief that teaching is more a talent or an art than a science. Partly for this reason, the value of educational methods courses is questioned by many teachers. But even talented artists can become better artists by conscientiously studying and applying the wisdom of experts—theorists, researchers, practitioners—in their field. Increasingly, it seems, results of research in different aspects of the process of learning hold significant implications for teaching that teachers now in the classrooms should know. Teachers need assistance in learning to apply these new insights to their own teaching methods, especially when changes in customary procedures may be required. The gap of decades between research and the classroom is generally recognized in education. An important aim of in-service education should be to reduce that gap by helping teachers become knowledgeable about important advances, especially as they affect competency in the classroom.

Goals 3 and 4 are specifically directed toward problems in the teaching of mathematics that in-service programs should be designed to correct. Teachers of mathematics, especially in the elementary grades, often look on mathematics as merely a necessary "tool" subject. They justifiably may lack an appreciation of the intellectual richness, the cultural significance, and the innate beauty of mathematics, its logical structure, and its varied processes. Frequently the product of uninspired mathematics teaching in their own early education, they convey to their students a similar lack of enthusiasm for, and satisfaction in, learning and using mathematics. One serious consequence is the acknowledged filtering of young women from advanced studies in mathematics. At the secondary level, a comparable lack of breadth and depth characterizes some mathematics teaching, especially if a teaching assignment is based on administrative convenience or fiat rather than personal choice and qualifications. Such "inadequately prepared" teachers of mathematics are prevalent enough in every school system to make this a major concern of an in-service program. In fairness it should be noted that these may be reasonably good teachers who need, and will profit from, direct assistance in widening their own mathematical horizons and in developing better methods of teaching mathematics. These concerns are summarized in goals 3 and 4.

3. *To help teachers expand their perceptions of mathematics.*

4. *To assist teachers in developing creative instructional approaches (a) that are meaningful and mathematically correct and (b) that inculcate in students an enthusiasm and a satisfaction in learning and using mathematics.*

The remaining goals for an in-service program may be referred to as system-oriented goals. These are goals that provide lasting benefit to the school system as a whole—local, regional, state, or national. They are important aids to decision making for those persons authorizing, planning, implementing, and evaluating in-service programs.

5. *To provide a means of maintaining quality in the existing curriculum.* For an educational program of high quality to continue to function well there should exist a means for the frequent review of curricular guidelines and updating of content and pedagogy. This could take the form of a series of seminars for members of a mathematics department or for teachers of specific mathematics courses or grade levels.

6. *To provide a means of assigning priorities to school problems and their need for solution.* In an established faculty, problem areas may easily go unnoticed for some time because of constant closeness to the problem. Within the framework of an in-service program, comparisons with other school systems—through teacher visitations or visiting speakers, for example—may help identify local weaknesses. This may in turn assist administrators, curriculum supervisors, and teachers themselves in deciding priorities associated with the problems and their solutions.

7. *To provide a mechanism for responding to problems of a curricular nature, to problems of an instructional nature, or to problems in human relations.* Some schools form special task forces to propose solutions to school problems. Other schools have no regular procedure for effectively dealing with problems. An in-service program can provide a natural setting for study sessions or workshops on new curriculum materials, a demonstration of microteaching using closed-circuit television, or sensitivity-training sessions.

8. *To facilitate a school's making full use of its resources.* The resources of a school can be classified under the headings *(a)* school plant,

(b) community, and *(c)* staff personnel. An in-service program is particularly suited to helping a school realize the creative and productive potential of its staff. In schools where departmentalization or general attitudes tend to isolate teachers in their classrooms, an in-service program may bring about cooperative ventures having considerable benefit to the entire educational program.

Further, an organized in-service program can help a school identify and develop leadership within its own staff. During the last two decades, thousands of mathematics teachers throughout the continent have attended workshops and institutes supported by professional associations, school districts, and various local and national agencies. Many teachers have returned to their own schools and shared newly acquired knowledge and techniques with other teachers. Many others, however, have returned to relative obscurity. There are at present in schools nationwide a cadre of teachers of mathematics, at all grade levels, who could become educational leaders, at least at a local level, if they were given the opportunity that a well-planned in-service program can provide.

9. *To implement significant innovative curricular and instructional practices.* This last goal might readily be considered the most important of all by critics of public education who are certain that schools need to do a far better job of educating youth. Hilda Taba, a recognized authority on curricular innovation, had this to say after reviewing her experiences in several major in-service training programs (1965, p. 475):

> The more radical the changes in teaching strategies that are expected, the greater the necessity that inservice training consider the sequential steps involved in producing such changes and provide both the time and the help in producing them. I am convinced that much of teacher resistance comes from the fact that exhortations to make changes are not always accompanied with the help to acquire the skills needed to make these changes with psychological comfort and without the threat and risk of making errors. . . . Reshaping curriculum and instruction is not a matter that can be accomplished in a 6-week summer workshop or a series of monthly meetings during the year. A more methodical way is required, plus time to change old habits and to develop new ideas and put them into practice.

More recently an investigation into strategies to promote innovation in the schools was conducted by the Rand Corporation under contract to the U.S. Office of Education. In its report, the study found (U.S. Office of Education n.d., p. 6)—

> that the implementation strategies selected to carry out a project vitally influence project outcomes.
>
> In particular, the strategies that significantly promoted teacher change included staff training, frequent regular meetings and local materials development. If any one of these elements was not present in a project's implementa-

tion approach the project's perceived success and amount of teacher change was reduced.

For elaboration of this study, see Berman and McLaughlin (1975) and Berman et al. (1975).

The matter of introducing innovative practices into the schools as a function of in-service education will be dealt with in succeeding chapters. The reader may find the ideas of the foregoing quotations interesting reference points for some of the findings of the survey of mathematics teachers and supervisors relative to in-service education that are reported in chapters 2 and 3.

What Are the Benefits?

The professional competence of the teacher remains an extremely crucial element in the educational process. In fact, the greatest impact per education dollar may be achieved when spent in professional development.

This statement by the Commission on the Education of Teachers of Mathematics was approved by the NCTM Board of Directors in September 1974. It states a point of view with which proponents of in-service education are bound to agree but for which hard statistical information is nearly impossible to obtain. In-service education for teachers is so readily justifiable on the basis of needs that its true cost effectiveness—although frequently questioned by school boards and taxpayer associations—is seldom, if ever, really determined.

Instead, the effectiveness of an in-service program tends to be evaluated on observable changes in the system, some measurable and some difficult to assess. The evaluation of an in-service program is the proper concern of a later chapter. But here, in terms of providing further reasons for expending substantial amounts of resources in staff development, are considered some benefits that may reasonably be expected from a school-based program.

Perhaps, above all else, a good in-service program for teachers should be expected to result in improved student performance. This would be consistent with the assumption underlying the goals of the previous section—that all goals are directed ultimately toward providing a better education for the students. The connection between in-service education for teachers and performance of students is very difficult to document and may prove quite misleading. Nevertheless, some studies do indicate that an expected improvement in students' performance is attainable. The Specialized Teacher Project, 1968–1972, was established and funded by the California state legislature for the purpose of providing "inservice training to elementary classroom teachers who would subsequently teach mathe-

matics to their own and one other class." During the project, some four
thousand teachers were involved in two- or three-week in-service sessions.
The evaluation report showed that "pupils whose teachers attend the
workshops perform significantly better on measures of comprehension and
computation than pupils whose teachers do not receive the training" (State
Board of Education 1972). As encouraging as a report may be, we must
be quick to point out that such an expectation cannot be taken as a criterion of the success or failure of an in-service program for teachers. Too
many variables exist that make reliance on measured student performance
an undependable indicator. The benefits to students of an in-service program for their teachers may occur over such a long term as to be not readily measurable or observable.

In industry, it is generally accepted that good employee morale leads
to higher productivity. Likewise in education, we claim that a satisfied
staff tends to produce education of high quality. As a group, teachers are
vitally concerned with providing the best possible education for their students. They recognize that in-service education plays an important role
in maintaining and improving their ability to teach. A good in-service program can be invaluable to developing self-confidence and self-concepts in
teachers, attributes that lend credence to their performance. An in-service
program in which teachers play significant roles in planning, implementing, and evaluating the program indicates that the school administration
and the school board consider teacher morale a high priority for good education.

One observable benefit that can accrue from an in-service program is
that a faculty can "come alive." The participation of teachers in in-service
activities inevitably brings about more staff communication, more exchange of ideas and information, and more cooperative efforts in the best
interests of the students. The view of a teacher solely as an imparter of
knowledge is not compatible with contemporary educational philosophy or
practices. Yet there are many teachers who do little more than act as foun-
tains of knowledge. Teacher-to-teacher contact, through in-service projects and programs, can do much to help all teachers discover better ways
to teach students how to learn. Through learning how to learn and how to
teach, teachers put knowledge to work.

Establishing Priorities

Finally, it should be observed that the reasons for having an in-service
program for mathematics teachers are as basic as the reasons for having
instruction in mathematics for the young. In-service education is a means
to an end. The priority that we, as a society, place on that end—that is,

the education of present and future generations—determines the priority we place on in-service education for teachers.

In this time of shrinking enrollments, inflation, a surfeit of teachers, and stabilizing faculties, we must guard against stagnation in education. The role of in-service education as a vitalizing agent becomes real.

If we could gain a view from above, we might observe that the reasons for in-service education, as well as its issues, its problems, and its goals, have a permanence that transcends the particular state of education at any given time.

Perhaps the most immediate, if not compelling, reason for in-service education for mathematics teachers is that teachers themselves want it and say that they need it. This is one outcome of the survey of teachers reported in chapter 2. As long as teachers of mathematics are sincere in wanting to do a better job of teaching mathematics to their students, they will want and demand a good in-service education program.

CHAPTER 2

The Context of In-Service Education

ALAN OSBORNE
J. MICHAEL BOWLING

THE CONTEXT of in-service education is changing. The purpose of this chapter is to report teachers' attitudes and perceptions about in-service education in this period of change.

The first part of the chapter examines some historical antecedents of this change. The evolution of the in-service "system" indicates some of the forces impinging on teachers and schools as new forms of in-service education are advocated and old forms are modified to serve better the learning and teaching of mathematics. The remainder of the chapter reports the results of the surveys of teachers as they consider the what-is and the what-ought-to-be for in-service education in this period of change.

A Historical Perspective for In-Service Education

During the latter half of the nineteenth century, most teachers were certified and hired by local or county boards of education, superintendents, or trustees, and many teachers held their office subject to political whim. Bush and Enemark (1975) report that as late as 1911 only fifteen states had control of certification. Most teachers had minimal professional training, if any, and tended to be young and inexperienced. They were poorly educated for their task of working with children and youth.

This sad state of affairs was recognized and documented thoroughly by a diverse set of people ranging from state superintendents of instruction to legislators to the popular press. Three levels of responses affecting in-service education evolved: (1) state legislative action, (2) response by institutions of higher education, and (3) action by local schools.

The response at the state level was two-fold in terms of legislation. First—and almost as an emergency, stopgap measure—legislatures passed legislation enabling teachers' institutes to be held at local and state levels. Legislators found money to sponsor one-day, Chautauqua-like in-service programs on an occasional basis. Generated to serve the needs and interests of the minimally competent, they served a significant purpose for the majority of teachers even through the 1920s and established a traditional form of in-service education that prevails even today.

The second form of state legislative response was to remove the control of certification from local school systems and to tie the financial welfare of teachers to that certification. By 1937, state control of certification for teaching had been asserted by every state. The emphasis on the academic degrees tied to salary schedules promoted preservice education to the level of the bachelor's degree. This has had two major effects on in-service education. First, because of increased education and the concomitant growth in professionalism, the effectiveness of the one-shot, Chautauqua-like institute has been considerably reduced. Teachers (and school systems) expect more than the typical inspirational and entertainment message that is possible in such programs. Teachers' proficiency in, and understanding of, the learning and instructional processes is such that they recognize the imperative for in-service education to be related to curricular plans and school needs. The short, one-shot institute is clearly inadequate for treating significant problems. In addition, most professional organizations—such as the NCTM and the School Science and Mathematics Association (SSMA)—have assumed, and richly extended, these functions of the one-shot institute to encompass more for the teacher at local, regional, and national meetings. This has caused many educators to question the value of the schools' investing resources in the short-term institute approach to in-service education.

The second effect of the degree-related certification by the state was to encourage the development of teacher education programs in institutions of higher education—the evolution of summer school programs being the most notable (Gibb 1970). Relatively new at the turn of the century, the summer school offerings in numerous normal schools, colleges, and universities provided teachers with a guaranteed mechanism for increasing their salary as well as acquiring new understandings and skills. Prompted and encouraged by legislative action, this form of post-baccalaureate in-service education has evolved to the extent that it warrants careful consideration in its own right. Indeed, summer school courses are the primary form of in-service education for the large majority of teachers. For many local school districts, continued academic study is the only available form of in-service education for a teacher; the local district provides none. Attaining a master's degree is required in some states to retain certification, but some recent trends have impinged on this form of in-service education.

Teachers are receiving their master's degrees earlier. Although many wish to continue their professional education, few institutions of higher education specifically tailor their in-service offerings to serve the needs of teachers who already possess a master's degree and who may not necessarily want another academic degree.

The response at the higher education level is incompletely captured when examined only in terms of certification, graduate programs, and the agency-sponsored, long-term institutes. Additionally, higher education is caught in a major quandary in terms of goals. An academic institution proffering graduate credit must respect academic goals, but these goals are not exactly congruent with teachers' needs in the schools. The post-sputnik revolution in mathematics education led to the creation of many institutes and programs oriented to subject matter. These programs did possess academic respectability at most institutions, but they were created when schools were coping with the effects of the postwar baby boom. Since then, the schools have moved through an era of stabilizing and declining enrollments, and more and more teachers are entering the profession with better credentials. Now colleges and universities are faced with the problem of attracting in-service enrollees at the master's level and beyond (desired for financial reasons because of declining college and university enrollments).

Market analyses at many institutions have convinced the institutions that the best way of attracting students is to build a program related more directly to the needs of schools and teachers. Since most teachers at the secondary level already feel comfortable with the mathematical content they are teaching, many institutions are discovering two problems. First, in-service education concerned with methodological and curricular problems and issues often requires attention at a level not consistent with the academic goals of graduate work. Many of the important problems and issues endemic to the schools require solutions that do not have the characteristic theoretical, research-oriented goals valued (appropriately) by institutions of higher education. Second, as an institution of higher education markets an in-service program based on need, it typically must operate on a very general level in order to attract students (i.e., teachers) from a large number of schools. But needs are specific to schools and vary from one setting to another. The in-service programs of universities and colleges are often taken to task by teachers because the generality of the program fails to meet the specific needs of a particular school.

The result of this recent history of declining collegiate enrollments and teachers' expectations of in-service education from institutions of higher education has been for higher education to look for other means to help teachers and schools. The shift is from mathematics to methodology, from the appeal to general needs faced by teachers in most schools and on-campus classes to programs marketed for one school (or a limited number of schools) and conducted in the school(s). In the authors' opinion, the new and creative ways that colleges and universities will use to package attractive and useful programs for teachers *in the schools* have only begun. Clearly, the impact of recent history—the demographic and economic forces impinging on both higher education and the schools— is forcing change on the traditional degree-certification-rate-of-pay system that has provided the impetus for, and the characteristic design of, the contribution of higher education to in-service education.

The third level of response for the provision of in-service education for teachers evolved in the schools themselves. As schools became larger during the nineteenth century, teachers assumed administrative and supervisory responsibilities. Richey (1957) documents the growing influence and responsibility of the supervisory personnel in providing in-service opportunities for teachers during the first half of this century. In 1951, the National Education Association (NEA) conducted a study of in-service opportunities in 1615 urban school systems, of which 1488 reported opportunities for in-service education and professional growth. Consistent with other survey data reported by Haas (1957), the interesting observation is that all the data concern urban schools. Generally, a school system must attain a particular size before the need for some control of the program is apparent and having a mathematics supervisor or coordinator becomes sensible and cost effective. Many large school systems did develop in-service programs and rewards for participation in them by teachers; but unfortunately, in times of economic hardship, such programs— and the supervisors who conduct and arrange them—are among the first items to go. And many rural and small school systems have never had such programs or personnel offering services to teachers (although recently cooperative district-level arrangements among small school systems have met this need). As apparent in the NCTM In-Service Survey data, having a responsible supervisor or coordinator appears to be strongly related to a school's providing a wide variety of in-service opportunities to teachers.

Supervisors have played a significant role in providing in-service education because of their capacity to relate in-service education directly to their schools' needs and long-range curricular planning and to provide responses to the immediate problems of teachers. The historical impact of supervisors on school mathematics and on teachers is difficult to assess or judge because data are simply not available. This level of response to in-service needs is apparently something that local schools can provide teachers during periods of economic well-being but is among the first of the "costly" items to be sacrificed if a school encounters bad times.

In summary, in-service education has evolved at three levels: (1) the states responded to needs of the last century by encouraging and funding one-shot, Cautauqua-like in-service programs and gaining control of certification and salary programs; (2) in-service education became intertwined with degree programs in higher education; (3) coping with in-service education began at the local school level through administrative responsibility for instructional and curricular leadership in the schools. Each of these levels of response has created a characteristic type and style of in-service education. Considerable variance between the program types and styles exists in meeting the needs of teachers and schools. Each type and style of program has created a set of traditions and expectations for the participants and for the providers of in-service education through the years.

Clearly, teachers are coming of age professionally. The overwhelming majority of teachers today have a bachelor's degree, unlike even twenty years ago. For many states, about half of the secondary teachers have master's degrees. In 1974, the Research Division of the NEA estimated that 45 percent of the secondary teachers and 33 percent of the elementary teachers had a master's degree. Teachers are staying in the profession longer. Corwin (1975) notes that since new teachers have gone through selective admissions and longer periods of training, they "demonstrate more career commitment." He states that "in the past decade the average length of teaching careers has doubled (from seven to fourteen years). The percent of teachers who have had a break in service has also declined (from 53 percent to 40 percent) during the past decade" (pp. 252-53).

But with increased professionalism has come increased militancy. Each of the traditional types and styles of in-service education was established prior to teachers being so well trained or before so much evidence of professional commitment was available. Do the traditional forms of in-service education satisfy teachers? What opinions do teachers have about in-service education as it is? As it ought to be? The changing nature of mathematics teachers—their professional aspirations, background, and experience—is the largest factor of change that needs to be accounted for in considering in-service education for the future. Thus, it was deemed particularly critical to collect evidence of teachers' opinions, attitudes, and perceptions about in-service education in order to adjust recommendations for in-service education to be consistent with the teachers' increasing professionalism and militancy as the schools enter the last quarter of the twentieth century.

The Surveys

The NCTM In-Service Surveys were designed to sample representative public school teachers across the United States at the elementary and secondary school levels. A maximal sample size of 7500 elementary and secondary teachers was within the budgetary limitations of the project. Projections based on the 1973–74 *Standard Education Almanac* indicated 1 113 000 elementary and 992 000 secondary school teachers for the 1975–76 school year. Sample sizes of 4000 elementary school teachers and 3500 secondary school mathematics teachers preserved this ratio of elementary to secondary school teachers.

The sample space consisted of all public elementary and secondary schools in the United States listed in the state education directories of each state for the 1974–75 school year. A map displaying the geographical distribution of respondents is displayed in Appendix 1 on page 231.

The sampling design involved two stages:

1. Stratified random selection of schools
2. Random selection of teachers within each of the selected schools

The sampling technique has been used extensively by the ERIC Information Analysis Center for Science, Mathematics, and Environmental Education for studies such as *A Survey of Science Teaching in the Public Schools of the United States* (1971), conducted for the National Institute of Education. The technique has well-verified characteristics in producing representative subpopulations and has been studied extensively.

Elementary and secondary school samples were generated independently, but using parallel techniques. The method of selecting the elementary schools is described in Appendix 1; the procedure for selecting the secondary sample was the same.

Once the selection of the school was completed, a letter was written to the principal of the school requesting cooperation in the survey and giving directions for selecting randomly (1) a teacher in the school if an elementary school or (2) a mathematics teacher if a secondary school. A copy of the materials sent to the principal—including the survey's questionnaire forms—is included in Appendix 1 (pp. 220–26).

In the end, 3964 surveys were mailed to elementary school teachers and 3482 to secondary school teachers (Rhode Island schools are not represented because of the lack of cooperation). Mailings were made in late fall and winter to all populations.

Returns were as follows:

Elementary	821	(20.7%)
Secondary	1431	(41.1%)

The rate of return for elementary and secondary school teachers is similar to rates of return for other uses of this sampling technique. We note the following factors that influenced the return rate:

1. Elementary school teachers (and principals) do not have the same familiarity with NCTM—its goals and purposes—as secondary mathematics teachers. Hence, they did not feel the same commitment for responding.

2. Some schools—particularly those in university towns and large urban centers—have rules requiring clearance from an administrative unit for participation in research projects. Letters were received from some school systems and principals indicating such clearance or permission would need to be obtained before the forms were released to teachers. But we suspect that many systems having such rules simply did not respond.

3. We expect that a better return rate would have been achieved if the mailing could have been made directly to teachers rather than through the intermediate stage of the principal.

4. The questionnaire was long enough to appear formidable to many busy teachers.

5. The majority of the mailings were made prior to the change in postage rates in December 1976. We feel that some teachers were bothered by the uncertainty of whether they should use a three-cent stamp, even though a prepaid stamped envelope was used.

Generally, we feel that the sample is representative of teachers in the United States. Prior experience with this sampling technique indicates that for science teachers, nonrespondents on follow-up mailings and calls did not respond significantly differently from initial respondents, except for the fact of nonresponse.

The low response rate for elementary school teachers is a matter of concern even though prior use of the sampling technique indicates nonrespondents are not appreciably different from the respondents. One reasonable conjecture about the differences between respondents and nonrespondents stems from the nature of the majority of the questions; namely, teachers were queried about their perceptions and value judgments concerning in-service education. We believe that nonrespondents are more likely than respondents to be negative about in-service, to have less commitment to in-service, and to feel that responding to the questionnaire is unlikely to produce any change or improvement in in-service education. The supposition is simply that they are less professional. Acceptance of this supposition suggests that the problems and issues are more extreme than are defined by the present data.

Instrumentation

The instruments for the teacher surveys were piloted in the spring of 1974 by the Commission for the Education of Teachers of Mathematics with a sample of every hundredth name of the membership roster of NCTM. The instrument was revised by the Advisory Committee for this project in the light of that sample's responses—subject to one major modification. The modification was to formulate many questions in a what-is/what-ought-to-be format in order that the discrepancies could be ascertained and analyzed.

There were 147 short-answer items on each form and 3 open-ended questions that were optional. One hundred thirty-eight questions were common to both the elementary and the secondary forms. The nine questions that were different were background questions reflecting the teachers' training or present teaching situation. Twenty-one questions ascertained the teachers' background and covered such diverse topics as salary, average number of students in classes, tenure status, types of in-service experience in the last three years, type of school, and the like. A common statement generated two questions for each of forty-nine items to examine the discrepancy perceptions between the *is* and the *ought-to-be* of in-service education. The questionnaires are exhibited in Appendix 1 (pp.222–26).

Survey Results

The results of the surveys of teachers are given in the next two sections. The first section provides a general description of the elementary and secondary teacher samples in terms of background, training, and the school setting in which the teachers work. Also included are responses to questions concerning satisfaction with present position and general experience with in-service education. The second section reports teachers' perceptions of the what-is and what-ought-to-be for in-service education and provides some interpretive discussion of the results and related statistical analyses.

The write-up of the results of the survey has been kept informal. Conclusions are given without the accompanying tables and statistical analyses on which they are based. (This information is on file in the ERIC system.) Chi-square and correlational techniques were used for most analyses.

The discussion and interpretation of the results is intermingled throughout the presentation of the survey's results. And at some points, implications and commentary are offered that extend beyond the results.

Because of the large number of variables, one would expect many significant statistics simply because of chance. The present interpretation of results is conservative. We have indulged in little random snooping through the data. Variables that were apparently critical in the pilot survey were used to generate hypotheses for analyses of data for these surveys. Unless noted otherwise, no chi-square statistic is reported unless at the .0001 level of significance or better. For correlational statistics, the level of significance used was .001.

Population Characteristics

The typical or modal teacher responding to the survey is well trained, has considerable experience, works in an urban setting with an average class size of between twenty-six and thirty pupils, and is satisfied with the teaching profession generally and his or her teaching situation specifically. Most respondents have had recent experiences with one of several types of in-service education but feel a need for more. Following are some specific population statistics supporting each of these statements. For each question, percentages are given, after being adjusted by deleting the number of teachers omitting the question.

Training

Three questions ascertained the academic training of teachers. The questions were general and requested, for example, the number of courses rather than the character or quality of the courses.

Mathematics Background—Secondary Teachers

43. The number of mathematics courses I have taken *after calculus* is

a) 0 to 3	b) 4 to 7	c) 8 to 11	d) 12 to 15	e) more than 15
15.7%	24.3%	21.3%	14.1%	24.9%

Mathematics Background—Elementary Teachers

43. The number of college mathematics content courses I have taken is

a) 0	b) 1	c) 2	d) 3	e) 4 or more
1.6%	8.9%	20.6%	23.6%	45.3%

Methods Background

44. The number of college courses, exclusive of student teaching, that I have taken concerned with *methods* of teaching mathematics is

	Elementary	Secondary
a) 0	10.8%	12.4%
b) 1	37.3%	29.4%
c) 2	26.7%	23.7%

d) 3	9.8%	13.8%
e) 4 or more	15.4%	20.6%

Degree

46. My highest earned degree is

	Elementary	Secondary
a) Bachelor's degree	61.7%	41.6%
b) Master's degree	35.2%	55.9%
c) Doctorate	0.3%	0.9%
d) Other	2.9%	1.6%

If this sample is at all representative of teachers, it deserves comment. First, it needs to be recognized forthrightly that in-service education addresses an audience very different from that of even twenty years ago. Teachers have a much better background in mathematics and in teaching methods. Also, their degree status is quite different. The task of in-service education during the 1950s and early 1960s was to update and strengthen the mathematical competencies of teachers and to suggest methodologies consistent with the new curricula. The large majority of teachers did not have a background that was close to what these samples exhibit. The authors suspect that elementary teachers who responded may have a somewhat better background in terms of mathematics teaching than the general population of teachers. However, it would have been difficult in 1955 to find a sample of elementary teachers reporting this background. Clearly, the recommendations of the Committee on the Undergraduate Program in Mathematics (CUPM) and modifications in state certification laws have had an effect. Although there is a significant number of teachers who have less of a mathematics background than is desirable and even though the number of courses says nothing about the quality and character of the understanding of the mathematics possessed by the teacher or the teachers' attitudes and perceptions of mathematics, it must be concluded that teachers have a significantly better background than twenty years ago.

The improved background of teachers is symptomatic of an increased sense of professionalism generally and has, in the authors' opinion, grown concomitantly with an awareness of what is critical and important in the classrooms. And with this sophistication has grown an expectation for a different level of answers to the questions and problems dealt with in in-service education. We suspect that some of the current dissatisfaction with in-service education stems from its being oriented to the sophistication and background characteristics of teachers in the 1950s and 1960s. This is not to say that teachers do not need what might be characterized by some as "lower level" help; it is, instead, to say that in providing "lower level" in-service education, the educator must be well aware of the impact of greater background on participants' expectations of the level of professionalism evidenced in the in-service program. (But it would also be a dreadful mistake for in-service educators to assume too much background and to operate at too high a level mathematically and methodologically.) In short, does one organize and conduct an in-service program based on a perception of teachers that dates to the early 1960s? If so, expect problems. Teachers are better trained and have higher expectations and aspirations.

A second conclusion based on these data is quite specific to the secondary school mathematics teachers' and higher education's participation in the in-service endeavor. Consider the responses to the degree question (number 46) from the standpoint of an institution of higher education making a market analysis for a new in-service master's program for mathematics teachers. Only 41.6 percent of the respondents report that their highest degree is a bachelor's. If you assume that one-third of that group would not qualify for any school's graduate program and that another one-sixth simply are not interested, then only about 20 percent of the mathematics teachers are potential enrollees in the envisioned master's program. But many mathematics teachers do aspire to different roles in the school; they become principals, guidance personnel, and the like. (Isn't it fortunate that a few people who have an understanding of mathematics and mathematics teaching enter these important phases of the school operation?) This reduces the potential market for the master's degree program to about 15 percent of the mathematics teachers. For areas of the country with many competing institutions of higher education, the population of prospective students is not sufficient to warrant the development and implementation of such a program. This conclusion is reinforced when the data are coupled with the increased professional commitment and job stability of teachers, the inclination of teachers to get their master's degree at an earlier age, and the present trends in decreasing secondary school enrollments. Thus, institutions of higher education must look to designing in-service opportunities for secondary mathematics teachers that are broader in intent and scope than simply providing an alternative master's degree.

Experience

		Elementary	Secondary
49.	I have taught		
	a) less than 5 years	22.1%	16.7%
	b) 5 to 9 years	27.4%	26.6%
	c) 10 to 14 years	21.5%	23.0%
	d) 15 to 20 years	15.3%	17.1%
	e) I'm an old pro; more than 20 years.	13.8%	16.5%

21. Do you have tenure?   73.6%   75.1%

School setting

	Elementary	Secondary
48. My school is		
a) urban	30.6%	32.4%
b) suburban	41.4%	41.9%
c) rural	28.0%	25.7%

47. The average number of students in my mathematics class(es) is

	Elementary	Secondary
a) 0–18	10.8%	6.9%
b) 19–25	30.2%	34.1%
c) 26–30	39.0%	42.0%
d) 31–35	18.0%	15.3%
e) More than 35	2.0%	1.6%

The survey inquired about the type and level of mathematics taught. For secondary teachers, the results indicate the diversity of teaching assignments. In particular, it may be inferred that junior high school teachers do not like to classify their courses as either college preparatory or non–college preparatory.

What mathematics do you presently teach?

5.	College preparatory; grades 7 through 9	42.6%
6.	College preparatory; grades 10 through 12	65.3%
7.	Non–college preparatory; grades 7 through 9	39.1%
8.	Non–college preparatory; grades 10 through 12	30.2%
9.	Other	11.4%

Statistical analyses using correlational and chi-square methods indicated weakly significant relationships ($p < .05$) between limited mathematics background and the teaching of non-college-preparatory mathematics at both junior and senior high school levels. If teachers had extensive mathematics backgrounds (question 43), they were much more likely to teach college-preparatory high school mathematics. A limited mathematics background at the junior high school level was strongly related to teaching non-college-preparatory mathematics at the junior high level and weakly related to teaching non-college-preparatory mathematics at the high school level ($\chi^2 = 10.6$, 4df, $p < .03$). Having a methods background did not have an apparent relationship to the teaching of either college or non-college-preparatory mathematics at either level.

On the one hand, this appears to be appropriate. The college-preparatory classes in mathematics should be taught by individuals who have better mathematical training. On the other hand, further analysis of the data indicates that the number of courses in mathematics is correlated with experience in teaching. At the junior high school level, experience in teaching correlates positively with teaching the non–college bound, but at the senior high school level, the correlation is negative. That is, the junior high school appears more likely to staff non-college-bound classes primarily with experienced teachers. One interesting result concerning the years of experience of the secondary teacher was that the number of years of teaching is positively correlated with the size of class.

Elementary teachers responded to the questions concerning level of teaching as follows.

5.	Preschool or kindergarten	4.1%
6.	Grade 1 or 2	21.7%
7.	Grade 3 or 4	32.1%
8.	Grade 5 or 6	43.4%
9.	Other	17.7%

The percentages sum to more than 100 percent, indicating considerable variation from the expected single-grade classroom teaching assignment. Teachers with a richer mathematics background tended to teach grades 3 and 4.

The salary level of teachers was as follows.

45. My salary is in the range (do not include summer school):

		Elementary	Secondary
a)	less than $8,499	7.4%	4.2%
b)	$8,500–$9,999	21.6%	12.7%
c)	$10,000–$12,499	33.1%	28.9%
d)	$12,500–14,999	20.5%	21.9%
e)	More than $15,000	17.8%	32.3%

As might be expected, these figures correlated significantly with experience, degrees, and other factors related to length of tenure in the profession.

Teachers were queried about whether they read the journals of the National Council of Teachers of Mathematics (NCTM) to gain some sense of their professionalism.

10. Do you read the *Arithmetic Teacher* magazine?
(elementary only)   31.8%

10. Do you read the *Mathematics Teacher* magazine?
(secondary only)   61.1%

The evidence is somewhat at odds with the subscription rates of each journal. However, many schools do have institutional subscriptions, and some teachers do share their journals with fellow staff members. Perhaps the most significant conclusion is that the NCTM—a professional group

with a subject-matter orientation—has a much greater potential for influencing the secondary school than the elementary school.

Satisfaction

Several questions related to teachers' satisfaction. The pilot survey
conducted by the commission indicated that questions in this category
had interesting relationships with critical variables concerning in-service
education programs. The NCTM teacher respondents were separated
sharply into two camps by the satisfaction-related questions. For in-service
education, the two camps were the "haves" and the "have nots." Teachers
who were satisfied tended to have more in-service experience and to work
in schools that provided more means of participating in in-service education and invested more money in a variety of in-service endeavors. It appeared that it was simply a case of the rich getting richer in terms of in-
service experiences. For this professionally oriented sample of NCTM
members, satisfaction was strongly related to most of the variables concerning in-service education. If teachers held a positive view about one
aspect of their professional life, they tended to be positive about all other
aspects of their professional life. A positive view of the profession, of their
school, and of their teaching responsibilities indicated ample experience
with in-service education and a positive perception of it. We decided to
explore this variable more throughly in this survey because of the apparent
robustness of the variable in the pilot survey.

Although many of the same relationships exist for the more generally
selected population, satisfaction does not appear to be as tightly related to
other variables, such as in-service education, as it was with the pilot population. Following are some results to questions concerning satisfaction of
the teachers with the profession, their teaching position, and facilities in
their school.

	Elementary	*Secondary*
	(percentage "yes" responses)	
1. If you had the opportunity to start again, would you choose teaching as your profession?	85.7%	78.4%
2. Are you satisfied with your present teaching position?	87.7%	80.9%
3. Would you prefer to teach at a higher level than you are teaching presently?	14.6%	35.2%
Are you presently satisfied with the following facilities for teaching mathematics in your school?		
11. Classroom	78.9%	74.4%
12. Textbooks	56.4%	67.5%

13. Library materials for students   53.2%   63.6%
14. Professional, personal-use library   52.5%   56.9%
15. Calculators   21.7%   38.6%
16. Laboratory or activity learning
    materials   43.5%   33.0%

To note that 14.3 percent of the elementary teachers and 21.6 percent of the secondary teachers would not choose to enter the teaching profession if they were to start again is disconcerting. For the majority of these respondents, it is hoped that there is little bitterness or rancor that affects their students. Interestingly, none of the satisfaction questions correlated at a significant level with pay for either the elementary or secondary samples.

A common perception of many teacher educators in mathematics education is that the level of teaching is a major source of dissatisfaction of secondary teachers. The belief is that many teachers would prefer to teach at a higher level. For this sample of teachers, the responses to the question about choosing teaching again for a career and the question about satisfaction with their present teaching position were negatively correlated with the desire to teach at a higher level. Chi-square analysis indicated that teachers of the non–college bound at the junior high school level were more unlikely to indicate satisfaction with their present teaching position than other teachers.

Responses to the question about satisfaction with their present position were related to the responses about facilities. Teachers at both the secondary and elementary levels tended to be satisfied with their texts if they were satisfied with their present position. Secondary teachers' satisfaction with their present position was also positively related to their satisfaction with their classroom and the professional library. Elementary teachers satisfied with their present position tended to be satisfied with the facilities for laboratory teaching.

One question that was on this survey, but not on the pilot, concerns teachers' perceptions of students and appears to have interesting relationships with several variables.

	Elementary	*Secondary*
20. Are students as excited about learning mathematics as they ever were?	(percentage "yes" responses)	
	67.7%	43.9%

The relatively more positive perception of their current students by the elementary teachers when compared to secondary teachers is intriguing. It suggests more questions than it answers. Is this related to the current concern for basic skills? In a subsequent section, data from this question will be related to preferences for topics for in-service education, gripes about it, and opinions concerning what-ought-to-be for it.

The responses to the student excitement question are related to teacher satisfaction. For secondary teachers satisfied with teaching (question 1), only 52.5 percent felt students were not as excited about learning mathematics, but for those who were dissatisfied, two-thirds believe students not to be as excited. For elementary teachers satisfied with teaching, 72.7 percent believe students are still excited about learning mathematics, but for those dissatisfied with teaching, only a few more than one-half perceive students as still excited by mathematics.

In-service experience

It was important to find out whether teachers had experience with in-service education on which to base judgments and opinions. An opinion based on some sort of reality is more valuable than one free of the bias induced by experience. In short, do teachers know what they are talking about when they render judgments about in-service education?

	Elementary	Secondary
22. Have you participated in any in-service program(s) since September 1, 1973?	82.9%	70.8%

Clearly, the question should have been worded in terms of in-service education in mathematics. But responses to the what-is segments of the discrepancy questions (50–98) yielded strong evidence that the respondents had a base of recent experience with in-service education for mathematics. The types of agencies providing this recent in-service education are indicated in questions 23 through 28.

If your answer to 22 was "yes," indicate the sponsoring agency(ies) who conducted the in-service program(s). If no, omit 23 through 28, and proceed to 29.

	Elementary	Secondary
23. My school system	88.3%	82.0%
24. A state educational agency	24.5%	23.7%
25. A district or regional educational agency	32.7%	25.7%
26. A college or university	37.9%	35.9%
27. A private concern such as a publisher	35.6%	13.0%
28. A professional group such as the NEA or NCTM	20.6%	29.4%

The only major difference between the agencies servicing elementary and secondary teachers appears to be private concerns. There were few interesting interrelationships between the data from questions 23 through 28. One that should be noted is that if a school system provides secondary teachers in-service education, then the teacher is much less likely to have in-service education with a college or university than the teacher with no in-service opportunity from the local system. Another notable observation is that the high percentage of people who had recent in-service experience participated in an in-service program sponsored by a school system.

A final observation relating to in-service participation by secondary teachers is that participation appears related to salary. Teachers earning below $12 500 are more likely to have participated in in-service education of some form than those earning more than $12 500. For elementary teachers, the experience of the teachers is correlated positively with their participation in in-service programs. These two statistics are somewhat at variance with each other but perhaps are indicative of differences in the elementary and secondary mathematics teachers' attitudes.

Two questions (4 and 29) indicated teachers' satisfaction with in-service education. The responses to these questions correlated highly.

		Elementary	Secondary
4.	Are you generally satisfied with the in-service education you have had in the past?	50.0%	37.2%
29.	On the whole, have your experiences with in-service education been positive?	63.7%	53.8%

Elementary teachers appear to be somewhat better satisfied with their in-service work than secondary teachers.

The satisfaction with in-service education (question 4) for elementary teachers correlated positively with fifty-one variables. It correlated positively with the responses to all forty-nine of the what-is questions and with satisfaction with present teaching position, classroom facilities, library facilities, and laboratory teaching materials. It correlated negatively with the responses to five questions about in-service gripes. For the secondary teachers, the questions produced almost an identical pattern. The secondary teachers who had participated in in-service education recently (question 22) tended to have had a positive experience.

Three questions (17-19) on the form ascertained the degree to which teachers felt a need for in-service education, how the teachers felt about the availability of it, and whether they would require it of all.

		Elementary	Secondary
17.	Do you feel a need to participate in mathematics in-service education?	77.1%	80.2%
18.	Should each school system have an organized in-service education program available for all who teach mathematics?	86.3%	83.3%
19.	Should in-service education be required of all who teach mathematics?	62.9%	59.3%

The responses show that secondary teachers have about the same positive expectations for in-service education as elementary teachers. This is worth noting, particularly since their experiences are not as positive about in-service education as those of the elementary teachers, according to questions 4 and 29. Many supervisors and university mathematics educators observe that secondary teachers are harder to work with and harder to satisfy in in-service education. It should be noted that as a consequence many supervisors do work more with elementary teachers than with secondary teachers. (Do they receive more positive feedback and reinforcement from elementary teachers for what they do?) Secondary teachers do want in-service education even though their experiences are not all that positive (question 17). Perhaps two conclusions should be drawn: (1) supervisors and college people should not favor the elementary teachers with in-service experiences simply because they are more appreciative of efforts, and (2) it is necessary to work harder to satisfy the needs and interests of secondary teachers.

Complaints about in-service education

The pilot version of the survey—used with the NCTM teacher population in the spring of 1974—had two open-ended questions requesting teachers to identify gripes and complaints about in-service education or to make suggestions to improve it. The respondents "unloaded" their perceptions in no uncertain terms, often couching their statements in colorful, poignant language. These responses were used to generate a set of thirteen questions (30–42) about gripes in in-service education. Responses of teachers are given below, along with the relative ranking for the gripes.

My major gripes about in-service education in the past have been

	Elementary percentage		Secondary percentage	
	yes	rank	yes	rank
30. It has not fit my needs in the classroom.	58.0%	1	65.5%	1
31. I did not help select the topics.	42.7%	4	44.0%	5
32. The leaders have not taught classes like mine.	42.0%	6	46.8%	4
33. The program was poorly planned and disorganized.	30.1%	8	31.8%	8
34. The program was too theoretical.	51.1%	2	47.0%	3
35. Everything was old-hat; I had seen it all before.	29.3%	9	30.6%	9.5

36. It was inconvenient; too far and at the wrong time.	27.7%	11	30.6%	9.5
37. The program was so general it did not help in the teaching of math.	45.5%	3	52.4%	2
38. The only reward was the personal element of self-satisfaction.	26.6%	12	29.7%	12
39. The leaders had other things on their minds than my problems.	18.1%	13	25.4%	13
40. Too much method and too little mathematics.	39.8%	7	35.7%	6
41. My fellow participants were so bored and uninterested that it discouraged me.	28.3%	10	33.1%	7
42. Materials used in the in-service were too expensive for practical classroom use.	42.5%	5	30.2%	11

The gripes appear to be of the same relative importance to the two populations. A Pearson correlation coefficient for the two populations was found to be 0.885, with the probability of the relationship occurring by chance less than .001. Item 42 perhaps is testimony to the different types of teaching and levels of mathematics encountered by elementary and secondary school teachers.

It was hypothesized that for each sample of teachers, there would be many significant pair-wise correlations between gripes. That is, if a teacher had one gripe about in-service education, he or she would probably have several others. This was the case; indeed, so many intercorrelations were significant that it was decided to see if using the gripes as a subscale would be justified. (Hoyt reliabilities were generated for this thirteen-item subtest; for the elementary teachers and the secondary mathematics teachers, reliabilities of .79 and .77, respectively, were found.) One interpretation is that each item was measuring the same attribute that the other items taken together were measuring. Item 36 concerning inconvenience seemed somewhat at odds with the others. This is clear on examination of the statistical analyses of the contribution of the various items to the reliability. This might be expected; rather than relating to an attribute of the in-service program's planning and content, it relates to location and time. Although this is an important characteristic of inconvenience for teachers and one affecting their participation, apparently it is not a measure of the quality of the experience of the teachers.

Teachers' satisfaction with in-service education (question 4) and their experiences with it having been positive (question 29) are related to their gripes. If they have a gripe, then they give negative responses to these two satisfaction questions; if they do not have a gripe, then the responses are positive. The chi-square statistics are dramatic. A chi-square value of 17 was sufficient to assure the probability that the relationship could be attributed to chance was one in 20 000. The larger the chi-square statistic, the less likely it could be attributed to chance. The following table gives the chi-square statistic (rounded to the nearest whole number) for each of the thirteen gripes. Note the number of very large statistics. We conclude that these gripes are very significant factors in the design and implementation of in-service programs.

SUMMARY TABLE: CHI-SQUARE STATISTICS FOR
"GRIPES" ITEMS WITH SATISFACTION WITH IN-SERVICE (4)
AND POSITIVE IN-SERVICE EXPERIENCE (29)

Gripes Item No.	Elementary		Secondary	
	Satisfaction	Positive Experience	Satisfaction	Positive Experience
30	81	167	199	281
31	37	63	43	54
32	$(p < .001)$12	22	34	65
33	55	74	104	156
34	30	28	56	54
35	18	49	34	88
36	$(p < .1)$ 3	$(p < .2)$ 2	$(p < .2)$ 3	$(p < .2)$ 3
37	48	92	140	190
38	$(p < .0005)$13	19	18	17
39	24	33	48	97
40	35	42	28	58
41	37	70	96	163
42	$(p < .005)$10	$(p < .01)$ 8	19	$(p < .2)$ 3

All statistics except those with a given probability level have $p < .00005$.

The factors of most significance for a large number of teachers are directly related. Item 30 (fitting in-service education to classroom needs), item 34 (the program was too theoretical), and item 37 (the program was too general) appear strongly related. The two factors of the theory and generality of the in-service program can be major mechanisms of assuring that the in-service education does not deal with classroom issues and problems at a level of practicality. All who have conducted in-service programs have at times assumed that teachers can and would make the connection to what happens in their classrooms. But many teachers are so busy with lesson planning, homework grading, extracurricular activities, and the like that they are hard-pressed to make the connections of good theory and generality to their own teaching situations. The in-service educator needs to consider carefully the demands that the program places on teachers. It appears safe to conclude that the major category of important gripes for the teacher relate quite directly to what happens in the teacher's classroom as a result of the in-service program.

Question 31 concerning participants helping select topics for in-service programs reflects what is often considered a major approach for assuring that the program does fit the teachers' needs and, on a different level of importance, is a strategy for making teachers feel the program fits their needs, whether or not it does in actuality. The chi-square test relating the needs gripe and the topic-selection gripe indicates that people not having the latter gripe are much more likely not to have the needs gripe than those who help select the topics. It is quite unlikely that this relationship between in-service education fitting classroom needs and teachers having helped select topics occurred by chance.

Secondary teachers share many of the perceptions of the elementary teachers. The gripe of not helping select the topics for in-service programs was significantly related to all the other gripes, except the final gripe concerning pay for in-service participation. The contingency tables for the chi-square analyses indicated that if the teachers had the topic-selection gripe, then they were quite likely to have the other gripe; if not, not.

Clearly, topic selection is a critical variable—most of the chi-square statistics considerably exceed the level that says the relationship is due to chance at the $1/10\,000$ probability level. It is difficult to say what is cause and what is effect. Participation in topic selection was important for the elementary school teacher; it appears to be even more important for the secondary school mathematics teacher. It is related also to how the leader's experience is perceived, the level of disorganization sensed by the teacher, whether there is too much perceived emphasis on methods, and whether the in-service education is viewed as fitting classroom needs. The gripe of leaders of in-service education not having comparable experience was significantly related to all other gripes for secondary teachers, but for the elementary teachers it was not significantly related to the gripes of disorganization (question 33), inconvenience (question 36), peer boredom (question 41), or pay (question 42).

There is a need for researchers to examine carefully what works and what leads to specific types of dissatisfaction within an in-service program in terms of the differing responsibilities and backgrounds elementary and secondary teachers bring to the in-service setting. In-service educators need to consider carefully means of reducing these gripes in their own programs. In-service educators who work with both elementary and secondary teachers must note the distinct differences in the two sets of teachers.

The gripe of fellow participants being "so bored and uninterested that it discouraged me" was important to both elementary and secondary teachers and was related to general satisfaction with in-service education. Secondary teachers who read the *Mathematics Teacher* are less likely to find peer boredom a gripe. Secondary teachers who have had in-service experience provided by the local school system are more likely to have peer boredom as a perceived gripe than those whose experience with in-service is other than with a local program. For both elementary and secondary teachers, it is significantly related to feeling positive about past in-service experience (question 29). Both elementary and secondary teachers are less likely to have the peer-boredom gripe if they do not feel *(a)* that they are excluded from in-service topic selection; *(b)* that there can be no application of in-service topics to classroom needs; *(c)* that leaders were not aware of their type of class; *(d)* that there was disorganization and poor planning; and *(e)* that in-service topics were too general. Teachers who do not perceive an overemphasis on methods also are less likely to feel that peer boredom is a major gripe.

Interestingly, the probability that a teacher would identify peer boredom as a major gripe decreased with experience (question 41) for both elementary and secondary teachers. This factor was related significantly to other factors also measuring experience, such as salary, but at a less significant level statistically. The results might be explained by the fact that the younger teacher has a stronger expectation for reward from in-service participation but that the more experienced teacher is more likely to be disappointed by past experiences. The older teacher may simply feel that it is inappropriate to tie the appreciation for in-service education to other people's reactions.

In any event, all teachers have a profound responsibility to examine their own attitudes about in-service education and how they display these attitudes. Their attitudes appear to be strongly related to other mathematics teachers' perceptions of in-service education. It is particularly critical for the older teacher to provide a good model for younger peers.

Thought-provoking relationships are to be found between specific gripes and the general background information that the teachers provided. If elementary or secondary teachers perceived students as being as excited as they were about learning mathematics, then they tended not to have the gripe of in-service not fitting classroom needs, or the gripe of the leaders of the in-service education not having taught classes like their own, or the gripe of too much method and too little mathematics. In addition, at the secondary level, negative correlations of the perception of student excitement about mathematics and the gripes about generality and theory were found.

For secondary teachers, experience correlated negatively with having had positive experiences with in-service education and positively with the gripes of not fitting classroom needs, being too general, and being affected by the boredom of fellow participants. For elementary teachers, experience correlated positively with the gripes of too much method and too little mathematics and peer boredom.

The gripes about the in-service education section of the questionnaire appear to be significant and important. Perhaps the most appropriate conclusion is that the gripes are factors profoundly affecting the success or failure of an in-service program. Teachers at each level want to participate in topic selection, want their in-service experiences to fit their classroom needs, and note the effect of their fellow participants' attitudes, as well as the specific characteristics of the in-service program.

In the next section, the factors considered in this section—experience, satisfaction, background, teaching situation, prior experience with in-service education, and gripes—will be used as the foundation for examining teachers' perceptions of what in-service education should be like and the discrepancies between what-is and what-ought-to-be.

Discrepancies: What-Is and What-Ought-to-Be

A major goal of the survey process was to compare teachers' perceptions of current in-service practices with their opinions of what should be in-service practice. Forty-nine item pairs served as the base for making the comparisons. A teacher was asked to respond twice to a stem like the following: first, for what-is, and, second, for what-ought-to-be.

82. Money is budgeted for in-service education in my school district.

What-Is	What-Ought-to-Be
SA A D SD	SA A D SD

Likkert scales (SA—strongly agree, A—agree, D—disagree, and SD—strongly disagree) were used and assigned values of 0, 1, 2, and 3 respectively. A mean response was calculated for the Is portion and for the Ought portion of each item pair for all populations. The discrepancy was found by subtracting the mean Ought response from the mean Is response for a population. Thus for the elementary teachers, the mean was 1.62 for the item 82 Is response and 0.72 for the Ought response; the discrepancy for item pair 82 is 0.90. All discrepancies are graphed on line segments from 0 to 3 in Appendix 2 (pp. 233–39).

Each of the discrepancies was examined statistically to see if the observed discrepancy was significant. Hotelling's t provided one analysis employed for those individuals responding to both sides of the item pair. For all but four item pairs, the hypothesis that the mean responses were equal was not supported.

Before specific items are examined, a few cautionary remarks are in order. First, in order to produce a mean for an item, the sum of the responses of all the individuals in the sample was found. But is it appropriate to say that the average from the scores assigned to an Agree statement (1) and a Strongly Disagree statement (3) corresponds precisely to $(3 + 1) \div 2 = 2$, or a Disagree statement? There is an assumption of linearity and uniformity in the scaling, and, consequently, interpretations must be considered as gross indications of what teachers are thinking.

Second, in looking at the Is decisions of respondents, it is hard to distinguish what is the difference between an Agree and a Strongly Agree response. To query a teacher whether a school system budgets money for in-service education is to ask a question of fact; either the school does or it does not. The shade of meaning between Agree and Strongly Agree is hard to understand. Thus, for most analyses and discussion, the four-point scale has been collapsed in the obvious way to a two-point Agree-Disagree scale. However, for the opinions of respondents to the what-ought-to-be items, we felt that the shades of response from a four-point scale were necessary to gain a more robust perception of the strength of opinion of the respondents. The decision to make the what-is scale a four-point scale was made in terms of providing uniformity for the two scales. Responses to specific items warrant discussion and analysis because they are particularly informative. Much of the discussion will be in terms of the percentage of responses rather than discrepancies per se. Hence, Appendix 2 must be examined if the mean responses to either part of the item pair are to be considered or the discrepancy examined.

Both elementary teachers and secondary mathematics teachers perceived a large discrepancy between practice and what-ought-to-be for most items. The average discrepancy was .98 with a standard deviation of .31 on all forty-nine pairs of items for the secondary population. With the maximum possible score on an item being 3 for Strongly Disagree and the minimum being 0 for Strongly Agree, one senses considerable variance between the teachers' perceptions of what-is and what-ought-to-be.

Sixty-two percent of the elementary teachers and 53 percent of the secondary teachers report that their schools have in-service programs. (*Note.* Strongly Agree and Agree responses have been lumped.) This sounds promising, although one must wonder how the in-service needs of teachers in the schools without in-service programs are being met. But one must inquire about the nature of these programs; many teachers apparently feel a need for in-service education specific to the teaching of mathematics.

Two questions (61 and 62) were directed to determining whether the in-service programs were general in character or specifically for mathematics teaching.

	Elementary	*Secondary*
	(lumped Agree percentages)	
61-Is. My school district has an in-service program designed specifically for teaching mathematics.	21%	16%

The discrepancy for item-pair 61 was the largest for any item pair for secondary teachers (1.47) and for elementary teachers (1.30). For elementary and secondary teachers, question 4 (Are you satisfied with in-service education you have had in the past?) correlates positively with item 61 Is and with the values of the discrepancies. The latter correlation is subject to a variety of interpretations. One explanation is simply that the higher a teacher's satisfaction with in-service education, the more likely that he or she will perceive or feel there ought to be more mathematics-specific in-service education than there is.

Secondary teachers in a school system not having an in-service program specific to mathematics (61 Is) are about twice as likely to have the gripe that they have participated in a disorganized, poorly planned program (item 33), about half as likely to have had a satisfying experience with previous in-service programs, and typically have a lower percentage of participation than teachers in a school with a mathematics-specific in-service program. The ratio of teachers stating that in-service education should be required of all who teach mathematics (item 19) to those who would not require it is approximately 7:4 for those agreeing that a school should have a mathematics-specific in-service program (61 Ought). For those disagreeing with item 61 Ought, the ratio is reversed, 6:10. A significantly higher percentage of teachers agreeing with 61 Ought indicated a need for in-service education (item 17) than those disagreeing with it.

Interestingly, teachers agreeing with item 61 Ought tended to have as a gripe that fellow in-service participants were bored. Responses to 61 Is correlated negatively with the gripe of being excluded from the in-service topic selection.

The second question relating to in-service education specific to mathematics teaching was

	Elementary	Secondary
	(lumped Agree)	
62-Is. My school district has an in-service program, but it is not designed for mathematics teaching specifically.	64%	58%

(Note. The number of omits was not counted in the percentage. More secondary teachers responded that their schools had this sort of program than any program at all for question 50-Is. The number of omits more than makes up this difference.)

The discrepancies for item-pair 62 between the Is and the Ought responses for both elementary and secondary teachers were the smallest of those for any of the forty-nine item pairs. Indeed, for the secondary teacher sample, the discrepancy was a negative number, indicating that they were participating in more general in-service education and less in-service education specific to mathematics education than they wanted. This is perhaps an understandable reaction by teachers at the secondary level; their business is teaching mathematics. They find it more difficult to see the benefit of general in-service education in terms of mathematics learning and teaching. Indeed, each of us has encountered secondary mathematics teachers so committed to mathematics teaching that they have difficulty in seeing the quality and usefulness in a sound but more general in-service program. However, most schools do have some major problems that extend across most classrooms transcending particular disciplines and that are in need of attention. For example, student discipline and vandalism are major problems in some schools—certainly they are not specific to any subject matter and can be the theme of productive in-service work. Are the many teachers who react adversely to such transcendent in-service topics simply saying, "Let mathematics teaching and mathematics teachers be the focus of *some* of my in-service work?"

Item pairs 57, 60, and 55 concern who should conduct in-service programs.

	Elementary		Secondary	
	(lumped Agree percentages)			
	Is	*Ought*	*Is*	*Ought*
57. There is an individual in my building or in my school system responsible for inservice education in mathematics.	32%	84%	28%	83%
60. In-service education programs are conducted by personnel within my school system.	64%	73%	54%	71%
55. My school district depends on neighboring colleges and universities to provide the majority of opportunities for inservice education.	42%	52%	53%	50%

Teachers appear to want a person in their own school to have the major responsibility for their in-service program. The general trend in the United States appears to be for local school systems to acquire more legal sanctions to provide in-service education for their teachers. Both Pennsylvania and Minnesota, for example, have relatively recent laws allowing local schools or professional organizations to identify, design, and implement in-servie programs that can offer master's equivalent credit for purposes of earning an increment on the salary schedules. This trend appears consistent with teacher preferences.

Chi-square statistical tests indicate that secondary teachers who are in a school system with an individual responsible for in-service education (item 57 Is) are less likely to have the gripe of in-service education being too general (item 37); are more likely to have participated in in-service education (item 22); are more likely to feel in-service education should be required of all who teach mathematics (item 19); and are more likely to be satisfied with their in-service experience (item 4). Those who feel there ought to be an individual in the school system responsible for in-service education favor in-service education being required (item 19); are more likely to state they need in-service education (item 17); and are more likely to be readers of the *Mathematics Teacher*. Teachers who feel in-service education at their own school is preferable (60 Ought) are significantly more likely to have participated in in-service education (item 22) and to have participated at the school system level (item 23).

Two items (88 and 91) examined the critical variable of how topics for in-service education are identified. The gripes section (question 31) indicated this to be a critical variable.

	Elementary		*Secondary*	
	(lumped Agree percentages)			
	Is	*Ought*	*Is*	*Ought*
88. I participate in identifying topics for in-service education.	44%	93%	35%	92%
91. Achievement data of students in my school are used to determine needs for in-service education.	26%	84%	13%	82%

For elementary teachers, if the teacher indicated having helped identify the topic, then it was about four times as likely that the teacher had participated in an in-service program (question 22) than if the teacher had not identified a topic. Elementary teachers who would require in-service education (question 19) in mathematics were more likely to have participated in identifying in-service topics. Elementary teachers who helped identify in-service topics were significantly more likely to have realized satisfaction (question 4) and have had a positive in-service experience (question 29) than those who had not. For secondary teachers, if they indicated a need for in-service education (question 17) or an inclination to require in-service education of all (question 19), then they were more likely to want to help identify in-service topics. Teachers at both levels were more likely to be dissatisfied with in-service education (question 4) if achievement data had not been used to determine in-service content (91 Is) than if achievement data had been used for topic selection. Of the elementary teachers having a positive in-service experience (question 29), two of seven had had achievement data used to determine in-service topics, but of those not having positive experiences, only two of ten had had achievement data used for topic identification. For both elementary and secondary teachers, the perception of students being as excited about learning mathematics as they ever were (question 20) correlated negatively with the teacher's perception that achievement data should be used for the identification of in-service topics!

Secondary teachers who have not participated in topic selection (88 Is) are about twice as likely to express dissatisfaction with previous in-service education (question 4) and are much more likely to feel that in-service education has not fit their needs (question 30) than those who have participated in topic selection. Teachers with fifteen years of teaching experience are about twice as likely to have participated in topic selection than those with less experience. A positive perception of in-service experiences (question 29) is about twice as likely if the teachers have participated in in-service topic selection (88 Is).

The organization of the in-service program

Four questions (59, 58, 64, 63) addressed the problem of the format or organization of in-service education.

	Elementary		Secondary	
	(lumped Agree percentages)			
	Is	*Ought*	*Is*	*Ought*
59. I give some of each of my summers to in-service work.	32%	47%	26%	48%
58. Single-topic, all-day in-service programs are available five or six days during the school year.	14%	71%	10%	68%
64. In-service education programs consist of several short, weekly meetings all organized around a single theme or topic.	24%	58%	17%	58%
63. In-service education programs are short and to the point.	36%	93%	25%	90%

Clearly, the summer in-service option is not popular with teachers at either level. The most strongly correlated variable with the avowal of teachers that they participate in in-service work during the summer or should participate during the summer was that of teachers stating they needed in-service education (question 17). If a teacher at either level indicated that they read the NCTM journals, they were more likely to have participated in summer in-service work and to indicate that they ought to in the future. Secondary teachers who had the gripe that in-service education had not fit their needs (question 3) were less willing to say that they should give summers to in-service work than those who did not have that gripe. For secondary teachers, the number of methods courses taken (question 44) was negatively correlated with the feeling that summers should be given to in-service work.

The availability of in-service days five or six times a year was more of a significant factor for the elementary teachers than for the secondary teachers. If such in-service was available, they were more likely to be satisfied with their in-service experience (question 4), to have had a positive experience (question 29), and to be earning a larger salary ($\chi^2 = 28$, 12df, $p < .005$). In terms of the Ought part of the question, teachers at each level who felt in-service education should be required (question 19) or that they had a need for it (question 17) were significantly more likely to feel the five or six in-service days a year were appropriate.

Questions 64 Is and 64 Ought were intended to give some feel for whether teachers preferred a continuing experience with a single topic scattered over several in-service days during a year. For both elementary and secondary populations, participation in this sort of continuing in-service experience made satisfaction with in-service education more probable (question 4) and a positive experience (question 29) than if the teachers did not participate. For secondary teachers, three gripes correlated negatively with their perception of whether they should participate in such a continuing program: peer boredom (41), too general (37), and needs (31).

The short-and-to-the-point characteristic appears important to both secondary and elementary teachers. Short-and-to-the-point in-service programs are for some teachers more likely to produce positive in-service experiences (question 29) and satisfaction with the programs (question 4). Teachers at each level who do perceive students as being as excited about learning mathematics as they ever were (question 20) are significantly more likely to perceive the in-service experience as short and to the point than those who do not ($\chi^2 = 14$, 6df, $p < .005$). Gripes affect whether teachers perceive in-service programs as short and to the point; those who have the gripes do not have that perception, and those who do not have the gripes do. This is apparent in the chi-square tabulations for the gripes of too much method (40), too general (37), too disorganized (33), leader's experience (32), needs (30), and selection of in-service topics (31) for both elementary and secondary teachers. The interesting question is, of course, what is cause and what is effect.

The questions concerning the format and organization of in-service programs are not formulated tightly enough to give definitive answers to the pressing matter of how in-service experiences should be arranged. A continuing thematic program of several in-service experiences should probably consist of short-and-to-the-point segments. Some in-service topics probably require the leisure of a summer program free from the distractions of grading papers and planning lessons. The data do suggest, however, that the arrangements for the program are important.

Many teachers noted a need for follow-up to in-service experiences on the open-ended questions of the pilot NCTM survey in the spring of 1974. Consequently, the following question was placed on this survey.

	Elementary		Secondary	
	(lumped Agree percentages)			
	Is	Ought	Is	Ought
54. Systematic follow-up in the classroom is provided after an in-service program.	18%	83%	9%	79%

Elementary teachers have more follow-up activities than secondary teachers and feel that they are more important. For both elementary and secondary teachers, follow-up activities appear to build a significantly greater feeling of satisfaction with in-service education (question 4) and to provide for a positive experience (question 29). Many of the individuals indicating gripes about in-service programs (questions 31 through 42) feel that classroom follow-up of in-service activities is a strong ought-to-be-factor, whereas individuals not having the gripes are not so concerned with having follow-up. This is an expensive extension of in-service education. Little information concerning what kinds of in-service programs most require follow-up activities or the desired characteristics of that follow-up activity is available.

Usefulness of in-service activities

The use factor has important bearing on why in-service education is important to teachers and to schools. Two questions (89 and 90) looked at how teachers perceived the use factor for the mathematics and the methods they encountered in the in-service setting.

	Elementary		Secondary	
	(lumped Agree percentages)			
	Is	Ought	Is	Ought
89. I can use in my teaching most of the mathematics I learn in in-service programs.	30%	92%	52%	97%
90. I have been able to use in my teaching most of the methods demonstrated in in-service education.	28%	90%	49%	95%

For the secondary teacher, the use question (89 Is) provided significant chi-square relationships for twelve different variables: satisfaction with in-service, positive in-service experience, nine of the thirteen gripe statements, and the respondents' methods background. The latter variable is the only one in which the relationships are not easy to predict; we comment on it. Individuals with a weaker methods background tend to have a perception that the mathematics they learn is less useful in the classroom than those with a stronger methods background.

The elementary population chi-square analyses were remarkably similar to those for the secondary teachers, but one analysis deserves particular comment. The teachers responding to question 22 (I have participated in in-service education in the last three years) exhibited a 3:2 ratio for finding the mathematics of in-service programs useful compared to those finding it not useful; for those whose in-service education was not recent, the ratio was only 1:2.

The question about the use of in-service methods (90 Is) produced results that were quite similar to the question about the use of in-service mathematics. Nine statistically significant chi-square statistics were found in the analyses of much the same patterns. In addition, it should be noted that participation in in-service programs correlates significantly with whether the teachers find the methods useful in the classroom. Secondary teachers with higher salaries tend to find more use of the methods they experience in programs than those with lower salaries (?).

A recent feature of mathematics education at both elementary and secondary levels has been a reawakening interest in activity or laboratory learning. Responses to question 16 indicated that 45 percent of the elementary teachers and one-third of the secondary teachers were satisfied with the laboratory learning materials in their schools. Question 56 focused on in-service education related to activity learning indirectly.

	Elementary		Secondary	
	(lumped Agree percentages)			
	Is	Ought	Is	Ought
56. Teachers complete in-service programs with materials for classroom use that they have made themselves.	53%	83%	33%	77%

Both elementary and secondary teachers apparently feel a need for specific, usable materials as a result of in-service programs. Were teachers reacting to the use factor or the materials factor in responding to question 56? That is not clear. In any case, the factors of satisfaction (question 4) and positive experience (question 29) are significantly related to the factors item 56

Is measured. Senior high school teachers were more likely to feel 56 Ought was unimportant than junior high school teachers (as might be expected).

Two strong conclusions can be drawn from the use of in-service mathematics and in-service methods questions. First, these are critical variables that affect the teachers' perceptions of the power, reward, and gripes about in-service education. Second, every teacher feels that the practical use factor is most important.

In-service topic preferences

What kind of topics do teachers prefer for in-service education? Do teachers prefer mathematics over methods? Are these preferences related to any background characteristics or previous in-service experiences of the teachers? The pilot survey suggested that the balance between methodological and mathematical content was a critical variable to examine.

One Is-Ought item was pointed most directly at the question of the balance between methods and mathematics (51).

	Elementary		*Secondary*	
	(lumped Agree percentages)			
	Is	*Ought*	*Is*	*Ought*
51. In-service education is about teaching methods rather than mathematical content.	63%	68%	54%	65%

Approximately 40 percent of the elementary teachers and 36 percent of the secondary teachers had indicated that too much method and too little mathematics was a major gripe in responding to question 40. None of the chi-square analyses for question 51 were significant, except those relating to question 40.

The listing of in-service topics (questions 65 through 77) gives more insight into the type of in-service emphasis that teachers prefer than the methods-versus-mathematics questions.

The topics for in-service educa-tion in mathematics that re-ceive emphasis in my school are	*Elementary*			*Secondary*		
	Is	*Ought*	*Ought Rank*	*Is*	*Ought*	*Ought Rank*
65. Computational skills	39%	89%	8	24%	83%	7
66. Motivation	42%	94%	1	37%	94%	2
67. Applications of mathematics	37%	94%	3.5	22%	95%	1
68. Mathematical structures	30%	76%	11	19%	70%	12

69. Metrication	45%	92%	6	39%	86%	5.5
70. Use of calculators	8%	58%	12	20%	77%	10
71. Students with learning difficulties	42%	94%	2	35%	92%	4
72. Diagnosis	37%	90%	7	19%	83%	11
73. Evaluation	39%	87%	9	26%	81%	8
74. Transformational geometry	12%	44%	13	9%	49%	13
75. Transition between grade levels	31%	85%	10	26%	79%	9
76. Remediation	40%	94%	3.5	33%	86%	5.5
77. Improving student attitudes about mathematics	33%	93%	5	22%	93%	3

Teachers at both elementary and secondary levels are interested in those topics that relate to student attitudes and basic skills. The same pattern was evident in the listing of topics in the pilot survey of NCTM members in the spring of 1974. Because there were forty-two topics listed on the pilot survey, the inclination to select topics in these two areas was even more evident.

Some specific analyses are of interest. Topic 65 (computational skill) was related to teachers' feeling positive about or satisfied with in-service education for both elementary and secondary teachers. Sixty percent of the elementary teachers in in-service programs addressing computation were satisfied with their programs, but only 43 percent were satisfied in the programs that did not address computation. For secondary teachers, just more than one-half of the teachers in programs stressing computational skill indicated satisfaction with in-service education, but fewer than one in three were satisfied if the in-service program did not have that emphasis. Responding that programs ought to be concerned with computational skill was related to teachers generally feeling that they needed in-service education (question 17).

The variable of teachers perceiving students as being as excited about mathematics as they ever were (question 20) was strongly but negatively correlated at the secondary level with the following topics:

   66-Ought: motivation; 67-Ought: applications
   69-Ought: metric; 73-Ought: evaluation
   76-Ought: remediation; 77-Ought: attitudes

The same variable was positively correlated with these:

71-Is: student learning difficulties; 72-Is: diagnosis;
77-Is: attitudes

Secondary teachers perceiving students as less excited now than in the past were twice as likely to specify motivation as an Ought topic of importance as those who saw students as excited about learning mathematics as they ever were. Secondary teachers were less likely to have gripes about the in-service leader having appropriate experience with classes like they were teaching (question 32) if they were receiving in-service information concerned with motivation.

Applications as an in-service topic was strongly related to both elementary and secondary teachers' perceptions of satisfaction with in-service education and having a positive in-service experience. Many gripes were weakly significant in their relation to the Is portion of the responses. If the topic did not receive attention, then the teachers were more likely to have the gripes.

The topic of structure was important in in-service education a few years ago. One-third of the secondary teachers with more than nine years of teaching experience indicated that they had had in-service experiences with mathematical structures as the topic, but only two out of fifteen teachers with fewer than nine years of teaching experience indicated in-service experience concerned with structure. The chi-square analysis for elementary teachers indicates differences in the same direction, but only at the $p = .03$ level. An even smaller portion of teachers with fewer than five years of teaching experience has had in-service education on the topic of mathematical structures. This may indicate a waning of interest in mathematical structures per se for school mathematics. Secondary teachers not having the gripes of disorganization and of in-service being too general are less likely to have had in-service experience concerned with mathematical structures.

For each of the rest of the topics—69 Is through 77 Is—satisfaction with in-service programs (question 4) produced significant chi-square analysis for both the elementary and the secondary teachers. Generally, if the teachers had experienced in-service education for the topic, then they were more likely to be satisfied than if they had not.

Two alternative conclusions may be offered by way of explanation. First, topic selection for in-service education has a somewhat faddish character. Needs may be "discovered" because the neighboring school system offers an in-service program that teachers hear good things about, as well as recognizing the relation to legitimate classroom needs in their own school. The topics listed in the survey are or have been the popular topics for programs. Teachers may be testifying to the popularity of the topic and to the fact that since the topic has been the source of so much in-service education, some fairly effective programs have evolved.

The second alternative explanation is simply that teachers are appreciative of in-service efforts in the direction of needs that are real. One feels that the faddish factor is missing if significant chi-squares are present for the ought-to-be segment of the questions. For secondary teachers responding to the question 17 indicating a need for in-service education, the topics —computation (65), motivation (66), applications (67), metric (69), calculators (70), learning difficulties (71), diagnosis (72), evaluation (73), articulation between grades (75), remediation (76), and attitudes (77)— yielded significant chi-squares. Teachers indicating a need for in-service were much more likely to specify that these topics ought to be the focus of in-service education than the teachers who specified that they felt no need for in-service education. The teachers who stated that in-service education should be required of all who teach mathematics specified much more often than those who did not that appropriate in-service topics were learning difficulties, diagnosis, evaluation, articulation, remediation, and attitude.

The elementary teachers produced almost identical what-is topic reactions to the secondary teachers in terms of satisfaction, the topic of calculators being the only exception. In terms of the what-ought-to-be topics for in-service education and the chi-square analyses of need (question 17) and requiring in-service education (19), only the topics of diagnosis and attitude produced at the same level of statistical significance as the secondary teachers, although the other topics did have significance levels between .05 and .0001.

We conclude that the topics of computation, motivation, applications, learning difficulties, diagnosis, evaluation, articulation, remediation, and attitudes are quite important to teachers today. Their interests in these topics extend well beyond faddish awareness.

Basic skills and turning students on to mathematics appear to be the current important categories of in-service topics for teachers. Elementary teachers who favor future in-service topics in evaluation were those who have more methods-course background (question 44). The greater portion of the secondary teachers who indicated a need for future in-service education concerned with attitudes (77 Ought) or remediation (76 Ought) came from the set of teachers who felt students were not as excited about learning mathematics (question 20) rather than from those who felt students are as excited as they were in the past.

Purposes of in-service education

Is the in-service topic selection of teachers consistent with their views of the purposes of in-service education? Several questions (78–86) were asked concerning what the perceived purpose of in-service education is and what it ought to be.

	Elementary		Secondary	
	(lumped Agree percentages)			
	Is	*Ought*	*Is*	*Ought*

The purposes of in-service education reflected in my school include:

78. Keeping "alive" professionally.	63%	90%	47%	88%
79. Learning about new curricula.	70%	95%	44%	95%
80. Learning new mathematics.	45%	85%	24%	78%
81. Studying new methods of teaching mathematics.	45%	96%	28%	96%
82. Analyzing problems, such as discipline, faced by all teachers; not just teachers of mathematics.	46%	90%	43%	88%
83. Facilitating the use of a new text or text series.	62%	92%	35%	83%
84. Providing opportunity to share ideas with other mathematics teachers.	44%	96%	48%	96%
85. Building enthusiasm for teaching mathematics.	39%	94%	25%	90%
86. Describing new materials and information of direct use in my classroom.	55%	96%	34%	95%

The items describing the purposes of in-service education are "motherhood and apple pie" statements. In terms of the what-ought-to-be, practically all teachers at each level agreed with the statements. Of greatest interest is the proportion of teachers who indicate that a particular purpose of in-service education *is not* being met in their school and the size of the discrepancy between what-is and what-ought-to-be perceptions.

An examination of the raw data indicates that secondary teachers have apparently been in in-service programs respecting these nine purposes less than elementary teachers. An examination of the discrepancies in Appendix 2 indicates that the what-is means for secondary teachers fall to the right (in the Disagree direction) of the means for elementary teachers in all but one of the purpose categories. The one exception is that of keeping "alive" professionally (item 78 Is).

These results may be interpreted several ways. One alternative is that secondary teachers participate less often in in-service programs than elementary teachers. Examining the portion of elementary teachers (82.9%) indicating recent participation in in-service programs (question 22) and the percentage (71.3%) of these participating in programs conducted by local school systems (question 23), we note that about 59 percent of the total sample has participated in local in-service programs. For secondary teachers, the respective percentages are question 22, 70.8 percent, and question 23, 57.4 percent, indicating about 41 percent participation in locally conducted in-service programs. Since the question is formulated in terms of "in-service education reflected in my school," the results may reflect this almost 20 percent difference in participation. Is there that much difference in the availability of elementary and secondary in-service programs across the United States?

Another possible interpretation is that the elementary teacher has a much broader responsibility for learning, curricula, and the total school operation than the typical secondary school teacher. The elementary teacher's responsibility covers all facets of the students' life in the school, whereas the secondary teacher's responsibility is generally limited to mathematics. Thus, the elementary teacher can realize these nine purposes in a variety of in-service programs devoted to any one of several different topics. The responses may reflect the specialization of the secondary teacher.

A third alternative explanation is that the relatively greater training and specialization of the secondary teacher has made the secondary teacher a more discerning critic of what happens in the in-service program. For example, knowing more mathematics—indeed, having the specific lifetime commitment to doing mathematics that led to an undergraduate major in mathematics—may make it harder for the in-service educator to "build enthusiasm for mathematics" (85 Is). Or having specialized methods work in only one area—coupled with exclusive attention to the teaching of mathematics—may lead to a greater expectation for the purpose of learning new teaching methods (81 Is).

In any case, there is little difference between elementary and secondary teachers' mean responses to the what-ought-to-be questions for the purpose items. The correspondingly greater discrepancies of the secondary teachers arise from the secondary teachers' responses to the what-is portion of the questions. Two particular items deserve attention because of the magnitude of the discrepancies for secondary teachers: studying new methods of teaching mathematics (81) and building enthusiasm for teaching mathematics (85).

The purpose for in-service education of learning methods of teaching mathematics seems obvious to most mathematics educators. But only 28 percent of the elementary teachers and 14 percent of the secondary teachers responding to both question 4 (on their satisfaction with in-service education) and question 81 Is (concerning methods as a purpose) indicated that methods was a purpose of in-service education in their school system. But for those elementary teachers reporting satisfaction with in-service education, 38 percent reported the purpose was methods; and of those stating methods was not the purpose, only 22 percent indicated satisfaction. Teachers reporting positive experience with previous in-service programs were more likely to have had programs devoted to the purpose of methods than those who had not. Only 56 percent of the teachers reporting that their present in-service program's purpose was methods reported the gripe of in-service education not fitting their needs (question 30), but 70 percent of the teachers who participated in programs without this purpose had the needs gripes. Thirty-two percent of the teachers participating in programs whose purpose was methods had the gripe of the program being too general (question 37), but 56 percent of the teachers had this gripe if the program was devoted to purposes other than methods. The Ought portion of the question of purpose correlated positively with teachers recommending that in-service education be required and their personal perception of a need for in-service education.

The enthusiasm variable is particularly intriguing. One might hypothesize that secondary teachers should have enthusiasm for teaching mathematics because of their career choice and all the necessary experience required to enter the career. Would these respondents have taken on the average eight to eleven mathematics courses (question 43) and have gone through extensive undergraduate and graduate professional courses without strong commitment to mathematics teaching, indeed, enthusiasm for mathematics teaching? It is hard to imagine an undergraduate participating two or more years in intensive preservice work without some feeling of enchantment with mathematics and with teaching. But we have the strong evidence of experienced teachers stating that they need renewal for mathematics teaching. Does this mean that they entered the profession with an unrealistic impression of mathematics teaching? Of mathematics? Of their role in the schools? Perhaps they imagined doing mathematics of challenge and significance at the advanced secondary levels and are frustrated by teaching what they perceive as routine, basic computational skills requiring little analytic thought or problem solving? Perhaps they do not feel a sense of respect for their profession by the community in which they live.

One-third of the secondary teachers who have participated in in-service programs addressing enthusiasm report a positive in-service experience, but only one-sixth of the teachers who have participated in programs without this purpose report a positive experience. For satisfaction with programs, the enthusiasm characteristic splits the population into 35 percent being satisfied versus only 20 percent being satisfied for programs without the enthusiasm purpose. Fifty-four percent of the teachers in programs they characterize as addressing the goal of enthusiasm for teaching mathematics have the gripe of in-service education not fitting their needs (question 30), but 69 percent have this gripe if they are from the population not participating in such programs. About one-half of the teachers participating in programs not addressing the purpose of enthusiasm have the gripe of not helping select topics, but only one-third have this gripe if their experience is with programs addressing enthusiasm. Of those teachers indicating that the enthusiasm purpose ought to be a goal of in-service programs, the ratio was 9:2 for those who did indicate a need for in-service education compared to those who did not. The ratio was 3:2 for those not indicating that enthusiasm was an important purpose. Comparable ratios are 2:1 and 1:2 for requiring in-service education split on the base of the enthusiasm purpose. But what is cause and what is effect? The analyses concerning the enthusiasm purpose for in-service education indicate the importance of this purpose for the secondary teacher but yield little insight into the factors involved.

Judging from the collection of descriptions of in-service programs submitted for this project, we found that few, if any, secondary teacher in-service programs have as the direct and primary goal of the in-service program the building of enthusiasm for teaching mathematics. More typical is for this purpose to be of a secondary, informal character. We suspect that the large majority of teachers responding yes to item 85 Is have participated in in-service programs whose leaders have been sufficiently dynamic and enthusiastic to make this purpose seem premier.

We opine that the message from the statistics about the enthusiasm purpose is not to design in-service programs that address this purpose as the primary objective of the program. In our opinion, teachers would react negatively to a Pollyanna style of in-service program focused uniquely on building enthusiasm for teaching mathematics. However, for almost any topic or primary objective, the in-service experience may be designed and implemented to feature entertainment and novelty. In-service programs can be designed to offer teachers respite, renewal, recuperation, and relaxation. Many in-service educators who enjoy a fine reputation among teachers avow that they give particular attention to this feature of program design.

The purpose of building enthusiasm for mathematics teaching may be served well by the type of in-service program that a professional organization—such as the NCTM—is eminently suited to provide. Few professional organizations can offer the need-specific and program-specific in-service education needed at the local school level. Organizations can, however, bring to teachers the people with recognized and proved talent for building and renewing enthusiasm for teaching mathematics.

The factor of building enthusiasm as a purpose of in-service education needs more research. Some authorities such as Kozol (1968) and Silberman (1970) comment specifically on the tremendously debilitating atmosphere of many typical schools and how this operates on the attitudes and self-concept of not only the pupils but also the teachers. If this be true, then a school system might expect the need for programs that build enthusiasm to be the greatest early in the career of teachers. This suggests designing special in-service programs for teachers in their first five years of teaching. It also suggests that preservice teacher education programs need have some concern for helping students assess realistically their motivation, interest, and abilities for teaching.

Table 2.1 indicates the relationships between variables found signifi-

TABLE 2.1
SUMMARY OF PURPOSES*

*This table indicates statistically significant χ^2 relationships between variables without indicating their direction or interpretation. The direction is predictable from or similar to those discussed in the text. The level of significance is $p < .0001$.

| Purpose Variables | *Other Variables* | | | |
| | Secondary | | Elementary | |
	Is	*Ought*	*Is*	*Ought*
78. Keeping alive professionally	Satisfaction with in-service (4)	Needs in-service (17)	Satisfaction with in-service (4)	In-service required (19)
	Recent in-service experience (22)	In-service required (19)	Experience positive (29)	
	Experience positive (29)		Salary (45)	
	Gripe—disorganized (33)		Gripe—does not fit needs (30)	
79. Learning about new curricula	Satisfaction with in-service (4)	Needs in-service (17)	Satisfaction with in-service (4)	
	Recent in-service experience (22)	In-service required (19)	Recent in-service experience (22)	
	Experience positive (29)		Experience positive (29)	
	Gripe—disorganized (33)			
	Gripe—too general (37)			
80. Learning new mathematics	Satisfaction with in-service (4)	Needs in-service (17)	Satisfaction with in-service (4)	
	Experience positive (29)		Experience positive (29)	
			Gripe—does not fit needs (30)	
			Salary (45)	
			Experience (49)	
81. Learning new methods	Satisfaction with in-service (4)	Needs in-service (17)	Satisfaction with in-service (4)	Needs in-service (17)
	Recent in-service experience (22)	In-service required (19)	Experience positive (29)	In-service required (19)

No.	Purpose				
		Experience positive (29) Gripe—does not fit needs (30) Gripe—too general (37)		Gripe—leader's experience (32) Gripe—too general (37) Gripe—no reward but satisfaction (38)	
82.	General problems	Recent in-service experience (22)	In-service required (19) Student excitement (20)		
83.	New text adoption	Satisfaction with in-service (4) Recent in-service experience (22)	Needs in-service (17) In-service required (19)	Satisfaction with in-service (4) Recent in-service experience (22) Experience positive (29)	
84.	Sharing ideas	Satisfaction with in-service (4) Recent in-service experience (22) Experience positive (29)	Needs in-service (17) In-service required (19)	Satisfaction with in-service (4) Experience positive (29) Gripe—did not help select topics (37)	
85.	Building enthusiasm	Satisfaction with in-service (4) Experience positive (29) Gripe—does not fit needs (30) Gripe—did not help select topics (31)	Needs in-service (17) In-service required (19)	Satisfaction with in-service (4) Experience positive (29) Gripe—too general (37)	Needs in-service (17) In-service required (19) Experience (49)
86.	Using new materials	Satisfaction with in-service (4) Recent in-service experience (22) Gripe—did not help select topics (31) Gripe—too general (37) Experience positive (29)	Needs in-service (17) In-service required (19)	Satisfaction with in-service (4) Experience positive (29) Gripe—too general (37)	

cant at the $p < .0001$ level. The direction of the chi-square relationship is stable from one purpose variable to another. For example, the elementary teachers who participated in an in-service program designed for learning new mathematics (question 80 Is) tended to find in-service programs relatively more satisfying (question 4) than teachers who were in programs not perceived as serving the purpose of learning new mathematics.

The elementary or secondary teachers participating in programs for the purpose of facilitating the adoption of new texts (question 83 Is) were relatively more satisfied (question 4) than teachers who did not. Generally, all the satisfaction (question 4), positive experience (question 29), and recent experience (question 22) relations with purpose statements "behave" in the same way. However, a note of caution must be made: the people responding yes to the in-service satisfaction question (4) and agreeing with the purposes question (79) may not be the same as those responding yes to both the satisfaction question and question 85.

Two observations are of sufficient strength to be considered generalizations about teachers' perception of purposes in in-service education. First, each of these purposes has been important to a number of teachers recently. Each has been sufficiently important to generate a feeling of accomplishment and satisfaction for some program designs. Second, the exception in terms of having a relationship with the in-service satisfaction and positive in-service experience is the purpose question 82: "Analyzing problems such as discipline, faced by all teachers, not just teachers of mathematics." This type of general orientation to in-service education apparently does not generate satisfaction or positive experiences in in-service education with teachers.

The interactions of gripe variables with the purpose variables also generated predictable common patterns across the purposes variables. Generally, if the teachers have not participated in a program for the purpose indicated by the variable, then they are more inclined to have the stated gripe than those who were in a program for the purpose indicated by the variable. For example, only 25 percent of the teachers agreeing with 78 Is had the gripe of the program being disorganized, but 37 percent of the teachers disagreeing with 78 Is had this gripe of disorganization.

The results of gripe variables are subject to several interpretations. Teachers may be reacting to the character of the program that is entailed by respecting a specific purpose. Or it may be that the relationship of a specific gripe to a purpose variable simply indicates a lack of acceptance or a lack of understanding of the purpose by a significantly large subset of the teachers. Perhaps the best interpretation is that if a gripe is intrinsically related to a program's purpose (that is, appears in the table) and if a program is designed or implemented for the purpose, then one must realize that teachers are prone to have that category of gripe and must allow for that inclination in the planning.

Some specific variable interactions require comment. For elementary teachers, the interaction of building enthusiasm for teaching mathematics (85 Ought) and experience indicated that the teachers with fewer than ten years of experience viewed this purpose differently from teachers with more than ten years of experience. A greater portion of the younger teachers were inclined to say this purpose was not important.

The reactions of elementary teacher samples to learning new methods as a purpose for programs in the future (81 Ought) and the gripes of the leader's experience (32), excessive generality (37), and no reward by self-satisfaction (38) indicate a potential causal relationship. Teachers agreeing with the methods purpose were less likely to have the gripe than those not agreeing with this purpose.

Finally, the items relating to a teacher's perception of need for in-service education (17) or the willingness to require in-service education for all teachers of mathematics (19): if teachers agreed with the purpose, then they were likely to have responded positively to items 17 and 19; if not, then not.

The willingness of teachers to require in-service education was checked in three different questions (19, 52, 53). A cynical appraisal of the results is that teachers think that such a requirement should apply to the less-than-competent teacher down the hall rather than thinking of the requirement as applying to themselves. The questions and response data are

	Elementary		Secondary	
	(lumped Agree percentages)			
	Is	Ought	Is	Ought
19. Should in-service education be re-quired of all who teach mathematics (yes-no)		63%		59%
52. In-service education is required to maintain certification.	27%	54%	18%	46%
53. In-service education is required to maintain tenure.	17%	43%	11%	40%

The pairwise correlations between questions 19, 52 Ought, and 53 Ought were significant for both populations. It must be noted that the type, amount, and intensity of the in-service experience was not specified. These percentages are about ten percentage points below the responses of the NCTM sample on the pilot survey. Teachers indicating they read the *Arithmetic Teacher* or the *Mathematics Teacher* (question 10) were more inclined to require in-service education than those who did not for the present samples.

Teachers who would require in-service education were inclined to indicate a need for in-service education (question 19) at both the elementary and the secondary levels. Teachers at the secondary school level earning more than $10 000 were less inclined to require in-service education for maintaining certification than teachers earning less than $10 000. The requirement of in-service education for maintaining tenure produced parallel results, but at a lesser significance level ($\chi^2 = 31$, 12df, $p = .0021$).

Mechanisms for encouraging in-service participation

Requiring in-service education suggests a host of political and practical problems. Many of these questions become bargaining points when and if the local teacher group negotiates a contract. A particularly sore point for teacher groups—if in-service education is required—is the mechanisms and rewards that schools use to encourage or to accommodate participation in in-service. For the schools and teachers without union-negotiated contracts, such encouragement mechanisms do not have the same critical importance; the system is more permissive. For the schools with union-negotiated contracts, mechanisms for encouraging in-service education have often been bargained away by teachers in order to get benefits more directly related to the teachers' financial welfare, particularly if the in-service program has unhealthy and inconvenient features in the teachers' perceptions.

Following are questions that concern the mechanisms that teachers responding to the pilot NCTM survey perceived as critical in encouraging in-service education. The pilot sample teachers frequently mentioned these factors in responding to open-ended questions.

	Elementary		Secondary	
	(lumped Agree percentages)			
	Is	*Ought*	*Is*	*Ought*
My school encourages in-service education by				
93. Providing release time from classroom duties.	44%	92%	39%	90%
94. Paying expenses for in-service education offered by agencies other than school.	36%	88%	33%	90%
95. Paying me to participate in in-service education.	25%	74%	24%	76%
97. Giving credit toward promotion.	20%	62%	17%	57%
98. Participation in in-service can result in being placed in a higher pay bracket.	29%	73%	32%	70%

Examination of the data in questions 93–98 indicated a high percentage of significant pairwise correlations between the six Is items for each population. (A Hoyt reliability estimate for each population for these six items was computed as if these items constituted a subtest. For the elementary teachers, $r = .77$; and for secondary teachers, $r = .70$. Reliability is computed by examining whether the responses to each individual item are in agreement or correlate with responses to the remainder of the scale.) The fact of moderately high internal consistencies for this subtest is interesting, not for any testing purposes, but rather because it provides evidence that if teachers are in a school that encourages in-service participation in one way, they are in a school that encourages it in a wide variety of ways. It is an embodiment of the statement that the rich get richer and the poor get poorer. School systems that initiate one form of encouragement of in-service education apparently come to use many forms of encouragement.

An examination of the discrepancies in Appendix 2 between the teachers' perceptions of what-is and what-ought-to-be indicates considerable consistency of the views of elementary and secondary teachers. Teachers are more concerned with means of facilitating in-service participation than in having continuing financial reward because of in-service participation. Item 98 Ought is the only item that concerns a continuing impact on the teacher's bank account. The mean response for 98 Ought was less than it was for items 93 Ought (release time), 94 Ought (paying expenses), and 95 Ought (paying for participation).

Release time is a favorite issue for teachers and supervisors in discussing the why's and why not's of in-service participation. Of the elementary and secondary teachers indicating recent in-service participation (question 22), almost one in two are in schools that provide release time for in-service education. But for the elementary teachers in schools not having release time, only one in four have participated in recent in-service programs and for secondary teachers only one in five. For both elementary and secondary teachers, the chi-square analyses indicate a weak relation to satisfaction with teaching ($p < .005$) and satisfaction with in-service programs ($p < .003$); release time apparently contributes to the teacher's satisfaction. For every three secondary teachers in a school providing release time who would not require in-service education (question 19), there are six who would require it, but for those in schools without release time, there are three who would not require in-service education for every four who would require it. Secondary teachers in schools with release time have greater satisfaction with their in-service experience ($\chi^2 = 17$, 3df, $p = .0008$). Both elementary and secondary teachers are more inclined to say they need in-service education (question 17) if they say that release time ought to be provided than if they don't.

Secondary teachers' satisfaction with in-service education correlates positively with a provision of higher pay (98 Is), credit toward tenure (97 Is), and credit toward promotion (96 Is). For elementary teachers, satisfaction with in-service programs correlates with each of the six encouragement factors.

Money and in-service education

The mechanisms for encouraging release time cost money. They are profoundly related to the teachers' sense of satisfaction with in-service education. They are bargaining points. Teachers' perceptions of whether they ought to be available in their school relate to their previous satisfaction with in-service education, many of their specific gripes, and their perception of whether in-service education should be required. Clearly, expense is a major factor. Question 87 examines the teachers' perceptions of whether money is budgeted for in-service education.

	Elementary		Secondary	
	(lumped Agree percentages)			
	Is	*Ought*	*Is*	*Ought*
87. Money is budgeted for in-service education by my school district.	68%	96%	57%	95%

If the Is responses are accurate, many teachers are left to their own devices to acquire in-service education experiences. The disparity between what the secondary teachers and elementary teachers perceive as current in-service expenditure is disconcerting if the samples are representative. If teachers believe in in-service education and if they think the schools should provide funds for the support of it to the extent indicated by these survey results, then teachers must become more politically aware and aggressive.

In this era in the United States, it appears that cost effectiveness and accountability are major political issues. To get support for in-service education, evidence of the effectiveness of the in-service program appears a necessity in many areas of the country and desirable in the remainder. Only one question on the survey (92) was directed toward this politically sensitive area.

	Elementary		Secondary	
	(lumped Agree percentages)			
	Is	*Ought*	*Is*	*Ought*
92. Achievement data of students in my school are used to evaluate the effectiveness of in-service programs in my school.	17%	68%	9%	69%

Teachers with satisfying or positive in-service experiences are more likely to be in schools that have used student achievement as a criterion of in-service education's effectiveness than teachers whose experience is negative or nonsatisfying. (Would you use student achievement as a criterion if your teachers were not evidencing positive attitudes about the in-service experiences?) Teachers who perceive students as less excited about learning mathematics than they were in the past are less likely to feel that the achievement of students should be used as a criterion of the effectiveness of the in-service program than their peers who feel students are still excited by mathematics (secondary: χ^2 = 12.5, 3df, p = .0058; elementary: χ^2 = 11.1, 3df, p = .0114). Further, belief that achievement data ought to be used depends on a variety of gripes. If teachers have the gripe of topic selection (31), leader's experience (32), or needs (30), they are not so inclined to want achievement data to be used for the evaluation of in-service education. This is sensible; why prefer achievement data to be used if your gripes lead you to suspect the program is ineffective? Generally the teachers satisfied with the teaching profession (question 1) or satisfied with their present teaching position (question 2) were more inclined to the use of student achievement data for determining in-service program effectiveness.

Summary

The results of this survey contain few surprises. Teachers want in-service programs. In-service satisfaction depends on a variety of factors subject to the control of program designers and implementors. The complaints of teachers appear to be the potent and lethal genes that profoundly affect teachers' reactions to in-service programs; among these, planning the program's content to fit classroom needs appears particularly important. Planning is a major factor contributing to teachers having a positive perception of in-service education. Teachers do have definite opinions about how programs should be conducted and the topics and content that they need in order to be more effective in the classroom. There appears to be a strong concern for motivation, for basic skills, and for teacher participation in the selection of in-service content. Follow-up is a key variable. Methods are a prime concern. Teachers feel strongly that schools need to apply mechanisms, such as release time, to make it possible to participate easily in in-service education without the penalty of inconvenience or the expenditure of personal resources.

CHAPTER 3

Supervisors
and In-Service Education

ALAN OSBORNE
J. MICHAEL BOWLING

THE SUPERVISOR has many responsibilities in serving the needs of a
school mathematics program. Traditionally in schools that have a mathematics supervisor or coordinator, in-service education has been one of
these responsibilities. Although the policies and procedures for realizing
this responsibility vary considerably from one school system to another,
two types of evidence from the survey of teachers' attitudes and perceptions reported in chapter 2 indicate that the supervisor does make a difference in the in-service program. First, there is direct evidence that recent participation by teachers in an in-service program was more likely if
there was a person in a local school system responsible for in-service education. The second type of evidence is indirect but more compelling. The
teacher surveys indicate that many factors contribute directly to the success of the in-service program: an assessment of needs, follow-up, direct
relationship of the in-service activity to the school mathematics program,
and the ready availability of an in-service program. Each of these factors
appears to be controlled most readily by an agent of the school system.
The argument may be made that each of these crucial factors for successful programs needs a person in the local school system—such as a supervisor—because the administrative demands for managing these factors is
made more simple and met more efficiently within the school system. The
existence of a supervisor can provide the margin between an in-service
program that serves well the needs of teachers and the mathematics program and one that does not.

It is appropriate, therefore, to examine how supervisors perceive in-service education and their opinions of the factors that teachers identify as critical to the success of an in-service program. The supervisors that were surveyed were selected from the membership roster of the National Council of Supervisors of Mathematics (NCSM). Given the professionalism of mathematics supervisors, it was believed highly likely that the majority of supervisors would be members of NCSM. It should also be noted that it is quite difficult to prepare a list of addresses of mathematics supervisors independent of the NCSM membership roster; many state directories simply do not list that level of school administrative or service personnel.

Survey forms were mailed to the 742 members of NCSM residing in the United States who were not staff members of institutions of higher education. The response rate was 74 percent (549 surveys returned).

The questionnaire for supervisors contains many items in common with the questionnaires for teachers. After the response patterns to questions describing the supervisor population and their capability to participate in in-service education are reported, responses to questions concerning some variables identified by teachers as critical to the in-service process will be examined.

The supervisors' questionnaire is given in Appendix 1. The supervisors responded to 49 is-ought discrepancy items; the supervisors' discrepancies are reported along with the teachers' discrepancies in Appendix 2.

Participation of Supervisors in In-Service Education

Supervisors serve in a variety of school settings. They work with "mostly rural schools" (20.2%), "mostly urban schools" (38.3%), or "mostly suburban schools" (38.1%). Almost a third (31.2%) of the supervisors are found in the southeastern region of the country: Maryland, Delaware, the District of Columbia, Virginia, West Virginia, North Carolina, South Carolina, Tennessee, Alabama, Georgia, and Florida. This yields an NCSM supervisor for about every 56 000 students in the southeastern region as compared to a supervisor for approximately every 108 000 students in the rest of the country. This difference between regions would hold correspondingly for teachers. It suggests the possibility of exploratory research to search for and identify effects of this degree of supervisory attention. An analysis of the data from the teacher surveys suggests that some regional differences in in-service education may be attributable to the greater number of supervisors in the southeastern region. However, the surveys do reveal regional differences in characteristics of teachers and other factors that need careful control before interpretations can safely be made.

Many supervisors worry that their attention to teachers is spread so thin that they have little probability of significant impact. Eight questions (5–9, 45, 49, and 43) concerned this variable. Most supervisors work with large numbers of teachers. Only 20 percent reported working with 50 or fewer teachers. Thirty-five percent report working with more than 500 teachers, and 26 percent work with between 150 and 500 teachers. It would appear that the majority of supervisors cannot afford the luxury of providing individual attention to each teacher in their system. When coupled with the fact that 56 percent of the supervisors must work with, and learn the characteristics of, more than twenty schools, it is easy to realize the problem a typical supervisor has in simply being familiar enough with a local school's problems to provide service tailored to that school. More than half of the supervisors have responsibility for all schools in their district, K–12.

The statistics paint a picture of a typical supervisor needing to be familiar with all levels of a school mathematics program, knowing the staffs of several different schools, and being able to know well only a portion of the teachers with whom he or she works. Given the other responsibilities entailed by supervision, how much attention can be given to in-service education? The supervisors were asked to "estimate the closest percentage of their time given to administrative tasks (i.e., filling out forms, budget, meetings, paper shuffling, . . .)." Responses to this question (44) were as follows:

a. 10% of time   10.7%
b. 20% of time   28.3%
c. 40% of time   32.0%
d. 55% of time   16.5%
e. 70% of time   12.4%

The responses to question 46, "What percentage of your time do you estimate is given directly to in-service education?" were negatively correlated with these responses. The response pattern was as follows:

a. 10% of time   53.7%
b. 20% of time   26.3%
c. 40% of time   10.3%
d. 55% of time   7.0%
e. 70% of time   2.7%

These results indicate that supervisors have much more to attend to than in-service education. The supervisor must have adequate support services and manage time well to function effectively as an in-service educator. Thus, it is critical to have not only adequate clerical help but, more importantly, a cadre of individuals who can assume a helping, leadership role in providing in-service education. About 75 percent of the supervisors reported (question 41) that one or more teachers were to be found in most of their schools who could be depended on to assume leadership in in-service education—an important potential for a multiplier effect that the supervisor must encourage. The supervisor must also address the problem of finding and using resource people other than teachers. Eighty-nine percent of the supervisors reported that resource people, such as district or state personnel, were available to use in the in-service effort, but only 79 percent of those 89 percent made use of them. Only 62 percent of the supervisors indicated that they would depend on neighboring colleges or universities to provide opportunities for in-service education.

The statistics concerning the number and variety of schools, teachers, and classrooms for which a typical supervisor has responsibility makes it imperative that the administration of local schools be cooperative and supportive. Seventy-eight percent of the respondents reported local school administrators were generally helpful in establishing and implementing in-service programs (question 40), but 28 percent noted that a lack of administrative cooperation at the local school level (question 21) constrained in-service education.

In providing in-service education, the supervisor has many significant problems to cope with above and beyond the fact of needing to deal with so many schools, people, and types of programs. A perennial problem is the budget. Slightly more than 75 percent of the respondents noted that the budget was a constraint on their current in-service program. The supervisors were asked in question 47 to estimate how much their school invested in in-service education per teacher, exclusive of the salaries of supervisory personnel. Their responses were

    a. 0¢ per teacher   10.4%

    b. 25¢ per teacher   14.6%

    c. 50¢ per teacher   10.2%

    d. $1 to $5 per teacher   41.3%

    e. more than $5 per teacher 23.6%

One must question the quantity and quality of in-service education that can be provided in those schools (35.2%) that invest less than a dollar a year per teacher for in-service education. A supervisor must operate shrewdly to seek and find funds for in-service education, and once a source of funds is found, the supervisor must conduct the program in such a way as to maintain that source. Only 28 percent of the supervisors indicated control of discretionary funds for in-service education.

Interestingly, 60 percent of the supervisors reported that the teachers' contract stipulates that a few days be given to in-service education, but

65.8 percent pointed out that their state did not provide money that was "protected" or that could be used only for in-service education. Thus, it appears that about 25 percent of the respondents are in states whose legislators think that in-service education is a good activity for teachers but are unwilling to provide the necessary financial support. The picture appears somewhat worse when it is noted that only 26.3 percent of the respondents indicated access to monies for in-service programs that "are generated from non–local school tax sources."

The data suggest that the supervisors responding to this questionnaire serve more than 150 000 teachers of school mathematics and between nine and ten million students. Since they are a prime enabling mechanism for in-service education, the fact that 35.6 percent of the respondents to the survey indicated their school system was considering doing away with supervisory personnel "because of budgetary problems" is not to be taken lightly. If the position of supervisor in mathematics is terminated, who will watch out for the interests of mathematics for teachers and children? Who will minister to the in-service needs of teachers?

Thus, we argue that it is important for supervisors to be sure to conduct themselves in a politically aware fashion. This means part of their responsibility is to have available evidence of what they are doing to improve the effectiveness of the mathematics program for students and for teachers. In particular, they need evidence of teachers' participation in in-service programs and their views of the effectiveness of the programs. Supervisors also need to be able to speak realistically to the curricular needs of the system correlated with the in-service needs and preferences of teachers. At points, supervisors may even find it appropriate to publicize their school system's program and program needs beyond the educational establishment to build and maintain support of the mathematics in-service program.

The political aspect of being a supervisor is a reality. It is an uncomfortable burden for some. It is reassuring to note that most of the evidence for program effectiveness and needs assessment is needed in order to design and conduct an effective in-service program. The political issues boil down to how should the supervisor use the information and with what audience. We are of the opinion that the supervisor should use information to increase support of the mathematics program. This means operating in a manner to increase the attention, resources, and time given to critical responsibilities such as in-service education, but to decrease the attention, time; and resources given to paper shuffling and other "administrivia." Thus, the interests of teachers can be protected.

An economic reality that the supervisor must face is that in-service education and other supervisory services are negotiable items in collective bargaining. Teachers' groups, administrators, and school boards have often allowed in-service education to intrude into the collective bargaining process. In-service education was reported as a "point of negotiation when teacher groups bargain for new contracts" by 35.2 percent of the supervisors.

The intrusion of in-service education into the collective bargaining process has assumed two different forms in the past. One form of intrusion is in terms of teachers seeking to gain control over the organization, content, and implementation of the in-service program. For example, one question (28) on the survey inquired whether teacher contracts provided a constraint against "after-school" in-service education (33.4% of the supervisors indicated they did). The political activism of many teachers' groups is leading them to a participatory planning function for in-service education and an attempt to control factors in this planning that they believe significant. This can be a healthy factor in in-service education and, in some schools, is testimony to a high order of professionalism by the teachers. At least two states—Minnesota and Pennsylvania—have recently modified their postbaccalaureate certification laws to allow teachers a greater voice in the planning and approval of in-service programs. If the collective bargaining concerns substantive matters of in-service program design and implementation, it is usually evidence of supervisors needing to attend more directly to participatory planning, to needs assessment, and to relating in-service education more specifically to program and teacher needs.

The other manner in which in-service education becomes involved in collective bargaining is more invidious. This form is a financial trade-off of in-service resources for teachers' welfare benefits, such as salary or fringe benefits. To modify a salary or fringe benefit package takes considerable money. Operating expenses tend to be fixed and predictable. Salary is about the only major modifiable factor. In-service education has little apparent, direct effect in the classroom. Therefore, some school boards and a few administrators reason that the only slack in the budget is in supervisory salaries and the expenditure of those monies that affect the classroom the most indirectly. This translates to: Do away with in-service education. And with recent inflationary trends in the economy, teachers' trading in-service funds for personal, "pocketbook" money is quite understandable. Three conclusions are in order:

1. Supervisors need to be sure to collect evidence that demonstrates their impact on teachers and the school mathematics program in order to provide a rationale for the continuation and maintenance of the program.
2. In-service programs need to be established on a "protected dollars" financial base.

3. Supervisors need to accept and use the teachers' desires for full professional partnership in planning and implementing in-service programs.

Several administrative variables that serve to describe supervisors and how they participate in the in-service education program in their school system have been examined. Two summary conclusions are compelling:

1. Supervisors typically have such a variety of responsibilities to so many people and programs that given their limited resources, they must be very careful to marshall them wisely if they are to have any impact on in-service education.

2. The supervisor must face the political realities of finding, using, and maintaining resources in terms of both the preservation of their in-service programs and the encouragement of the professional participation of the teachers with whom they work.

Supervisors' Management of Critical Variables

The survey of teachers' opinions and attitudes about in-service education identified several factors that contribute to the success or effectiveness of in-service programs. Some of these factors will be examined in terms of the supervisors' perceptions of how these factors operate in their school systems and how the supervisors would manage them. Five categories of factors are explored:

1. Availability of in-service programs
2. Mechanisms used to encourage teacher participation
3. Participatory planning and needs assessment
4. Evaluation of the in-service program
5. Supervisors' views of teachers' needs

In-service availability

Teachers indicated a desire to have readily available in-service programs that were tied to school needs. Their perceptions were most positive, and the probability of their participation was improved if the in-service program was conducted by their own school system. Only 28.9 percent of the supervisors indicated that their schools had an organized, regularly scheduled in-service program in mathematics for elementary teachers, and only 24.9 percent of them indicated comparable availability of a program for secondary mathematics teachers. Chi-square analyses indicated that the variables related to availability were primarily financial and in the expected directions. Predictably, the capability of providing release time was a highly significant factor; if the provision of release time (question 20) was not a constraint, then the likelihood of an available program was considerably better at either elementary or secondary levels. Interestingly, if a school system had an organized plan for assessing needs (question 22), or if they had in-service offerings related to long-term curricular plans (question 23), then they were more likely to have in-service available at either level.

Teachers indicated that a pet peeve about in-service education was its generality or its being nonspecific to mathematics teaching. Of the supervisors responding to a question about the availability of a general in-service program not specific to mathematics teaching, 54.4 percent indicated that their school system had such programs, and 58.1 percent indicated that their schools should have such general programs available.

Is the available in-service program throughout the year related to a single theme? Only 19 percent of the supervisors conducted such a program, but 30 percent indicated the availability of several weekly in-service meetings organized around a single topic. About 17 percent of the supervisors are in systems using the single-topic, all-day in-service meetings up to half a dozen times a year, although 65 percent would like such program availability. Interestingly, 63.4 percent of the supervisors avow their programs are short and to the point. (Would that square with the teachers' perceptions?)

Mechanisms used to encourage participation

Teachers' responses to questions about encouraging participation in in-service programs indicated *(a)* that if their school had one means of encouraging participation, the school used several; *(b)* that release time was a critical factor; and *(c)* that immediate, here-and-now financial rewards, such as pay, were important. The supervisors' responses to parallel items—questions 50 through 55 Is and Ought—indicated comparable judgments for the most part. Two major differences occurred, however, in how the teachers and the supervisors would rank these six mechanisms for encouraging participation. Teachers ranked the paying of expenses for in-service education offered by nonschool agencies as more significant than supervisors (question 51 Ought). It is as if the supervisors attribute an importance to keeping control of resources and what they produce. Secondly, supervisors ranked placing the in-service participant in a higher pay bracket (question 55 Ought) greater than teachers did. An apparent interpretation is that teachers are concerned with the here-and-now of rewards, but supervisors were more oriented to rewards that would endure over several years.

Nearly all these mechanisms for encouraging participation in in-service education require money. Only 39.7 percent of the supervisors indicated that teachers in their district participated as other than unpaid volunteers (question 27). One nonbudget item was noted as a major factor in determining teachers' willingness to participate by 63.6 percent of the supervisors—the location or convenience of the in-service program. This appears to be less important to teachers than to supervisors.

The factor of release time is of major significance both to supervisors and to teachers. Eight percent of the supervisors noted as a major constraint the inability to provide teachers with release time in conducting in-service education (question 20). Only 40.2 percent indicated they could use this as a mechanism to encourage participation (question 50 Is), but 94.4 percent felt they ought to be able to use this as a mechanism to encourage teacher participation. Conducting in-service programs at the end of a long and taxing school day is more than a challenge—it is a prime difficulty.

The evidence of the teachers' responses indicates that providing follow-up activities is a critical variable affecting their perception of the in-service program and is a mechanism that encourages participation. Thus, it is reassuring to note that 64 percent of the supervisors do provide follow-up activities after an in-service program. However, it needs to be noted that the nature of the follow-up activities was not specified by the questionnaire for either population. Chi-square analysis indicated that the capability of the supervisor to offer follow-up activity was related to how much time the supervisor invested in administrative tasks (question 44).

Supervisors were asked to respond to four items concerning the ultimate means of encouraging in-service participation. Their responses were as follows:

Should in-service education be required of all who teach mathematics?	Percent yes
13.	85%
In-service education is required to maintain certification.	Lumped Agree and Strongly Agree percentages
90 Is	24.1%
90 Ought	64.6%
In-service education is required to maintain tenure.	
91 Is	14%
91 Ought	58.5%
I can require a particular teacher to attend an in-service program.	
97 Is	18.1%
97 Ought	64.5%

Supervisors in suburban school settings appeared to be somewhat less inclined to want to require participation in in-service education than either rural or urban supervisors.

Participatory planning and needs assessment

Responses to a large number of items on the teachers' survey indicated that the teachers' perceptions of in-service program effectiveness, satisfaction with those programs, gripes, and program success were significantly related to factors of participatory planning and needs assessment. It should be observed that these factors are critical to supervisors for reasons other than the teachers' perceptions of program effectiveness. First, the multitude of responsibilities other than in-service education—and the sheer number of schools, people, and programs with which a supervisor must interact—argues that the supervisor must have leadership at the school level on whom he or she can depend. Needs assessment and participatory planning are mechanisms for sharing the leadership responsibility. They can build into the in-service program a multiplier effect. They can help teachers realize their professionalism and may mean that the teachers have an egocentric involvement or stake in the success of the program. Participatory planning requires management skills and an ability to delegate responsibility. How do supervisors regard teacher involvement in assessing needs and planning?

Question 22 inquired whether the supervisor used an organized process of needs assessment to define and justify in-service program content. Only 42.1 percent of the supervisors responded in the affirmative. Chi-square analyses indicated that they were more likely to respond in the affirmative if they based in-service programs on long-term curricular plans (question 23), if they had control of some discretionary funds (question 43), and, interestingly, if their supervisory responsibilities were limited to the junior high school level. Only 37.6 percent of the supervisors indicated that needs assessment was based on the achievement data of students (question 88 Is), although 72.5 percent responded to the Ought portion of the question that it should be.

But do supervisors believe teachers know their own in-service needs? Forty-four percent of the supervisors indicated they believe "teachers are so inclined to the practical, what-can-I-use-tomorrow attitude that in-service education loses its effectiveness" (question 94 Is). Are these 44 percent of the supervisors willing to give teachers a voice in needs assessment? Question 24 inquired whether teachers' perceptions of in-service program needs were consistent with long-term curricular plans; 59.6 percent of the supervisors responding to this question said not. Does this define a problem for supervisors? Do supervisors need to share more information with teachers in order that their participation in assessing needs and long-range planning is more realistic? Sixty-two percent of the supervisors indicated that their in-service offerings were based on long-term curricular plans (question 23), and 75.5 percent indicated that the teachers with whom they work do participate in long-term curricular planning (question 26), although the nature and extent of this participation was not specified. Almost 83 percent of the supervisors indicated that teachers help them select the topics for in-service education (question 36), and 48.6 percent stated that teachers helped select the organization or administration of the implementation plan for in-service education (question 37).

Supervisors were queried about topics that are and ought to be stressed in in-service programs in their schools. The same topics were used on the teacher surveys. Teachers and supervisors prized the same topics, generally favoring methodological, motivational, and attitudinal topics over mathematical topics. Applications and basic skills were also points of considerable interest.

Evaluation of in-service programs

The evaluation of in-service education is important. It is the base for determining the effectiveness of the program and its efficiency, which, in turn, provide the substance for arguing for the continued support and maintenance of the program by a school board or a school administration. An evaluation of this year's program can also be part of a needs assessment for next year's program. The evaluation may provide the evidence needed to gain resources for a new program or a change of direction in the present program.

A second use of evaluative information is for redesigning the program rather than for seeking resources. To ask teachers to evaluate their in-service experiences provides the supervisor with feedback to modify or re-design the program to fit the needs of teachers better. This sort of information can be used to encourage teacher participation. If you can advertise that 91 percent of the participants in the program last year found it effective, then that will encourage participation in a comparable program this year. Or if you can say that 27 percent of the teachers participating in the program had a gripe and that the program has been redesigned to alleviate that gripe, then potential participants have more reason to expect payoff and good use of their valuable time. Seventy-three percent of the supervisors indicated that they regularly ask participants to evaluate their in-service programs (question 30). A question of significance is whether supervisors consider all the different ways in which that evaluative feedback can be used productively.

A touchy political issue is what should be evaluated. The teachers split into two camps in responding to the question of whether it was appropriate to use data on student achievement to evaluate in-service programs.

Teachers who held the opinion that students were not performing as well in mathematics as they did in the past were opposed to using student achievement data for this purpose. Only 10.3 percent of the supervisors indicated that their school system presently required that student achievement data be included in the evaluation of in-service programs (question 29). Only 37 percent responded that student achievement data should be part of the evaluation (question 89 Ought). With the present orientation to accountability, this will remain an issue. Perhaps the critical problems are who should have access to the student achievement data and for what purpose should they be used. Even though some in-service education program content by its nature may be somewhat removed from a direct effect on student achievement, student achievement data are, at the least, symptomatic of the program's effect. Supervisors should note this information even if it is only for their personal use.

Supervisors' views of teachers' needs

Supervisors have pronounced views of teachers' needs in in-service education. Five items were directed to how secondary and elementary teachers differed. Of the supervisors, 86.6 percent avowed that secondary teachers needed a type of in-service program different from elementary teachers (question 31). Interestingly, the more time a supervisor invested in in-service education (question 46), the less likely the supervisor was to exhibit this opinion. Eighty-four percent of the supervisors believe a methods-oriented in-service program is a greater need of the secondary teacher than a content-oriented program (question 33). Content was judged a greater need for elementary teachers than methods by 57.7 percent of the supervisors. Seventy-two percent of the supervisors indicated that their perception was that elementary teachers wanted in-service for mathematics teaching, but only 39.4 percent believe that secondary teachers want in-service education. It should be noted that this latter perception is in profound disagreement with the evidence of the survey of secondary teachers. The supervisors' judgment of the elementary teachers' wants is somewhat at variance with the supervisors' responses to question 18, "Do you find a constraint on in-service education today because of lack of interest on the part of teachers?"; 63 percent of those responding to this question answered yes.

Three questions inquired about new teachers. Fifty-three percent of the supervisors do not perceive new teachers as being well prepared to teach mathematics (question 10). However, chi-square analyses indicate this perception is more likely to concern elementary teachers and to be held by supervisors in rural and urban school settings. But almost 55 percent of the supervisors report that their school system has a special in-service program above and beyond orientation for new teachers (question

82 Is). However, only 40.7 percent of the supervisors perceive that new teachers expect to participate in in-service education throughout their professional life (question 98 Is).

A final note about supervisors' views of teachers' needs: supervisors responded to the same set of questions concerning the purposes of in-service education as the teachers. There was no appreciable difference between the supervisors' opinions concerning purpose and the secondary teachers' perception of purpose except that supervisors tended to show more realization of the importance of problems faced by all teachers rather than only those relevant to the mathematics teacher. Generally, each of the purposes was important to all the respondents.

Conclusion

Supervisors' views of in-service education in their schools are important to more people than the supervisors themselves. They have first-hand information and experience in marketing and conducting in-service education within the school setting. If in-service education by external agencies, such as colleges and universities, is to move in the direction of more closely relating their in-service programs to school curricular programs and teachers' perceived needs, this first-hand experience is an important consideration.

The two overwhelming factors that appear to relate to practically every response are budget and the number and varying nature of responsibilities of the supervisor. Clearly, the supervisor must be a political animal to be successful. The supervisor must constantly address the problem of building and maintaining resources for the in-service program. Equally clear is the supervisor's task of building on the professionalism of teachers to develop leadership capability within the school staff in order to share those responsibilities.

CHAPTER 4

Guidelines for Designing the In-Service Program

RICHARD WILKES
DWIGHT COBLENTZ
DOROTHY STRONG

IN-SERVICE EDUCATION in mathematics encompasses all activities involved with improving the school mathematics program *and* the continuing development of the mathematics staff members. Planning an in-service program can be complex, since it requires the work and wisdom of many professionals, the consideration of the curriculum, and the marshalling of resources. The purpose of this chapter is to stipulate the major factors that must be accounted for in the planning process. Since planning necessarily touches on all phases of the development and implementation of an in-service program, the principles and processes described in this chapter foreshadow the content of each of the remaining chapters in the handbook.

The chapter begins by examining the setting for in-service education in order to highlight the critical components of the planning process. In the second section of the chapter, these components are related to each other in a decision-making model of the planning process. Needs assessment—as well as other important components of the decision-making process—are highlighted.

The Setting for Planning

The purpose of local educational agencies in providing in-service education for mathematics teachers should include the following goals:

1. To provide teachers with the opportunity, the time, the means, and the materials for improving their professional competencies

2. To assist teachers in applying to themselves new insights into the learning process

3. To help teachers expand their perceptions of mathematics

4. To assist teachers in developing creative instructional approaches that—

    a) are meaningful and mathematically correct

    b) inculcate in students an enthusiasm and satisfaction in learning and using mathematics

5. To provide a means of maintaining quality in the curriculum

6. To provide a means of assigning priorities to school problems and their need for solution

7. To provide a mechanism for responding to problems of a curricular nature, an instructional nature, or to problems in human relations

8. To facilitate a school's making full use of its resources

9. To implement significant, innovative curricular and instructional practices

The planning of mathematics in-service programs should be shared among those who are to receive the service and those who are to provide the service. Administrators traditionally set policies that indicate broad purposes, authorize the allocation of funds and facilities, and provide for the participation of personnel in the school system's in-service program. Once the policy for the mathematics in-service program is set, it should be publicized. This will enable the citizens of the school district to realize the purposes for which funds for in-service education are being used and will help them to be aware of the efforts school mathematics personnel are making to improve the learning of students.

The in-service program should be designed to meet the needs of the locality in which the service is rendered. It should be related to problems that actually exist, that are relevant, and that are of vital concern to teachers. The mathematics teacher's role should not be restricted to instructional decisions alone. Mathematics teachers must contribute to the planning, implementation, and evaluation of the mathematics in-service programs. It is detrimental for any group of teachers, supervisors, curriculum directors, principals, superintendents, or boards of education to consciously or unconsciously clutch power to themselves, assuming that they are so expert and wise that they can bypass others in planning, implementing, and evaluating mathematics in-service programs. Of the messages teachers receive, none are more powerful than those that tell them how much their professional judgment is valued.

An in-service program is not likely to be effective if it is built on imaginary problems. The in-service facilitator must know the needs of the teachers and provide in-service opportunities to address those needs. The program should provide time for growth in understanding, systematic progress in the modification of curriculum and teaching methods, and a gradual reshaping of purposes and objectives for mathematics programs. An element of flexibility must be evident in an in-service program so that it can be adapted to the needs of local systems. Cooperative, goal-directed planning opens the way for flexibility.

The mathematics in-service program must stand up to the test of usefulness. The teachers and administrators must be convinced that the time, energy, and financial resources devoted to the in-service program are yielding benefits and strengthening the mathematical program where it is most needed.

The personnel who take primary responsibility for planning and implementing the mathematics in-service program must be capable of making decisions and must have the authority to do so. The participant's role in the program should be an active one. The program should be financed so that all teachers in the school system will have an opportunity to receive the services essential to the effective operation of the mathematics program. Each participant must have a desire to grow professionally and profit from the in-service experience.

Components of an In-Service Design

The in-service program should be planned to prepare mathematics teachers to implement specific local improvement activities that are directed toward locally determined student needs.

The major components of the system include—

1. the major theme or goal of the in-service program;
2. the rationale for the program;
3. an assessment of needs;
4. a statement of clearly defined objectives and expected outcomes;
5. an implementation model;
6. evaluation procedures.

A model of a relationship between the components of the in-service design process is exhibited in the flowchart in figure 4.1. The flowchart suggests an appropriate order for collecting information, making decisions, and taking action in the process of designing an in-service program. This model will be referred to by the word *systemic* throughout this handbook.

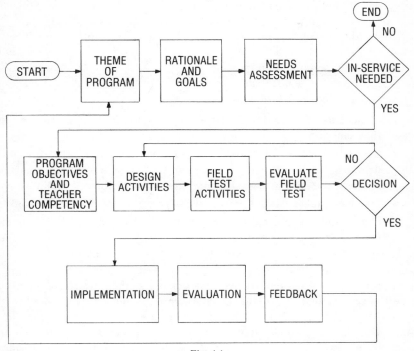

Fig. 4.1

When a school system begins planning a mathematics in-service program, all components of the systemic plan should be considered. On deciding the theme of the program, a rationale for it should be prepared. The rationale should state specific problems in the mathematics program and why they should be solved. The rationale should include empirical and philosophical support for the reasons for the in-service program. It should be formulated in terms of the long-range curricular goals of the school mathematics program.

Needs assessment

An apparent discrepancy between what is desired (goals) and what in fact exists in a mathematics program (performance) defines a problem area for in-service education. The process of finding and verifying the discrepancies and formulating a refined, precise description of them is called *needs assessment*.

The discrepancy approach to needs assessment assures the in-service program planner that two important characteristics are part of the needs assessment. First, needs assessment is related to the curricular program in mathematics. Second, needs assessment is related to performance. Often needs assessments have been based exclusively on opinion. Although personal opinions of apparent needs can be very accurate, they should be verified by data, such as test scores, surveys, and inventories. Needs supported by objective data are realistic needs, which is not always so if needs are identified by personal opinions.

One format for a needs assessment program that could be used by a local school district is the following:

1. Collect data from schools regarding the mathematics program in that school.

2. Compile separate data profiles for high- and low-achieving students.

3. Analyze the data as compiled and draw conclusions of findings.

4. Describe the needs that exist and assign a priority to these needs.

5. Determine the objectives for the in-service program that, if met, meet the needs that exist.

The first three steps in this process are objective in nature; that is, an attempt should be made to gather objective data, compile the data, and draw conclusions from the data without being judgmental. The data need not be limited exclusively to student characteristics but can and should encompass objective information about teachers and the school community setting. The last two steps involve an element of subjective judgment in moving from raw data to statements of the desired objectives. The format assumes that curricular plans for the mathematics program exist. Each statement of need—according to assigned priority—will be translated into a specific objective for an in-service program. These objectives become the blueprint for a comprehensive course of in-service action to improve mathematical achievement.

The needs assessment process is facilitated if the school system has collected and maintained descriptive information about the school mathematics program through the years. Data thus collected provide a comparative benchmark for the discrepancy analyses. An example of a form that could be used to initiate a descriptive collection of baseline data to provide a useful basis for discrepancy analysis is given at the end of the chapter. The form is designed for an elementary school, and the information can be supplied by the principal. A form of parallel design should be used for the secondary school in order that a department chairman can provide the designer of an in-service program comparable information.

After such an initial effort at data collection is begun, the form should be modified and shortened to request only information concerning changes from the previous year and data unique to a given year. Information already available in central office files should not be sought again. The form is long enough that repeated usage without modification might lead principals and department chairmen to make pointed suggestions about appropriate filing techniques.

INSTRUCTIONS FOR COMPLETING
THE SCHOOL MATHEMATICS PROGRAM SURVEY

1. *Please provide only data from your school.*
2. *Please indicate each of your responses with an X, unless numbers or words are required.*
3. *Wherever possible, please provide exact data. If exact data are not available, please estimate carefully.*
4. *Unless specified otherwise, please provide data from the last school year.*
5. *Please respond to each item. If the data requested are unavailable or an item is not applicable, please indicate by the letters UA (unavailable) or NA (not applicable).*
6. *Questions dealing with clarification of items should be directed to:*

     (person designated)
7. *Please return the completed survey questionnaire to the following address within ten (10) days following receipt:*

     (Name)
     (Address)

SCHOOL MATHEMATICS PROGRAM SURVEY

School _____ Date _____

Name of Person Completing Questionnaire _____

Title _____

Administration and Organization

1. Last year, what was the total pupil enrollment for the school? _____
2. Last year, what was the pupil-teacher ratio by grade?

Grade	Ratio	Grade	Ratio
K	_____	4	_____
1	_____	5	_____
2	_____	6	_____
3	_____		

3. Indicate below the number of teachers in your school by the years of assignment to your school.

No. of Years of Assignment to Your School

	1–3	4–7	8+
No. of teachers	_____	_____	_____

4. Last year, the principal was a

      Teaching Principal _____

      Supervising Principal _____

5. In the chart below, indicate the percentage of the principal's time used in the performance of each of the listed duties:

Categories of Duties	Percentage of Time
Administrative duties (including office routine, school plant, business, food services, and transportation)	
Pupil activity programs	
Teaching	
Organization, administration, and improvement of instructional programs, excluding mathematics (includes supervision)	
Pupil personnel (includes evaluation, records and reports, counseling, conferences, discipline)	
School/community relations	
Other _____ (specify)	
TOTAL	100%

6. In the chart below, mark all school organization patterns that apply to your school.

Organization Patterns	Grade					
	1	2	3	4	5	6
Self-contained Classroom						
Team Teaching						
Departmentalization						
Differentiated Staffing						
Nongraded						
Graded						
Multiage						
Other _____ (specify)						

7. In the chart below, mark the dominant grouping used for classroom mathematics activities.

Dominant Grouping	Grade					
	1	2	3	4	5	6
Individualized Instruction						
Small Group (five or fewer students)						
Large Group (six or more students)						
Total Class						
Other _____ (specify)						

8. What was the average number of minutes the teachers in your school devoted to daily mathematics activities?

_____

(Minutes per teacher per grade level)

9. Do you have a mathematics specialist on the school staff? _____ _____

yes   no

If yes, mark the functions the specialist performs:

Curriculum development _____
Remedial mathematics _____
Diagnostic testing _____
Supervision _____
Other (specify) _____

_____

10. Do you have a written curriculum plan for your mathematics program?
_____ _____ If yes, indicate the school year when last revised: _____
yes   no

11. During the past year, have you devoted a staff meeting to the study and review of the mathematics program? _____ _____
yes   no

12. Are remedial mathematics services available to students? _____ _____
yes   no

If yes, who provides the services? _____

13. How many pupils received remedial mathematics services this year?

Grade	Number	Grade	Number
1	_____	4	_____
2	_____	5	_____
3	_____	6	_____

14. Please mark each of the following items that are an integral part of your school's remedial mathematics program.

Released time for remedial activities _____
Coordination with the basal mathematics program _____
Interaction with parents _____
Evaluation activities with teachers or teacher teams _____
Diagnostic testing _____

Supervision

15. Within the school, who supervises mathematics instruction? _____

16. During the last school year, what was the average number of hours each teacher was observed in mathematics instruction?

By school-level observer _____
                                    hrs.
By county-level observer _____
                                    hrs.

Decision Making

17. Who decides the basic approach to be used in mathematics instruction?

_____
(Title)

18. Who decides on the selection of supplementary books and materials?

_____
(Title)

19. Who decides on the testing and evaluation of the mathematics program?

_____
(Title)

20. Who decides the type and length of mathematics in-service training programs to be available to the teachers?

_____
(Title)

21. Who decides how the available teacher aides or volunteers will be used?

_____
(Title)

22. Who decides how much time will be used in mathematics instruction?

_____
(Title)

23. Indicate on the chart below the location of supplementary instructional materials for mathematics.

Location	Supplementary Mathematics Materials	
	Books	Other Than Books
Central		
Classroom		
Central and Classroom		
Other _____ (Specify)		

24. Are periodicals used as a basic resource in mathematics instruction?

      _____ _____

      yes   no

In-Service Training in Mathematics

25. What was the total number of hours of in-service education related to the basal program available to teachers and principals? _____

26. What was the total number of hours of mathematics-related in-service education (excluding in-service training for the basal program) available to teachers and principals? _____

27. How many teachers attended at least one mathematics in-service program?

_____

28. Identify those areas of the instructional program in mathematics that are most in need of in-service attention. _____

Testing Programs

29. Which mathematics tests (standardized) were administered in your school last year?

Grade	*Test*	*Grade*	*Test*
K	_____	4	_____
1	_____	5	_____
2	_____	6	_____
3	_____		

30. Are the results derived from the mathematics tests used by the principals and teachers?

      _____ _____

      yes   no

If yes, indicate how the tests results were used.

_____

_____

_____

31. Did your staff identify strengths and weaknesses of the mathematics program based on the test results? _____ _____
                                                                yes   no
    If yes, please list them.
    Strengths _____
    Weaknesses _____

Finance

32. Last year the total cost/pupil of all instructional materials at the school was
    _____

33. Indicate the cost/pupil of the instructional mathematics materials (exclusive of the library) for the last year.

Purpose and Cost/Pupil of Mathematics Materials

Purpose of the Expenditure	Cost of Mathematics Material

Changes are to be expected in the type of information to be sought for such a collection of baseline data. If, for example, a problem area in the curriculum is identified, then information should be collected about performance in that area and the contributing factors to the problem. As the use of this survey process evolves through the years, the survey should request more precise evidence about strengths and weaknesses of the instructional program in mathematics. Thus, if basic computational skills appear to be a developing instructional problem, the form should be tailored to request specific information about computational skills. This could include information about the percentage of instructional time devoted to drill and practice, subscores of the standardized tests that concern computation, whether the difficulties concern whole number or fractional number understandings, the amount of in-service concerned with skill-building, and the like.

The natural evolution of the survey form through the years can provide a major avenue for realizing a discrepancy-based assessment of needs. The year-by-year comparison of data serves to identify discrepancies and problem areas. If adequate statements describing the school mathematics program goals are available, the discrepancies between performance and what is desired are readily identified.

The information thus collected provides insight and perspective for working with teachers to identify in-service needs. Since a major problem of teacher participation in assessing needs is their lack of information, parts of the information collected should be given to teachers for their consideration as they identify in-service needs. Needs assessment by teachers should be based on an informed professional judgment.

Other components of the design process

The determination of objectives for the mathematics program is another component of the system. Objectives are statements of intent for learner performance. They should describe who will do what, how well, and under what conditions. The objectives will help identify the expected learner outcomes of the mathematics program. An outcome statement describes what the learner should be able to do on completion of the program. As objectives become more specific, the problem becomes well defined and alternative solutions for the problem are easier to identify.

Each activity in the mathematics in-service program must be based on objectives. The objectives of the in-service program must be related to the teacher's classroom objectives if the program is to be a success in terms of student achievement.

Objective-based in-service programs can be more easily evaluated to determine to what extent the activities and instruction of the program affected the competencies attained by the participants. Further, the evaluation of the related student objectives can be measured to ascertain what effect the in-service program for teachers had on student performance. The objectives for the in-service program may need to be revised if the evaluation results indicate a need for different types of activities to insure success in future programs or future activities in the current program.

Once the program has been designed, essential teacher competencies must be identified. Competencies—like objectives—describe what needs to be accomplished, to what degree, and under what conditions. Competencies are statements describing the knowledge and skills about mathematics and mathematics teaching believed to be essential in facilitating the achievement of specified objectives by the learners. Since the mathematics staff may already possess most of the desired competencies, an assessment of staff competencies that are needed—but are found lacking—can form the basis of specific in-service activities. From the discrepancies identified in the assessment of desirable and existing staff competencies, activities need to be designed, screened, and organized to nurture the attainment of the desirable competencies.

One way of determining competencies is to establish decision points in the form of questions, such as the following:

1. What do mathematics personnel need to know in order to implement a program or enable students to achieve specified objectives?

2. What kind of decisions does the mathematics teacher need to be able to make in order to implement such a program?
3. What specific skills are needed by the mathematics teacher to implement the instructional program?
4. What attitudes are conducive to implementing the instructional program?

It is essential that the identification of the requisite competencies be comprehensive. Incomplete identification of competencies can be as hazardous as no assessment at all. Competencies may be generated by ideas that an in-service committee has about what a professional staff should be able to do. The competencies ideally have been identified and described by researchers in mathematics education. It is necessary to verify by objective data whether or not the teachers possess the competencies. Appropriate activities and resources must then be found or developed for the mathematics teacher to use to attain the specific competencies.

From the clearly stated objectives, activities can be identified that have the potential for fostering the behavior identified in the objectives. Not all possible activities are practical or feasible in a given mathematics in-service program. It is necessary to subject the activities to a screening procedure. A set of predetermined questions can assist in designing the most appropriate mathematics in-service program activities. The following questions will assist designers in selecting a practical and feasible in-service program:

1. *Financial outlay.* What is the cost of the activity? Will any present cost be eliminated? What new cost will be added? What source(s) of funding is available?
2. *Time variables.* Whose time and how much is involved? When is the best time to implement the activity? How long will the activity take to complete?
3. *Support services.* What will be required in the way of staff development, organizational change, instructional supplies, and equipment?
4. *Relative advantages.* Does this design meet the needs of teachers better than another? How much revision may be required?
5. *Facilities needed.* What will be the space requirements? What adaptation will be necessary to implement the activity?
6. *Equipment needed.* Does the program require specialized, expensive equipment?
7. *Complexity.* What has to be accomplished for the activity to be implemented? Are logistics a problem?

8. *Compatability.* Does the activity agree with the philosophy and values of the staff, parents, and community?
9. *Resource personnel.* Who will conduct and evaluate the program? Are personnel in the school system sufficiently knowledgeable and expert to staff the program?

These questions should help designers either to substantiate the worth of the activity they have identified or to help eliminate an activity that is impractical or not germane.

Implementation

Factors for implementing a mathematics in-service plan include designating responsibilities, allocating resources, constructing timelines, and establishing lines of communication. Four basic tasks should be considered in the administration and implementation of a mathematics in-service program:

1. *Designating professional staff responsibilities.* Many school personnel within the school system will not be directly involved in the training phase or members of a steering committee for an in-service program. Those involved directly may be concerned with the actual training of staff for the attainment of competencies. Of no lesser importance are those people who are indirectly involved with in-service education. These people provide the necessary support for the implementation, as well as the policy and administration supportive of the program. A clear delineation of responsibilities and roles of the primary personnel facilitates conducting the program, communicating about the program, and identifying the characteristics needed by key personnel.

2. *Assigning specific tasks.* Assigning specific tasks is accomplished after appropriate personnel are identified. They must be contacted and assigned specific primary and secondary responsibilities. It is important that they be informed about, willing to accept, and able to carry out each responsibility. They must realize how they fit into the total mathematics in-service plan and be accountable for those assignments they have accepted.

3. *Establishing timelines.* Timelines are important. Timelines identify when a specific task is to be completed and provide sequence and boundaries for the tasks. They can also provide one criterion for evaluating the progression of the plan.

4. *Establishing lines of communication.* Establishing open channels of communication is vital so that ideas and other inputs can flow among all personnel involved with the mathematics in-service program.

Student objectives and corresponding teacher competencies have been identified; activities for attaining the competencies have been planned and organized; and techniques for administrating the resulting in-service program have been developed. Prior to the implementation of the mathematics in-service program systemwide, a field test should be conducted, if feasible. The field test should simulate as closely as possible the exact conditions that will occur in the actual program. Selected staff should be trained in the desired competencies with appropriate evaluation of their performance. Field-testing provides a method for examining the design or prototype developed through a systems approach.

The last decision point—evaluation—provides a structure to make a judgment about the design or prototype. Evaluation is an important component of the program. If the results of the field-testing are satisfactory, the implementation of the in-service program appears to be sensible. However, evaluation may lead to a revised design. Evaluation and field-testing provide the information about the wisdom of the investment of valuable human and monetary resources. Even thoughtful and diligent planning can be misdirected.

Alternative designs

The description of the components of a systemic program-design process focuses on the local school system's actions and decision making for the in-service program. The capability of the school system for specific implementation activities may be limited. Designers of in-service programs may need to go outside the school system for a feasible program to implement. Some alternatives are considered below, although the in-service training of mathematics teachers is primarily the responsibility of the local school system. Size, resources, and availability of leadership personnel are some of the major areas of constraint that would force a system to seek implementation outside the school system.

Once a school system has identified problems in the mathematics program and has identified the objectives for its in-service program, the designers must select or develop activities for reaching the desired outcomes. This can be done in a consortium consisting of the local educational agency, the state educational agency, institutions of higher education, regional educational service agencies, teacher centers, the private sector of the community, and others. The local agency has the option of using any or all of the aforementioned agencies for information and assistance in implementing its mathematics in-service program.

Colleges and universities are a primary source of implementation outside the school system. Usually, college staffs are agreeable to providing services to a school system for meeting in-service needs of the school staff. For example, the local agency may enter into contractual agreements with the college to provide credit—or, in some cases, noncredit courses—to meet the in-service needs of teachers. Chapter 8 presents a variety of ways colleges provide in-service programs. These include extension courses, independent studies, workshops, certificate renewal programs, and college/ school system cooperative programs. The activities may be for mathematics content or methods for teaching mathematics or some problem that exists at the local level that a cooperative effort may solve. Many colleges will offer activities using the facilities of the local district and, sometimes, using an approved local instructor.

The local agency and college staff must plan, implement, and evaluate the cooperative effort together. The needs of the participants must be satisfied for this segment of an in-service program to continue over time. An existing graduate course in the college catalog does not always meet the needs of mathematics teachers. The college activities in a local educational system's in-service efforts must be planned to meet the needs of the local staff. If the school system can describe accurately and precisely the type of in-service program it wants, it helps college or university personnel to fit activities to the needs of teachers.

In-service implementation can be accomplished through creative use of media. Television and films have been used with some success in mathematics in-service programs. In some school districts, a film series has been used with a great deal of success. In West Virginia, the state department of education purchased the NCTM film series entitled *The Whole Numbers* for loan to local school systems for the in-service education of elementary teachers. The council also has a series of films titled *The Rational Number System.*

The use of televised in-service programs can be an important phase of a school system's in-service program. Television offers mass availability, reaching many sites conveniently and economically, without the distraction of setting up or taking down equipment. It can complement existing activities or initiate new ones. It can reflect in each presentation many hours of preparation, presenting in rapid succession alternative teaching strategies, techniques, and approaches to content. It can relate to teachers' experiences or introduce experiences not yet familiar to them.

Television presentations can provide a full auditory and visual experience, overcoming the traditional dependence on the spoken and written word. Television can motivate teachers by claiming their interest with compelling presentation of content. It can dramatize the importance and usefulness of what is being taught. It can set up intriguing opportunities for application and illustrate convincingly different teaching strategies.

If local school districts possess television cameras, videotape recorders, and receivers, teachers may decide to use the equipment to observe themselves in follow-up activities with other teachers in order to strengthen their classroom techniques. Many colleges are using microteaching techniques with preservice teachers. These techniques are applicable in the in-service setting as well.

Visitation programs can provide a stimulating alternative in-service experience for teachers. One phase of a mathematics in-service program may include visits to other teachers, classrooms, or schools. The observation of a new mathematics program, new organizational design, or another teacher's method of teaching with immediate follow-up discussions can be a meaningful in-service experience, especially for inexperienced teachers. The observations may be within the teacher's own department or in a science room where mathematics applications can be observed. A teacher may observe differing methods of teaching as well as content development in other schools or school systems. Much planning is necessary for such observations and follow-up to be meaningful. Objectives must be predetermined and evaluated if the visitation program is to be considered a viable in-service activity for a local district.

The concept of the workshop has evolved over the past few years to what can be defined as a group of teachers studying common problems through small-group and individual sessions. For the most part, the workshop is flexible enough to permit teachers to work separately with assistance from consultants or other teachers. Workshops are of great value in many phases of an in-service program because of their flexibility. There are many types of workshops, ranging from faculty workshops that may continue all year to simply an afternoon session; summer work conferences of three to five days' duration to a three-hour session on Saturday. The one-time, three-hour workshop is not well suited for satisfying the desires and needs of in-depth study for teachers.

Summer workshops of extended duration concentrating on teacher-assessed needs are of great importance to many districts, since teachers have no teaching assignments and can plan for the coming school year. These summer workshops can be followed up with faculty workshops that continue through the school year.

Whenever workshops are conducted, they must be preceded by planning that is based on the problems, interests, and needs identified by the participating teachers. Each workshop should be designed specifically to solve one problem of the group. The evaluation of each workshop will provide feedback for future workshops to be conducted in the school system.

No activity is so effective in serving a given purpose or so broad gauged in its effectiveness for a variety of purposes that it should be used to the exclusion of other activities. Each activity tends to be distinctive in serving a limited array of purposes. Each activity should be selected for use in terms of its uniqueness. In-service plans should be structured for a diversity of activities, time schedules should be guidelines to progress, flexibility within structure should be encouraged, and there should be planning to revise the structure itself.

Some Cautionary Remarks about Implementation

In the previous sections, a systems approach to developing a mathematics in-service program has been expounded. Once each component of the system has been specifically planned, the planners must see that the system is properly implemented and evaluations of each component made to provide feedback for possible revisions of the implementation phase of the program.

The climate for open exchange of ideas and viewpoints is essential for the involvement of teachers. Means must be identified and used for getting the instructional staff actively involved as the subjects rather than merely as the objects of instructional improvement efforts. One of the few certainties in the field of human endeavor is the relationship between involvement in an enterprise and the commitment to its goals. Receivers of in-service education must be involved in the planning of the components of the system throughout the mathematics in-service program to insure relevance and continuity.

The success of an in-service program can stand or fall on the availability of materials. Two levels of availability must be considered. First, vicarious experiences are not enough. If teachers are expected to use certain materials in the classroom, the in-service program must facilitate "hands on" experiences with these materials. Second, and equally as important, the materials used in in-service programs must be readily available for use in the classroom. Too often in-service activities have ended with the in-service leader saying to the teachers, "Look what you could do if you had the materials I am using. However, since you do not have these materials, go back to teaching as usual with my blessings and no materials for your excuse."

It is fundamental that one does not get something for nothing. In-service education involves cost in terms of time and money for staff, materials, and facilities. Staff members must be freed by whatever administrative devices are necessary so that individuals and groups can engage in in-service activities in earnest. Staff members must be assigned in-service leadership responsibilities with high priority labels attached. Budgetary allocations must provide for payment for release time of the participants, visiting consultants, and materials.

Resources and conditions that need to be identified for an in-service program go beyond money, facilities, time, and materials. One must consider incentives for participation, teachers' skills and academic background, pupils' achievement, the instructional objectives of the school system and its evaluation procedures, and a climate conducive to the free exchange of ideas and values.

Incentives for teachers to participate must go beyond intrinsic motivation for personal development. Released time, advanced certification, college credit toward renewal or advanced degrees, stipends, and promotion are a few incentives that have been used successfully by some school systems. However, care must be taken to see that the incentives remain the incentives and never become the primary objectives of the in-service program. Where incentives become the primary objective for the participants, very little change in performance in the classroom may be observed. The in-service leader must be ever concerned with the question, "Is the in-service program worthy of the teachers' time and effort without the incentives?" Incentives in some form are necessary for participants, however; a successful in-service program must be a valuable experience for the participants and ultimately provide for a better classroom experience for the students.

Management of the Planning Process

Planning—the key to the management of any educational enterprise—has not always been of high priority in the development of mathematics in-service programs. A prime reason for this is that often no one is provided with the time and resources for the planning activity. The need to have individuals involved in planning in-service programs—both short- and long-range—is one of the best reasons for the existence of mathematics supervisors and coordinators in the local school districts. An extensive commitment of time is required to assess both the needs of the mathematics program and the teachers to set goals of the mathematics program and of the in-service program, to determine available resources, to implement the total plan of action, and to evaluate the effectiveness of the program. The number of different individuals and agencies involved indicates a need to plan for the articulation and cooperation among all agencies and individuals.

Planning is concerned with determining what is to be done so that practical implementation decisions can be made later. Planning is a process for determining the desired outcomes and identifying the necessary steps for getting there in the most effective and efficient manner possible. A systemic approach—or at least a modified version—is a useful attack on the problems of planning. A systemic approach is a planning process by which needs are assessed, problems identified, objectives set, implementation procedures outlined, and evaluation and feedback considered before the program is to commence. One should examine closely the total set of components of an in-service program in the planning phase. The whole system should be in focus at the beginning of the planning phase; that is, all components of the in-service system should be considered simultaneously and then each segment planned definitively. Individuals responsible for planning in-service programs may do it on their own or they may choose to use an advisory committee. The nature of mathematics in-service programs seems to make it most suitable for the use of an advisory committee. The committee should have more responsibility other than being a simple sounding board for the planner. The committee may make and carry responsibility for decisions and perform some of the tasks required in carrying out the in-service program.

To develop an in-service program, the planner is encouraged to employ some type of model of educational management. The components as listed in this chapter may be placed in two broad categories to add clarity to the process—(1) problem identification and (2) problem solution. Even if one does not adhere to a totally formal management process, the steps outlined in this chapter provide a sense of direction. They at least focus the action on the purpose of in-service education.

The first major task in developing a new in-service program or modifying an existing one is to conduct a thorough assessment of needs so that one knows what objectives the program should try to achieve. The second major task is to plan a program that will achieve these objectives. Once this is done, the developers of the new program should prepare a written plan. The plan must provide a clear description of what the design is to achieve, how it will operate, and how its progress and outcomes can be evaluated. This document should be developed—whether or not outside funds are being requested—because it makes the planners responsible for the program planning decisions. In addition, the act of writing such a plan helps the planners strengthen the rationale and encourages them to explore alternative programs, since they must justify their recommendations for the implementation of the plan. Even a "low budget" plan should have a written explanation of the reasons for its recommendations. This explanation should include the plans for the program's operation and evaluation.

The systemic approach to planning demands that (1) the objectives of the in-service program be clearly identified, (2) the possible alternatives for achieving each of the objectives be specified, (3) the cost related to the achievement of the objectives be specified, (4) a model be constructed that defines the relationships among objectives, alternatives, and costs, and (5) a means be developed for indicating, from the application of the model, the preferable alternative.

The preceding sections have provided an outline of educational systems planning. It is one way of assuring that relevant and practical solutions will be identified, selected, and applied to existing problems. Systemic planning prevents planners from concentrating on how to provide in-service education for teachers before identifying what to provide. Identifying the "what" must precede the "how" in systemic planning. An attempt should be made to apply these techniques to the problems of mathematics in-service education for teachers.

Finally, the principles and processes of systemic program design advocated in this chapter sound more than a little complicated and appear to require considerable investment of time and energy. Clearly, this is true when initiating this management system. However, employing these management procedures over a number of years has a cumulative effect; the orientation to information collecting and decision making becomes habituated. The majority of the participants in the planning process expect to use the systemic planning and management activities and find them natural and efficient in application.

Summary

A systemic approach to mathematics in-service programs lends itself to a properly balanced program that provides for input from all levels of the educational community as well as the lay citizens in a given school system.

The major components of a system to develop and insure a successful mathematics in-service program have been identified. The components discussed were rationales for the in-service program, needs assessment, student objectives, in-service program objectives, and evaluation and feedback. The systemic design processes advocated in this chapter may be completely adhered to or modified to meet local needs.

CHAPTER 5

Characteristics of Successful In-Service Programs

THOMAS E. ROWAN
ERNESTINE CAPEHART
GLYN H. SHARPE

THE PURPOSE of this chapter is to describe some of the ingredients that contribute to the success of in-service education programs. The first part of the chapter considers the process of identifying and meeting the needs of teachers. The second part discusses the process and problems of conducting the in-service program. Within this second section, the contributing factors of good leadership, program operation, and follow-up are considered. Finally, a summary section reviews the main points of the chapter.

Meeting the Needs of Teachers through In-Service Education

Fifty-one percent of the elementary school teachers and 37 percent of the secondary school teachers surveyed by the NCTM In-Service Project indicated they were satisfied with the in-service programs they had attended in the past. If satisfaction were the criterion, we would have to infer that the past in-service programs of the surveyed teachers had not been successful. Even if we declare that satisfaction, although highly desirable, is not the primary goal of in-service education, we still cannot be happy with the implications of these results. There definitely seems to be ample cause for seeking ways to improve in-service programs. First, though, we consider the criteria indicative of the success of an in-service program.

93

Most educators would agree that the ultimate goal of in-service education is to improve student learning. Unfortunately, this does not help much, since the in-service program deals with the teacher rather than the student. Other goals more directly related to teachers include satisfaction, improved professionalism, increased teaching skills, and improved knowledge of content. A discussion of goals is provided in chapter 1. The characteristics of successful programs that are considered focus on the goals of the teacher and therefore are likely to promote better student learning.

The characteristics that indicate success are almost certain to differ from one teacher to another simply because needs and expectations of teachers differ. They will even be different for the same teacher at different times and in different circumstances. This apparent ambiguity would seem to make the task of designing successful programs very complex. Fortunately, this is not the case. The ambiguity helps identify the first and most critical step in planning in-service efforts: the *identification of the needs* of the teachers who are to participate.

The survey found that 44 percent of the elementary school teachers and 43 percent of the secondary school teachers reported they had not been asked to help identify topics for their own in-service programs. At the same time, more than 92 percent of each group felt they should be asked. Since the identification of teachers' needs is vital to success, asking the teachers to help identify their needs would be a logical part of the process, but this is not occurring.

On the other hand, teachers are not in a position to be held totally responsible for identifying their own in-service needs. Many of the topics on which teachers may need in-service education are new. Teachers may not be aware of them. Ralph Tyler has said that both the teachers and the administrators must play a role in determining needed professional growth (Rubin 1971, pp. 3–17). That not only seems logical, it is essential. A national program such as metrication may dictate in-service needs, or data from a standardized test may point to an area of weakness in the school mathematics program that can be strengthened through an in-service program. Cooperative planning of in-service activities would minimize teachers' dissatisfaction while maximizing the effectiveness of the programs.

One reason for assessing needs is to inform and educate teachers. A teacher instructs a limited number of students in a small portion of the mathematics program. The teacher may not be aware of the contribution of his or her teaching to the total mathematical experience of the child and its impact on the needs and frustrations of other teachers. The junior high school teacher who stresses number concepts and skills almost exclusively may not realize the effect on students' geometrical intuitions and the consequent impact on instruction in graphing in first-year algebra. The needs assessment process should inform and educate teachers about the effects of their teaching beyond performance in their classrooms. It should broaden the perspective of teachers to the larger problems in the long-range curricular outcomes of the school mathematics program.

An in-service need that is completely outside the realm of a teacher's experience may develop. For some teachers, teaching about the metric system is such an example; prior experience provided little guidance concerning instructional needs. For such a completely new program, the purpose and nature of the in-service program should be communicated to the teachers prior to any decision to implement the program. This can be accomplished through minidemonstrations that provide samples of the program, through peer communication using teachers experienced with the program, or through a short awareness program that explicates the need and describes the program. Using these, the teacher can make judgments of need on an informed, rational basis.

There is evidence that in-service programs can change pupil performance. The Specialized Teacher Project, one of the California Miller Mathematics Improvement Programs, demonstrated over a three-year period that students achieved better when taught by teachers who had in-service training in the use of mathematics laboratories and manipulative materials (State Board of Education 1972). This large study extended over three years. The results certainly support the value of in-service education. Participation by teachers in a second summer's follow-up workshop produced substantial improvement in pupil performance. More research is needed to study some specific in-service problems, such as the appropriate balance between content and method in a program.

In *Improving In-Service Education,* edited by Louis J. Rubin, Lippitt and Fox declare that "most in-service activities should be carried on within a setting in which people who work together have an opportunity to learn together" (1971, pp. 133–69). Following this recommendation can increase the chance of identifying common needs or perceptions of teachers. If a need is identified, its probability of being recognized by the entire group is greater if there is close rapport within the group. Just a few individuals who realize the need can often cause the group as a whole to accept it.

Even though the team-of-teachers approach is an accurate and effective means for identifying and meeting needs, we cannot ignore the fact that many needs can be neither identified nor met in this way. Lippitt and Fox also recognize and speak to this fact. They suggest a variety of target groups for needs assessment and in-service education: *(a)* the administrators, *(b)* the school building staff, *(c)* teachers with a common interest, *(d)* the total school system, *(e)* individual teachers, *(f)* cross-role training groups, *(g)* continuing committees, *(h)* task forces, and *(i)* teaching teams (1971, pp. 133–69). A sound approach to a comprehensive in-service program for a school system should at some time consider the needs that might exist across any such groups or collections of individuals. Questionnaires, local discussion groups, surveys, analyses of student achievement, and other means should be used to help identify needs. These needs can then be categorized and priorities established. In-service program planning can then be designed in terms of the priorities.

National surveys can provide data that suggest in-service topics for further investigation at the local level. For example, the National Advisory Committee on Mathematics Education (NACOME) report cites a survey by the National Council of Teachers of Mathematics (NACOME 1975) that indicated that 37 percent of the elementary teachers in the survey had never used a mathematics laboratory and 10 percent had never used manipulative materials at all. Such data suggests the need for local investigation of this topic to determine whether to offer an in-service program to make teachers comfortable with, and improve their skills in, using manipulative materials. Such a course might be designed either for a school staff—all of whom have a common interest in it—or for an entire school system on an open enrollment basis.

Determining the needs of teachers is essential for successful in-service education. Teachers should be involved in the selection of topics and approaches. It should be a cooperative venture involving the teachers *with* the administration. Ultimately, the decision to implement an in-service program must be a joint decision if the probability of success is to be enhanced.

Conducting Successful In-Service Education Programs

There are many facets to implementing an in-service program that speaks to the needs of the participants and provides activities and materials that successfully serve those needs. Lippitt and Fox (1971, pp. 133–69) have posed several questions to be answered in improving teaching practice through in-service education:

1. What strategies will lead to institution of a program? What approaches can be used to involve the teachers in the need to participate in a program of learning opportunities?

2. Who are the appropriate targets of in-service training activities? Who needs to be reached by a particular training program?

3. Who should be the training specialists?

4. What framework is necessary in the training activities to provide continuity between initiation of a program and subsequent support efforts toward change? What will be the role of supervision?

5. What would be the content, methodology, and design of the learning activities?

6. What types of support materials are needed to facilitate and implement training activities?

We have discussed a part of the first of these six questions in the preceding section. The second part of that question deals with getting teachers to participate in the program once it is designed. If there has been cooperative planning and if the program really does meet the needs of the teachers, then problems of encouraging attendance should be minimal.

Teacher participation in in-service education programs can be encouraged through a variety of approaches. The NACOME report (1975) suggests that "possible factors might be release time, educational leave time, university credit stipends, credits toward other negotiated benefits, and incentive teaching materials." Poppen and Huelsman (1968, pp. 86–90) list six approaches:

1. **Extended service.** Under this plan teachers could be placed on an extended service contract for a pre- or post-school workshop. The teacher's salary would be prorated or a flat stipend would be paid.

2. **Overload.** The overload arrangement allows teachers to be paid on an hourly basis for attending inservice meetings after school and on Saturdays. Teachers could be paid on a basis which is prorated per hour according to the teacher's yearly salary or teachers could be paid on a flat rate basis. Overload meetings could be bi-monthly, weekly, or as needed.

3. **Substitute teachers.** Under this plan substitutes could be hired on a half-day or a daily basis to release one, two, or more teachers.

4. **Independent study by pupils.** Teachers could arrange for children to have one or two hours of independent study in the library under the supervision of some other staff member. Teacher aides could supervise the independent study of pupils for short periods of time.

5. **Visitation days.** (Visiting another teacher in the same, or a different, building.)

6. **Early school dismissal.** Under this plan students would be released from school early once each month. During this time, teachers would remain on duty for inservice opportunities.

Whatever the means, it is best for the school system to attempt some kind of adjustment in staffing patterns to encourage and facilitate participation if it really cares about in-service success. Probably the worst possible arrangement is having tired teachers come for long in-service sessions after their regular workday is completed and with no compensation other than professional growth. Some school systems presently release teachers on half or whole days one or more times a month. An interesting staffing mechanism is the "floating faculty." This is a group of ten to fifteen skilled teachers who are not assigned to a specific school in a system. They can go into any school in the system and release part or all of the teachers for a variety of in-service activities. Part of the in-service activity might include observing the "floating faculty" at work.

Once the arrangements are made and the teachers are in attendance, the success of the program depends primarily on three factors: the leadership, the nature of the program, and the follow-up.

Leadership

> Of the best leaders
>   The people only know they exist;
> The next best they love and praise;
>   The next they fear;
> And the next they revile.
>   When they do not command the people's faith
> Some will lose faith in them,
>   And then they resort to recriminations!
> But of the best, when their task is accomplished,
>   Their work done,
> The people all remark,
>   "We have done it ourselves."
> —Lao-Tze (ca. 600 B.C.)
> (Henry 1957, p. 157)

Obviously, the value—and perhaps the mystery—of good leadership is not a new concept. All too often, however, in-service leaders have a lesson to teach that seems so obviously important to them that the necessity of employing good leadership skills fades completely from view. The sad thing is that the lesson may well be just as important as the leaders think, but unless they employ effective methods, the participants may never know that. This is a particularly critical consideration for in-service education. Usually the participants in in-service education are themselves leaders in their classrooms and schools. Leading such a group of leaders requires more than ordinary concern and attention for the value of bringing them to feel that it is their program and it is being done by *them*.

Several points about leadership are pertinent. First, it has been pointed out by Coffey and Golden (1957, pp. 67–102) that groups progress toward change more effectively if they have participatory rather than supervisory leadership. At the same time the members of the group are more satisfied and persist in the group activity if the group really reaches decisions that seem important. This implies that the leadership, although participatory, should clearly *lead*. That is, participants need to feel they are learning and accomplishing. Finally, Coffey and Golden indicate that a group will be more productive if it feels the leader has institutional influence and can make needed changes at the system level.

All this is not to make the task of leading an in-service program seem impossible; it simply underscores the importance of thoughtful, considerate leadership. Parker (1957, pp. 103–28) lists twelve guidelines for in-service education that a good leader should employ:

1. People work as individuals and as members of groups on problems that are significant to them.
2. The same people who work on problems formulate goals and plan how they will work.
3. Many opportunities are developed for people to relate themselves to each other.
4. Continuous attention is given to individual and to group problem solving processes.
5. An atmosphere is created that is conducive to building mutual respect, support, permissiveness, and creativeness.
6. Multiple and rich resources are made available and are used.
7. The simplest possible means are developed to move through decisions to actions.
8. Constant encouragement is present to test and to try ideas and plans in real situations.
9. Appraisal is made an integral part of inservice activities.
10. Continuous attention is given to the interrelationship of different groups.
11. The facts of individual differences among members of each group are accepted and utilized.
12. Activities are related to pertinent aspects of the current educational, cultural, political, and economic scene.

Many of these guidelines may seem obvious, but the evidence—such as the responses to the surveys of mathematics teachers reported in chapter 2—indicate that many of these guidelines are often not employed in in-service courses.

A successful in-service leader makes the goals of the program clear to the participants and gives them a chance to modify those goals in a reasonable manner. Once the goals are clear and agreed on, the leader should give each participant the opportunity to select those goals to be stressed by that participant, according to his or her special needs. The use of this technique requires that the leader know the participants' strengths and weaknesses. Such knowledge will also enable the leader to make use of those individuals in the group who are respected by the others. They are leaders within the group and can be a valuable resource to the in-service leader.

Getting to know the strengths and weaknesses of the participants as early as possible is an important aspect of appraisal. Appraisal can be made an integral part of the in-service process in a variety of ways. Regular appraisal based on class activities, as well as more formal assessment, can help keep the in-service activities on target, as well as make growth apparent to the participants. Opportunities for self-appraisal and leadership appraisal will also contribute to the program's success. It cannot be stressed too much, though, that this appraisal should be brief, often informal, and to the point. Single-question written responses, observation during discussion, participant-designed procedures, and other means can be used to gather the necessary information without unduly interrupting the regular flow of activities.

The program

"Show teachers in an inservice activity how to make something for use in the classroom out of four pipe cleaners and they will go home satisfied, but try to give them anything related to learning theory and it's instant turn-off" (Dillon 1974, pp. 137–40). This is certainly an overstatement of the situation, but it does serve to remind us that teachers generally favor programs that are not overburdened with theory. In the survey of mathematics teachers, 82.5 percent of the elementary and 76.8 percent of the secondary school teachers expressed the desire to complete in-service programs with materials for classroom use that they had made themselves. Only 52 percent of the elementary and 33 percent of the secondary school teachers said this had really happened. Recent NCTM meetings have demonstrated a phenomenal interest by teachers in workshop sessions combining content, methods, and materials. Suydam and Riedesel (1972) found that among teachers, "the most agreement was expressed for courses which *combined* content and methods." One implication growing out of this desire of teachers is, as was stated in the NACOME Report, "that the background of instructors in both pre-service and in-service courses for teachers include not only the relevant mathematical competence but both current experience and interest in the mathematical curriculum of the level those teachers will teach" (NACOME 1975). This observation is supported by the results of the survey.

The NACOME Report weakly documents a point that is often cited and that also heightens the importance of good in-service leadership methods: "Teachers are essentially teaching the same way they were taught in school" (1975). NACOME also makes the point that more accurate descriptions of what teachers do are needed. If the techniques used by the leader are those that it is hoped the teacher will use, then the chances are greater that the teacher will in fact employ those techniques in the classroom.

There is evidence that in-service programs have not respected the judgment and needs of teachers in even the simplest ways. For example, the survey data indicate that 94 percent of the elementary and 89 percent of the secondary school mathematics teachers said that in-service programs should be short and to the point, but only 36 percent of the elementary and 27 percent of the secondary school teachers in the survey said this presently happens. Forty-eight percent of the elementary and 30 percent of the secondary school teachers in the survey said they could not even use the in-service mathematics in their teaching. In the pilot NCTM survey cited in the NACOME Report, 88 percent of the surveyed teachers felt a need for in-service education, but 61 percent felt that it had not fit their needs.

Several of Parker's guidelines for leadership bear emphasis here. Guideline 6 calls for multiple and rich resources. Do in-service programs generally meet this guideline, or are most programs of the lecture-exhortation type? Of course there should be some caution used in respecting this guideline. An in-service program brimming with resources that the teacher has little or no hope of obtaining for use in the classroom can be demoralizing. The answer, though, is to make the resources available in the classrooms rather than to make in-service programs dull and dry.

Guideline 8 suggests that teachers try out ideas and materials developed in the in-service program in the reality of their classrooms. Teachers who apply the materials and ideas in their classroom have performed a field-testing and can evaluate them effectively. If problems develop in the application, an opportunity to refine or modify the materials based on this experience is presented at the next session. The entire group of participating teachers can build their professional judgment by sharing their experiences of the benefits and the problems in using the materials and ideas. If the classroom techniques are new, the realization that other teachers are trying the techniques often encourages teachers to make a more thorough and enthusiastic test in the classroom. They are more likely to continue to use those ideas and materials that prove effective and beneficial. The trying out of ideas and materials is not complete if the results are not shared.

Making appraisal an integral part of the in-service program (guideline 9) is a sound and useful suggestion. Implementation of this guideline will encourage teachers to do the things we really want them to do. That is, it will encourage them to assess the operational level of each student and provide for individual differences. It will encourage them to make informal, formative judgments about the attainment of objectives during instruction and activity phases rather than always to resort to formal, summative testing. This is more likely to happen if appraisal is a routine part of the in-service program; it is not likely to happen if appraisal is merely discussed in the program.

One pitfall that some school systems fall into is failure to separate means from ends. In-service programs are a means to an end. Assessing needs is a means to an end. Methods of conducting in-service programs are a means to an end. If any of these means become the ends (i.e., the goals of the system), then the efforts have a greatly reduced likelihood of success.

Follow-up

In the survey of mathematics teachers, 84 percent of the elementary and 79 percent of the secondary school teachers surveyed said that systematic follow-up in the classroom should be provided after, or as a part of, in-service programs. Only 17 percent of the elementary and 9 percent of the secondary school teachers said this actually happens. Why should such a wide discrepancy exist? It seems logical that such follow-up would be vital to the lasting success of an in-service program. Another result of the survey indicated that 83 percent of the elementary and 84 percent of the secondary teachers felt that an individual in the building or school system should be responsible for mathematics in-service education. Only 32 percent of the elementary and 29 percent of the secondary teachers surveyed said this is actually true of their school systems. Obviously, one problem with follow-up is a problem of logistics and feasibility. Who will do the follow-up? How can follow-up be handled if there are a large number of teachers participating in the in-service program?

The amount and type of follow-up activity depends on the characteristics of the program and of the participants. A program designed to help teachers use new instructional materials and techniques in the classroom may require more follow-up activity than a program designed to teach specific content in mathematics. New teachers who are hesitant or tentative about the classroom application of unfamiliar teaching strategies may need more supportive follow-up than experienced, confident teachers operating at a sophisticated level of professionalism. The nature of the materials used in the program may require follow-up so that the materials can be thoroughly evaluated. Follow-up activities should be designed to serve at least one of the four purposes listed below.

1. To provide a supportive, consultive atmosphere for teacher participants
2. To refine, adapt, and modify the materials and techniques serving as the base for the in-service instruction to fit better the specific classroom needs of the teacher
3. To identify the needs and strengths of each participating teacher
4. To appraise the effectiveness of the in-service program and associated materials

Each of these purposes of follow-up activities is more readily accomplished if the teacher participates in the follow-up. The importance and significance of each purpose is a function of the type of in-service program and the characteristics of the participants. Green and others report the varied effects of follow-up activities for differing in-service program structures in a setting employing the Indiana Mathematics-Methods Project (MMP) teacher education materials in in-service education (Green et al. 1976).

If a program has been cooperatively initiated, developed, and conducted, the importance of the first purpose of follow-up is minimized. Teachers who feel that the in-service program's goals are really *their* goals have a less critical need for supportive follow-up and, in many cases, can plan its nature and frequency themselves. Follow-up efforts do tend to make the teacher feel that the program is really important.

There are a variety of possible ways to arrange for follow-up. Some school systems include half-days of released time for follow-up activities connected with summer in-service programs. Or follow-up may take the form of a newsletter that shares ideas between in-service participants in different locations. Another form of this kind of printed follow-up is the use of evaluation forms to have participants rate the usefulness of the program. Any method that is chosen will require careful planning. This planning should be accomplished in connection with planning the overall program.

Some in-service programs use television or film as the primary system of communicating ideas. Where this is done, follow-up efforts become even more crucial because of the impersonal nature of the delivery system. Personal and human follow-up is probably desirable in this type of program. One way in which this type of follow-up might be provided is through an established facility such as a regional teacher or curriculum center. Participants can be brought together to discuss and evaluate their experiences. Such centers can also be used for follow-up of other types of in-service education, as well as be the setting for the presentation of programs. Another valuable source of follow-up is the local mathematics specialist or supervisor. If these leaders are involved in the planning, implementation, and follow-up, it can greatly simplify all aspects of in-service program delivery.

Because of sheer numbers and the lack of specialized mathematical training, elementary teacher programs are often more difficult to provide and to follow up than those for secondary school mathematics teachers. Two solutions that can be applied to these problems are seldom used. First, the nature of the elementary school makes the team approach to in-service education particularly attractive and cost effective. If the team approach is used and if the elementary school has one teacher who has special skills in mathematics, then that teacher can be a participant and also share the leadership—with particular emphasis on follow-up. Another approach that is presently overlooked in many schools is the use of the elementary principal as a partner in the in-service leadership and follow-up. If the team approach is used, the principal should be expected to play this role for each in-service program undertaken by the teachers. This would enhance and build the principal's instructional leadership role in the school. Such a cooperative approach to instructional improvement through in-service education should have the mathematics specialist, the principal, and a classroom teacher with mathematics skills work together to implement the in-service process.

At the secondary level there are often department chairmen who would, if given adequate time and responsibilities, be able to facilitate the follow-up process within the school building. The effectiveness of this department leader might be increased if he or she were elected by the other members of the faculty on a regular cycle—perhaps every two years. Any teacher who met designated qualifications would be eligible for the position. Such election would give the department chairman more stature with the teachers. Appropriate qualifying requirements would assure that the teacher elected had the proper experience and training.

Summary

Ingredients contributing to successful in-service programs have been discussed. Education, including in-service education, is a complex process influenced by a myriad of factors. There are many factors that may contribute to success. The claim that many in-service programs are not viewed as successful by those who participated in them has been substantiated through the survey data. The belief that good in-service education does improve teacher performance and student learning has been supported by research.

A few of the more important ingredients contributing to the success of in-service programs are—

1. the identification of needs and cooperative planning;
2. the encouragement of participation in in-service programs through adequate funding and released time;
3. good leadership—the best is participatory but nevertheless leads to definite decisions and has the power to influence the system;
4. the team approach, which provides in-service programs for teachers who work together;
5. the proper combination of content and methods in the program;
6. having teachers take from in-service programs instructional materials that they can use in classrooms—the materials can be teacher-made or commercial;

7. the use of appraisal as an integral part of each in-service program;

8. regular and appropriate follow-up in the classroom and in subsequent progress review sessions.

Throughout this chapter the importance of cooperative activity has been stressed, but the onus for concern and action has been laid primarily on the supervisor or administrator. On the one hand, it is obvious that school system leadership is a critical factor. On the other hand, it should be quite clear that the role and responsibilities of the classroom teacher or in-service participant are equally vital. Rubin (1971, pp. 263-78) has spoken to this issue eloquently:

> Where the desired change is a matter of ritual, the difficulties are minor. Where it is a matter of value, or belief, or master craftsmanship, there is no easy way. The individual must fend for himself, negotiating among the available choices and anticipating that good intent must be conjoined with determination, that the chief rewards will come in the shape of intrinsic satisfaction, that success is not inevitable and the goal not permanent, that change is never free from stress, that skills enlarge with practice and atrophy with neglect, and that despite his best efforts he may fall short with some of his students. Even in the face of these risks, however, the vast majority of teachers will accept the odds if there is a reasonable opportunity to grow. They will accept them because the alternative is to be deprived of satisfying labor and to remain inert.

CHAPTER 6

Resources for the In-Service Program

DAVID DYE
ALEXANDER TOBIN

A VITAL, critical aspect for any in-service education program is to insure that resources are available and are used. This chapter will explore the resources—human, physical, time, and financial—that must be taken into account when a local program manager plans in-service activities.

Ultimately, the financial resources available for use will determine the character and extent of the in-service program. Hence, the person charged with providing the in-service experience for teachers must search for, and secure, these funds. At the same time, that person must be aware of the human resources available, both as leaders and as participants in the in-service program, whether from inside or outside the school system. The manager must also select the physical facilities and materials to be used so that they will enhance the learning opportunities for the participants. Likewise, the program manager must make good use of the time available in order for the in-service program to have a good chance of accomplishing its stated objectives.

These three kinds of resources—human, physical, and time—both affect, and are affected by, the availability and use of financial resources. The sections that follow in this chapter are organized so that the reader can identify these various resources and relate them to one another. The final section deals with financial resources and how they are identified and obtained.

106

Human Resources Needed

In order for an in-service program to be successful, the participants should be positive in their feelings about their participation. If teachers are forced to attend and participate against their will, most of the effectiveness of the program will be lost. It is imperative, then, that the sponsors of in-service programs be aware of the desires of the target population not only in both the process and the content of the program but also in the formulation of the policies under which teachers are asked to attend the sessions. Teachers' professional expectations are for participation in all phases of the in-service program; thus, they are an important, basic resource.

The teachers who responded to the survey indicated that they want and need in-service education that is relevant to their teaching situations. Although they state that they are in favor of having released time for their in-service education and would like to have any incurred expenses paid, they are not ready to say that tenure, promotions, or pay brackets should be tied to their attendance at in-service programs. Supervisors, on the other hand, tend to think that the long-term payoff is more important. Certainly these items are and should be negotiable when discussing teacher contracts.

Respondents to the questionnaire indicated that there is a need for all mathematics teachers to participate in in-service programs but that there should be an *organized* program available to these teachers. They said that they feel a need to participate, but they also indicated that in general the programs offered should be about the ways to teach mathematics more than the content of mathematics curricula. They strongly endorsed programs that help them keep alive professionally and that deal with the problems facing researchers in the classrooms across the nation. In addition to placing a high value on programs dealing with computational skills, metrication, and applications of mathematics, they indicated interest in such topics as motivation, students with learning difficulties, diagnosis, evaluation, transition between grade levels, remediation, and improving student attitudes toward mathematics.

More than half of the secondary respondents and about one-half of the elementary teachers responding indicated a dissatisfaction with the in-service education they had had in the past. Some of their gripes were that the programs did not fit the needs of their classroom situations, that the programs were too theoretical, and that the programs were too general.

All these survey results should be studied carefully by the designers and managers of in-service programs in order to determine priorities in the use of resources of all kinds.

From these responses, we can draw some generalizations about the kind of in-service programs that will appeal to teachers and make them want to be participants in the programs. In the first place, the program must be relevant to the classroom teacher and situation. It should be so constituted that it will allow the teacher to grow professionally, as well as answer the practical day-to-day questions about teaching methods and curricular content. Also, it would seem that the program should be held at a time when the teacher is not tired from a full day's work or preoccupied with the thoughts of upcoming classes. Participants should not be forced to lose monetarily as a result of attendance. If these rules are followed, it would appear that teachers will attend and participate enthusiastically in in-service programs in mathematics.

One of the very important aspects of any in-service program is the leader chosen to conduct the sessions. This choice can make or break the program. Leaders must be persons who, above all, relate well to the participants of the workshop. They must have the respect of those attending. To help insure this, those choosing the leader must look for one who has a mastery of the material that is a goal of the program. Nothing can be so damaging to a program as a leader who does not know the material being presented (this does not mean that the material must be "presented" in a formal manner; on the contrary, the leader might insist on a discovery or laboratory-activity approach by the participants).

The leader of the program need not be a well-known figure in mathematics education in order to be effective. Some of the most well-received in-service programs have been conducted by teachers from the buildings or school systems from which the participants come. When local leaders are chosen for a program, they must be teachers who have the respect of the other teachers in the system, perhaps because of their expertise in the area of teaching mathematics or maybe just because they are natural faculty leaders, well thought of by their peers. One must be careful, though, not to overexpose one faculty member by having the same leader for many in-service programs. Teachers can be just as jealous as any other group of people and might begin to resent having one fellow teacher constantly leading programs. If funds for in-service education permit, it is good to bring in occasionally a well-known mathematics educator to conduct the program for a school. This person should be one who has recognized expertise in the particular topic for the program. This is particularly important for any program dealing with advanced topics in mathematics, such as transformational geometry or applications of advanced content in mathematics. This may also be true if some particular pedagogy based on a learning theory is the topic. Leaders from outside the school district will typically expect more compensation for their services than a local teacher on the staff.

A local school administrator, when choosing a leader for an in-service program, might first look at the faculty members within the system. If someone in the school is qualified and able to do the job, the selection process is essentially complete. Otherwise, the administrator can turn to several avenues for a leader. A local or nearby college or university will typically have staff members qualified and willing to contract to do the job. The regional or state departments of education have consultants and supervisors who routinely conduct in-service programs or who will be able to supply the names of qualified people from nearby districts who may be willing to conduct the programs. Many large school systems have mathematics supervisors who can help the local administrators select leaders. Local and statewide professional educational organizations frequently have lists of people who could serve as leaders. Of course the local district must always be ready to provide stipends to the leader for contracted services.

The local district in-service manager who selects an outside leader has an important responsibility to provide a clear description of what is wanted and expected from this leader. Unless precise descriptions of these expectations are given, the school system may not receive full value for the expenditure of money involved. The systemic planning and needs assessment processes described in chapter 4 provide the basis for this description.

Once a leader is selected, he or she may or may not be ready to conduct the program. Certainly the leader must devise a program if one has not been developed. If this is to be so, then the selection of the leader is doubly important. The leader must have the necessary expertise to develop, as well as implement, the program. This means that the person selected must have a considerable knowledge of the subject matter and/or methodological background.

If the program involves a large number of workshops held for a large target population, then the in-service materials may have been centrally developed prior to the selection of the leaders. In this case, it is more important that the selected leaders are able and willing to learn the program content than to be expert in the subject matter. Of course, this means that the leaders must themselves undergo training in the use of the materials. One procedure for this training that has proved successful in many instances in the past has been for the leaders to go through the entire in-service experience in the same manner that the target population is expected to undergo it. This is the start of using what is called the multiplier, or ripple, effort in the in-service project.

Use of the multiplier effort

If the target population is large and includes teachers from many different buildings or districts and if the needed in-service education is essentially the same for all, the organizers of the in-service program should investigate the possibility of using the multiplier effort. This might be appropriate for a large district adopting new textual materials or when a new concept or idea—such as metrication or the use of calculators in the classroom—is to be incorporated into the instructional process. In this procedure, a number of leaders are trained to conduct the program at the local school or at district levels.

The Five State Consortium on Metric Education, funded by the U.S. Office of Education, developed a model for a program for elementary teachers based on the multiplier effort (1976). Part of the field test consisted of testing the hypothesis that leaders can be trained regionally to conduct a workshop for all the teachers in their building. Evaluation results showed strongly that the teachers trained by the multiplier effort did at least as well on a posttest as the teachers trained by the originators of the material. Hence, it was shown that the multiplier effort is a viable way of disseminating metric information to elementary teachers.

The organizers of the program must decide on the material to be used. They also must make a decision about how many teachers can undergo the in-service activities in one group. This will enable them to decide into how many groups to partition the target population in order to present the program in the best way. This will indicate the number of leaders that need to be trained in order to provide the in-service training to the entire target population. If this number is less than the number who can efficiently take the course, then there is need to train only that number to be leaders and let them do the in-service organization at the local level. However, if this number is greater, then it will be necessary to have more than one level of leaders trained. Thus, it may be necessary to train regional leaders, who will in turn train the local leaders who will conduct the in-service for the teachers. It is important that all the leaders at each level of training be identified before the training starts. This allows intermediate leaders to know who and how many people they will be responsible for in the further training.

As stated before, the most desirable way to train the leaders to conduct the program is to have them go through the entire program just as planned for the teachers. Some time should be taken to talk with the leaders and explain the procedures they should use and answer questions they may have about the program. The organizer should also make clear any logistical procedures employed to supply the in-service program at the next levels.

At least one state, Minnesota, has used the multiplier effort extensively for an in-service program for elementary teachers in the processes of metric education. The state was divided into fourteen geographical regions, each containing about thirty school districts. Each district was asked to submit the name of a District Metric Coordinator (DMC) and, if there were a large number of buildings in the district, the names of Building Metric Coordinators (BMC), one for each building. The fourteen Regional Metric Coordinators were trained at one session. A month later, they trained the DMCs from their regions at central sites. During the ensuing month, the DMC in large districts trained their BMCs. The effort was completed with the holding of local workshops by the DMC or the BMC. Through this multiplier effort, most of the elementary teachers in the state participated in an in-service metrication program based on a tested model of a workshop. Thus, all school staffs have similar knowledge and background for teaching the metric system and its use to students. It also produced an identifiable "expert" in the topic at the local level, one who can do other things to further the cause of metrication. The expert can be relied on to provide follow-up and consultive service to teachers.

In general, the multiplier effort is especially powerful if the topic of the program is one that is new and innovative, having wide applicability in the schools. However, this does not delimit its use and applicability. The procedure can be used in a large system when the needs assessment demonstrates that an in-service program on a common topic is needed by many teachers in several settings. The multiplier effort can represent an efficient and cost-effective plan for in-service education.

Physical Facilities Needed for In-Service Sessions

The kinds of facilities needed for holding successful in-service sessions vary according to the kind of program to be presented. If the program calls for a lot of "hands on" activities, then more space—and perhaps different kinds of space—will be needed than if the program is to be largely oral. Some in-service topics might require outdoor spaces for the activities planned.

Whether the in-service manager is from the target school or system or is an outsider will also help determine the selection of the facilities to be used. A local manager will probably use school buildings as the in-service site, whereas an outsider might tend to use a commercial facility. The affected school district personnel must be aware of any financial arrangements made by the in-service manager. If there are financial constraints of sufficient urgency, the manager is advised to use the school facility.

The organizer of the program must take into account the kind of space available. The availability may dictate the type of in-service program to be held, although every effort should be made to see that space does not restrict the program. An on-site visit to the space is almost a necessity, particularly if the program is to be held in a commercial establishment. If a commercial location is to be used, the organizer must be careful to specify exactly the arrangements needed. Sales personnel from hotels and restaurants are not always familiar with the needs of educators. Once they know what is desired, however, the facilities are usually provided in complete compliance with the request.

If a school is to be used, the best rooms to use are those in which the teachers can be the most comfortable. These may be an auditorium, a cafeteria, or simply classrooms. Combinations of these rooms might be best for an activity-based workshop. Teachers usually prefer to have tables for writing and taking notes. If the design requires teachers to do things together, one must provide for movable seating. The program manager should check the scheduling of facilities to assure that other groups do not expect to use them at the same time as the in-service group.

There are times and situations where it is necessary to use facilities with particular characteristics. For example, if the session is one in which leaders are being trained as part of a multiplier effort, one cannot use a school building when school is in session, since the students might be bothered by a large number of strangers in the building. Other facilities must be found, such as a central office building in a large school district or a commercial establishment. In another instance, when the program is to be for an entire staff, the school building will be ideal, since the students are not likely to be in school if all the teachers are attending the meeting. Some examples of commercial establishments that have been used in past in-service situations follow. Hotel meeting rooms are usually ideal because they are versatile in that they can be made into different configurations: classroom style, tables and chairs, chairs in rows, and so on. In addition, hotel managers are able to provide refreshments, such as coffee or lunch.

Restaurants are convenient places for some in-service sessions, particularly for an all-day session where lunch is a necessity. Restaurants that are not generally open to the public except for the dinner hours are usually appropriate for an all-day session. Other restaurants that are open to the public all day might have separate rooms where meetings can be held. If meals are served, there is usually no charge for meeting rooms in either hotels or restaurants.

The meeting rooms of service clubs—such as the American Legion, Veterans of Foreign Wars, Elks Club, or Moose Club—are available in many communities. These sometimes are able to serve meal functions, but at other times the participants must go to some other nearby facility for meals. In some communities, the local bank has meeting rooms in its building. Many in-service sessions have been held in church basements during the weekdays, and usually there is at least one organization in the church that is willing to serve meals. Public libraries often have meeting rooms that can be used for in-service sessions.

Holding in-service sessions in commercial facilities almost always requires some financial outlay, whether for room rental or food services. The in-service manager must take this into account in planning.

Equipment and materials

The equipment and materials needed for the in-service program are included in the category of facilities. These can be divided into three categories—audiovisual aids, printed materials, and nonprinted manipulatives. Of course, the program's content will dictate the kinds of materials that are needed. Planning for these needs is quite obvious, and little need be said about this aspect. However, many commercial establishments do not have such specialized equipment as overhead projectors, slide carousels, and computer terminals. They can usually be counted on to have screens and chalkboards. It is advisable to check on the availability of needed materials when arranging for the space requirements with the establishment.

Most in-service programs do have a base of materials for teachers to use. If this is to be prepared or printed locally, the organizer must be aware of the time it takes to get the material finished, printed, and delivered. Enough lead time must be allowed for this phase of the operation. The developer is cautioned to order more than a bare minimum of printed materials so that all participants can have the needed copies.

The same statements apply to other nonprinted materials. If commercial manipulative materials are needed for the program, the leader must gather them early or order them with enough lead time to allow for any contingencies. It is unfortunate if the program must be started without the necessary materials on hand.

Survey results indicate that teachers like to make use of materials in their classrooms that are either distributed or developed at in-service sessions. Leaders should be aware of these desires and provide for the application of the program's topics by insuring that teachers leave with usable materials.

A word should be said about the custom of "scrounging" for in-service materials. This is a much used procedure and is effective in showing teachers what they can do in their classroom—and do effectively—without a large expenditure of funds. For example, a workshop on the topic of measurement might need a large number of containers of different sizes. The wise teacher will ask students to bring in different containers for use in learning about capacities. Tools of various sorts can be borrowed rather than purchased. Also, scraps of wood, metal, and plastic often come in very handy for special purposes. They can be found in many places if one will take the time to look for them.

The organizer must prepare for the program so that the physical facilities—including needed materials—are available for the leaders. It might be well for the organizer to establish a checklist of these needed facilities. If a multiplier effort is to be used, the organizer should provide for the material needs at all levels of the in-service model. If these materials are ready at the time the leaders are trained, then it will not be necessary to mail the materials later on. In some instances, it may be necessary to send materials to local leaders. Arrangements should be sufficiently simple for a clerk to take care of the logistics; otherwise, the disorganization can impinge on staff time needed to complete the in-service program.

Time as a Resource

The purpose of an in-service program is to provide teachers with learning experiences that will in turn help them become more effective in the classroom. Workshops and courses for elementary teachers—who typically have little formal training in mathematics—are usually designed to instruct teachers in mathematical principles and to acquaint them with effective teaching strategies. Workshops and courses on the secondary level usually provide mathematics teachers with opportunities to learn about successful teaching techniques and to expand their already substantial knowledge of mathematics.

Often, in-service programs include workshops or courses in which participants have sufficient time to delve into significant topics. Courses provided by universities usually carry credit. Workshops conducted by school districts sometimes do also. Some in-service experiences for teachers are organized much like formal courses. Others have a workshop format whereby teachers engage in activities designed to help improve their teaching.

When should in-service programs occur?

In-service programs can occur at any of the following times:

1. During the school day
2. Before the beginning of the school day
3. At the close of the school day
4. Evenings
5. Saturdays
6. Summer
7. During the school year on a school day when pupils have been dismissed for that day
8. Released time

Eighty-one percent of the supervisors responding to the in-service survey indicated that they were unable to provide released time as a device for allowing teachers to participate in in-service education. At the same time, 94 percent felt that they ought to be able to use released time as a mechanism to encourage teacher participation.

Times during the school day can be arranged through a series of devices. Principals can arrange to cover classes and release at one time a limited number of teachers to work with an in-service course leader over an extended period of time. Another technique that has been found successful in certain districts is the use of substitute teachers who come into a school with the in-service leader. These substitute teachers release teachers from a particular grade or a number of grade levels to work with the in-service leader while they cover the classes. These sessions may run for an hour or an hour and a half. At that time, the teachers who are participating return to their classes and release the substitutes, who then move to other grade levels to repeat the process. Through the use of three or four substitutes in an average school, a significant number of teachers can be released for an in-service program during the course of a school day. This process can be repeated for one day over a series of consecutive weeks or can be used strictly on a one-session basis.

Another successful practice for in-service education during the school day is to use a substitute to go into a school and take over the teacher's classroom for the entire day. That teacher is then released to go to a central location to participate in an in-service education program with other teachers who are released in a similar fashion. A modification of this procedure is to have the substitute teacher release one teacher for a morning session and then substitute for another in the afternoon.

The use of substitutes to provide released time for teacher in-service education during the school day has many advantages.

1. It costs less money than paying teachers for after-school participation in most school systems.
2. It guarantees total participation, since it takes place during the working hours. After-school participation is voluntary, thus reducing the potential number of participants.
3. Teachers at the end of a full day are tired and thus cannot give their full energies toward participation at a higher level.
4. Many teachers have after-school, evening, Saturday, and summer commitments and thus are unable to participate, even if interested in doing so.

Many schools have offered opportunities for teachers to receive in-service education either before the beginning or at the end of a school day. In this kind of procedure, a group of teachers should indicate or express a need. At the elementary level, it might be the examination of the content to be taught so that it can be taught more effectively. At the secondary level, the stress might be on new programs or new ways of teaching regular, ongoing programs. In either case, once a group of teachers have indicated that they wish this kind of service, an in-service leader should be provided to meet with those teachers, either prior to the school day or at its close. These teachers do this on a voluntary basis. In-service leaders may either be paid persons or be part of a twelve-month supervisory personnel group, doing this as part of their ongoing responsibility. The amount of time to be spent should vary, depending on the content to be covered and the needs of the teachers being served.

In a similar fashion, groups of teachers—either from a particular school or from several schools within a given geographic area—might indicate a need that could be served through an in-service program conducted during evening hours. In this case, a particular building should be made available for the teachers and the in-service leader. The amount of time might be from one-and-a-half to three hours, with the duration of the program dependent on its content and design.

A popular time for in-service education for many teachers has been on Saturdays. In 1967, one of the most significant and effective city-wide programs of in-service education for elementary teachers of mathematics was conducted in Philadelphia by the Division of Mathematics Education. A thirteen-week workshop was designed to help elementary teachers become acquainted with what was then called the "New Math." The workshop was conducted on consecutive Saturdays and ran from nine o'clock in the morning to three o'clock in the afternoon, with one hour for lunch. The morning session was made up of two parts: one was a lecture on content, and the other was a classroom/workshop activity that indicated how the content could be translated into classroom instruction at every grade level. Teachers were grouped according to the grade in which they taught; the leader's part of the program was based on the level of instruction to meet the needs of the youngsters at a particular grade level. This process was repeated in the afternoon—first the lecture and then a workshop experience.

As a result of the thirteen weeks, five hours each Saturday, sixty-five hours of staff development was provided to 1000 elementary school teachers in a much needed area of in-service education. The lecture sessions were conducted by a university professor of mathematics education and a mathematics supervisor assigned to the Division of Mathematics Education. The workshop leaders were selected on the basis of their expertise and their involvement in in-service education in the school district.

Many successful programs have been offered over the years during the summer. Some of these took the form of National Science Foundation (NSF) grant programs. In this case, a particular need of a school district was identified and a proposal was submitted to the National Science Foundation for the funding of an in-service education program for the teachers so that the program could be initiated. At one time, these NSF programs provided stipends for participants. In more recent years the stipends have been eliminated, with reimbursement remaining only for lunches and travel. Despite the elimination of stipends, there have been many more applicants for these kinds of NSF-supported programs than available positions.

In addition to NSF-funded programs, school districts have provided in-service programs of their own. A very successful program is operating in the Philadelphia area under the Office of Staff and Leadership Development of the School District of Philadelphia. It is called the In-Service Certification Master's Equivalency Program. This program is a planned, competency-based program whereby professional educators can renew initial certification, obtain permanent certification, attain a master's degree equivalency certificate, or simply improve skills. The master's degree equivalency certificate is obtained by completing a total of thirty-six approved semester hours. A minimum of eighteen graduate credits earned at a university and a maximum of eighteen in-service credits provided by the school district may be applied toward the attainment of this certificate. The program has been operating for four years in the School District in Philadelphia. To this date, approximately twenty-five hundred teachers have benefited from the program. It affords them the opportunity of accelerating completion of the twenty-four additional credits required to make their teaching certificates permanent. The courses are offered in the fall, the spring, and the summer. During the year, most courses meet once a week in a two-hour block and yield two in-service credits for thirty hours of instruction. During the summer, the in-service courses run for two hours a session for a series of fifteen consecutive days.

Arrangements have also been made with local universities to offer graduate credits, at a reduced tuition rate, for teachers who need such credits toward the master's equivalency certificate. Courses yield three semester hours of credit. A minimum enrollment of twenty persons in a course is required by the university before a course can be offered at an off-campus location. Thus, universities and a school district become cooperative partners in an educational enterprise to enable a school district to upgrade its instructional program.

Although some of the references cited here are specific to a given school system, all of them are possibilities for other school systems as well. Some may require adaptation or modification to fit the requirements of a particular district. It is hoped that mathematics supervisors will use this information as a catalyst and generate their own ideas for meeting the needs of the teachers in their particular district. In the last analysis, an imaginative, resourceful, and persistent supervisor will find a way, despite the many constraints and roadblocks.

Many concerns were expressed when programs that formerly provided funds for staff development of teachers were wiped out as a result of the financial problems in large school districts. Many people felt that once the money was no longer available, teachers would stop attending these in-service courses. In fact, this has not happened. In many school districts across the country, in-service education continues to operate despite the absence of funds for the payment of teachers. In all cases, the real criteria for the successful operation of the program are the creation of courses designed to meet the needs of the teachers and the selection of in-service leaders based on their ability to offer a course that not only meets teachers' needs but also produces enthusiasm and a desire to attend the programs.

How long should in-service education be?

State supervisors of mathematics, city mathematics coordinators, and college faculty members receive thousands of requests each year to serve as consultants or speakers for meetings referred to as in-service education programs. Many school districts set aside a certain number of days a year for "one shot" in-service activities. Outside consultants are often brought in to serve as group leaders for teachers in their specified disciplines.

The very nature of such sessions—the shortness of available time and large groups of teachers with which to work—forces consultants into presenting inspiring messages that offer teachers new ideas applicable to their classroom situations. One-shot in-service programs must be considered inspirational and cannot be used as organizational devices to satisfy the needs of teachers for in-depth study or to relate the program to the curricular needs of the school.

The ideal length of time for an in-service program depends on the background and experience of the participants and the content to be covered. The optimum amount of time for the study of any content in depth would seem to be between a minimum of twenty hours and a maximum of forty hours. Courses that are either too long or too short can produce adverse effects. The in-service course leader and those who have been working with in-service education are the best judges on the length of a particular in-service offering.

Another method of providing in-service education is through local and national professional mathematics education and mathematics associations. These groups provide professional conferences that enable teachers to participate in areas of their own choosing. These may take the form of section meetings, general sessions, or workshops. In every case, the opportunity for teachers is available, and only participation is necessary in order to have a meaningful learning experience. School districts and professional organizations are most anxious to provide in-service opportunities for the people in a particular school district or in a given geographic area. It is through the efforts, techniques, ingenuity, and persistence of professional educators that more and more opportunities of these kinds are provided.

Is staff development and in-service education a negotiable item? At the time of collective bargaining in many school districts, the question of in-service education is often raised as an item of discussion and negotiation. One obvious fact emerges from any discussion of this type; that is, in-service programs can quite legitimately be designed to meet the institutional needs of the school system on the one hand and the in-service needs of teachers on the other. The needs of teachers for in-service education are usually of quite a different order from those of the school administration and typically originate in a different way. A joint decision-making process is necessary to work out desirable arrangements for in-service education if collective bargaining is involved. It is imperative that teachers, as members of their professional associations, find the means to involve themselves in the formulation of policies for in-service education. Through a cooperative planning process, many representative teacher groups are willing—despite the lack of funds—to discuss establishing programs that would result in benefits to their members. The days of one group's making unilateral decisions that affect the working conditions of another group seem to be disappearing. The only successful programs are those in which there is a cooperative spirit and in which both parties have input into the decision making. For pupils in the classroom, the benefits derived from good in-service programs are so great that all efforts must be made to establish programs to meet the needs identified by teachers and administrators in school systems throughout the country.

Sources and Means of Obtaining Funding

Teachers in school systems all over the country are anxious to upgrade their skills in order to become more proficient in their ability to deliver instruction to their students.

Once a reason has been established for attendance at in-service courses and the right people to conduct sessions have been acquired, there is no need to demonstrate in great detail the advantages for teachers to be a part of this process. One of the most difficult aspects of in-service education for a school district is identifying sources of funding and then developing, in a logical and systematic way, a procedure for obtaining funding.

The search for funds is a continuous one. It mandates establishing and maintaining ongoing formal relationships with representatives of numerous governmental agencies and other possible sources of funding. Also, it is absolutely essential for the supervisor to participate in a wide variety of conferences, meetings, and discussions by school district personnel with personnel of federal programs and other people who are not on the staff of the district.

In planning for in-service programs, supervisors must assess needs, both immediate and long term, and then in light of their findings, set up priorities for expenditures based on the anticipation of the receipt of the funds. These priorities must of necessity be affected by the availability of resources, human and otherwise. If funds are limited, it becomes increasingly important to expend whatever funds that are available in a fiscally responsible manner.

Fiscal responsibility for in-service education means that there are many pitfalls to be avoided. One temptation is going with a current fad because of the availability of funds from certain agencies that have a particular idea, activity, approach, or product that they wish to sell. The desirable approach is to identify a need, devise a plan or proposal to meet that need, and then seek the necessary funds to carry out the plan or program.

The coordination of the search activities for monies involves contacts with central office staff, field personnel, representatives of various agencies and community groups, parents, and students. The gamut of activities includes providing ombudsman service; searching relevant literature—including the Federal Register and the *Congressional Record*—for indications of possible sources of funding; developing proposals; monitoring project activities; fulfilling liaison responsibilities in relationships with school district, federal, and state evaluation teams; preparing a budget analyzing project expenditures; and formulating and affecting phase-out procedures when a project's funding has been terminated. An important responsibility for a person in a leadership role is obtaining necessary funds to improve the quality of instruction so that the greatest benefit can be derived for the children served by that school district. This person should build skill in writing proposals.

Local sources

The first place to start in an effort to provide a vital and comprehensive in-service program for teachers is identifying and seeking out funding at the local level. For many years large city school systems provided many opportunities for teachers to grow in their professional capabilities. Often teachers were paid for attending these programs. Recently this practice has been eliminated because of the severe financial constraints that have been imposed on school systems as a result of the economy and the increasing cost of maintaining large city districts. Funds are still allocated in many large city systems for payment to leaders but are no longer available to pay participants. In some large districts, as an economy move, reducing payment for leaders is becoming the next step in the process of decreasing costs. This is being accomplished by involving twelve-month supervisory personnel and using them to serve as in-service leaders.

Small school systems have undergone the same process. However, the changes from the funding of in-service programs to no funding have not been so extreme or rapid for them. However, small systems are finding that in their list of priorities, the cost of supporting in-service education is one saving at which they can look before examining other items that seem to be more important to boards of education and leaders in the school system. In some states models are available that provide funding for leaders to conduct in-service opportunities throughout the state. Unfortunately, in large states this becomes a very difficult kind of in-service program to conduct because of the travel distances for participants. Sometimes funding is provided for leaders who travel from one section of the state to another to provide in-service opportunities for teachers on a regular basis.

A factor that increases the potential for success in obtaining funding at the local level is for the supervisor to establish an effective power base and to use it in time of need to have funds assigned, established, or maintained for in-service programs. Even with the existence of a power base, it becomes increasingly more important to produce a solid rationale and justification for the expenditure of funds for a particular program.

Supervisors must constantly be alert to the thinking and priorities of their superintendents and school boards. They must, on a regular basis, make a case for in-service education in mathematics and the necessity of allocating or maintaining funds to provide in-service programs.

One way to avoid the risk of having one's job "wiped out" is through an active, viable program of in-service education. This demonstrates the necessity of providing someone, such as the supervisor, to carry out an ongoing in-service program. It also argues for collecting evidence of in-service needs and using evaluative information that demonstrates a program's effectiveness.

School districts that remove funds for in-service education as a way of saving money are, in a sense, biting off their noses to spite their faces. Although the short-range effect results in a monetary saving, these savings end up costing more money in the long run. The better-trained teacher is able to deliver a more effective program of instruction, thus producing higher achievement levels from the students. An ill-trained teacher delivers an instructional program that produces lower pupil achievement levels. Thus, the need for a remedial program is necessitated. The cost of financing extensive remedial programs over an extended period of time is far more than the money saved by cutting out in-service programs. And the parents who support the school and vote for tax levies are less satisfied with the school's performance!

More and more, the in-service funding based on local resources is becoming a thing of the past. All school districts, both large and small, are starting to look for other sources of revenue in order to provide a viable in-service program for their teachers.

State sources of funding

For many years, opportunities were provided for school districts to submit proposals to the state for funding to carry on in-service programs for their teachers. The same problems that have beset local school districts have also beset state departments of education. Sources of funding have dried up at the state level. There are, however, some categorical efforts that are still bringing money into the local districts as a result of programs initiated by the state. Often programs have been brought about either by court decisions or by pressure from unique kinds of groups. One example of this is the Right to Education Act passed by the state of Pennsylvania. This act came about as a result of a lawsuit initiated by parents of youngsters in special education, who claimed that their children were being deprived of opportunities that were made available to "regular" youngsters. The court, in its decision, handed down a ruling that stated that all youngsters receiving special education must be provided with the same educational opportunities provided for regular school children. This necessitated, through state funding, programs being established to train teachers specifically in the handling of the unique needs of those students in special education. This involved working with resource room teachers and other specialized personnel to gain the necessary insights to produce a satisfactory program of instruction for youngsters being mainstreamed into the regular school program.

In many states very little resource is available on the state level to provide opportunities for upgrading the quality of teacher competence through in-service education. However, some states do provide funds for in-service education. It is up to the supervisor to search constantly for sources of funding at the state level and to encourage state departments of education to provide funds. Positive contacts with state legislators can go a long way toward the funding of in-service education through the state departments of education.

Federal funds

In general, the best outside source of revenue available today for school districts is the federal government. The federal government has provided aid to public education in some form since the beginning of the nation. During recent times, the allocation of funds for education provided by the Congress has grown rapidly, and the influx of new monies has influenced the nature of education throughout the United States. Federal aid to education is not a new phenomenon, but the growth in federal investment in education in the past twenty years has been astounding. In the single year 1965 to 1966, for example, federal funds supporting elementary and secondary education almost tripled, largely as a result of the passage of the Elementary and Secondary Education Act. The aforementioned period had the proper ingredients—political and otherwise—to facilitate the approval of legislation that literally drowned the objections that had previously accompanied the offer of federal funds to aid education.

In many cities across the country, the 1965–66 year marked the beginning of a new era of intense awareness that the way to meet the special needs of children was to turn to federal funds. In most cases, these special needs were met by retraining teachers in methods that seemed more successful in meeting these needs. Although the programs that had been aided by federal funds were sparked to some degree by the new money, the real impact developed among newly created educational projects. From then until now, there has been a steady nurturing of a multitude of programs. Usually, staff development and in-service education have been very heavy components.

In the information that follows, various acts under which school districts are able to obtain federal funds are described.

1. Title I Elementary and Secondary Education Act

This act provides the funds to meet the needs of educationally deprived children and to improve the education of delinquent and neglected children in state institutions. Training personnel involved in these programs is permitted when it is a part of the program approved by the state department of education.

2. Title IV Elementary and Secondary Education Act

Under part B, funds are distributed by formula to be used, at the discretion of each district, for the acquisition of school library resources, textbooks, other printed and published instructional materials, laboratory equipment, audiovisual equipment and materials, testing programs, and guidance and counseling services. Under part C, funds are available for state-approved supplementary and innovative projects and programs in almost all areas of elementary and secondary education and for strengthening the leadership resources of state and local educational agencies.

The act supports innovative and exemplary educational projects and provides funds to eliminate functional illiteracy for adults. It provides funds to improve state and local planning and evaluation of educational programs and to reduce the number of school dropouts.

3. *Education of the Handicapped Act*

This act provides aid to educational programs for handicapped children. In all the Title VI programs, a major component is the in-service education of teachers.

4. *Title VII Elementary and Secondary Education Act*

This act helps to fund the development and operation of programs for children aged three through eighteen who have limited English-speaking ability. Funds from this grant are used to provide staff development and supportive services in schools where the entire student body is involved in a bilingual/bicultural education program.

5. *Civil Rights Act of 1964—Title IV*

This act aids school districts in hiring advisory specialists to train employees and provide technical assistance in matters related to desegregation. A particular example of this kind of program is the establishment of an Office of Community Affairs. This office was established to enhance intergroup relations and address problems incident to desegregation. A further objective was to augment and sustain the proposed desegregation plan, and efforts towards this end were directed to teachers, parents, administrators, counselors, and community groups. In each school a crisis team was established to resolve conflicts. The team included students, principals, teachers, paraprofessionals, and community residents. Special workshops for administrators, guidance counselors, newly appointed teachers, paraprofessionals, and parents were conducted. These groups were trained in intergroup and leadership skills.

6. *Comprehensive Employment and Training Act*

The Comprehensive Employment and Training Act provides employment and training for the unemployed and the underemployed. The act was directed toward providing employment for unemployed individuals who are disadvantaged by poor educational background or lack of salable skills in finding employment in urban areas. As a result of the act, library instructional materials assistants were provided in Philadelphia schools. These persons were also encouraged to further their education and training to upgrade their skills. Under a Career Ladder Program, many of these people have become teachers and librarians. In addition to the library instructional materials assistants, attendance assistants and lunchroom aides were provided by the Comprehensive Employment and Training Act.

7. *The Community Services Act*

This act provides aid for improving educational programs for children in economically deprived areas. One of the most important programs funded under the Economic Opportunity Act is the Follow-Through Program. Sponsored by the U.S. Office of Education, Follow-Through is a research and development project that attempts to study, on a national scale, the comparative effectiveness of twenty approaches to the education of young children. The program was further designed to build on and augment gains children have made in Get Set, Head Start, and other preschool programs of high quality. All programs are based on a reduced teacher-student ratio, staff training and materials development for teachers, paraprofessionals, parents, and local supportive services by on-site instructional personnel.

8. *The Environmental Education Act*

This act encourages the development of environmental and ecological awareness and problem-solving skills through educational programs conducted by formal and nonformal educational organizations and institutions. Teachers are trained to act as guides and participators, and students are encouraged to conduct research, investigate environmental problems, evaluate their findings, and decide on appropriate courses of action to solve the problems.

9. *Higher Education Act* (Educational Professions Development Act)

This act funds projects that improve higher educational opportunities for children of low income families and that improve the quality of training programs for teachers and other educational personnel. One of the programs funded under this act is the Career Opportunities Program. This is a work-study program for professionals employed in early childhood education programs such as Get Set, Head Start, Follow-Through, and Title I Kindergarten Aids. Trainees attend community college or other colleges where they are enrolled in programs leading to a baccalaureate in early childhood, elementary, or special education. They are given released time of six to ten hours a week to attend the courses. They are given up to a maximum of twelve college credits by a community college for their work in the classroom. The practicum is supervised by resource teachers from the Career Opportunities Program who also conduct staff development workshops for trainees and cooperating teachers. An important feature of the program is the career ladder. Trainees receive automatic upgrading after accumulating the required number of college credits. In addition to salary increases, the trainees are gradually given more instructional responsibility as their education progresses.

Another program under the Higher Education Act is the Leadership Development Program. This program attempts to improve student performance by building into the system leadership ability, the capacity to implement change, and effective means of dissemination. The more immediate objectives are to consolidate and integrate previous leadership training activities and to improve the dissemination of training techniques in order to promote the greatest possible long-range impact on the school system.

A third program under the Higher Education Act is a National Teacher Corps program. This program was designed to provide improved educational services in regular classrooms to school-age children with special needs and thus to implement further the concept of "mainstreaming." College graduates participating in the program serve as interns in the schools. Their responsibilities include tutoring, participation in in-service training and a community work experience, instructing small groups, and demonstrating special assessment in instructional techniques to regular classroom teachers.

10. *The Housing and Urban Development Act*
    This act funds projects that promote more effective use of the nation's physical, economic, and human resources.

11. *Public Law 874—Aid to Federally Impacted Areas*
    This act provides payments to local school districts for current operating expenses. Entitlement to aid is based on the average daily attendance of pupils who reside on federal property or whose parent is employed on federal property.

12. *National Defense Education Act*
    This act provides school districts with matching grant funds for strengthening instruction in critical subject areas, such as mathematics, science, and social studies.

13. *Vocational Education Act*
    This act provides funds to maintain, extend, and improve vocational education programs and to develop training programs in new operations. This act covers a multitude of in-service opportunities for professional personnel. Among these are the following:

    1. Comprehensive career education
    2. Curriculum development—a multimedia, self-instructional, individualized instruction system
    3. Job placement centers
    4. Middle school curriculum development
    5. Mobile career development laboratory
    6. School district college cooperative program for vocational education personnel
    7. Vocational education staff development
    8. Vocational evaluation and diagnostic training facility

14. *The Indian Education Act*
    This act provides funds for local districts with Indian students enrolled.

15. *The Special Projects Act*
    This act provides grants for projects in the areas of metric education, gifted and talented children, community education, career education, consumer education, and women's equity in education.

All the federally funded projects above are indicative of the wide variety of opportunities that school districts have for obtaining funding for specific kinds of needs. The only bounds are the limits to the imaginations and the resources of the particular school district in seeking out programs that are available for funding purposes. In some cases these programs are very specific and are committed to very narrow guidelines. In others the funding is of a more general nature in a specific area, in which case the programs themselves are those that a school district designs within the general framework and outlines of the particular category under which funds are then received.

Supervisors must be aware that guidelines are in existence for the writing of proposals for funding. It would be advisable for these people to read and study such publications in order to be in an advantageous position when requesting funds from any source. Indeed, supervisors must develop their skills as writers of proposals.

The most frequent sources of governmental funding have been the National Science Foundation, the U.S. Office of Education, and the National Institute of Education. Each of these agencies publishes a catalog on a yearly basis outlining the wide variety of funding opportunities available for school districts. It requires the attention of designated personnel to seek out these opportunities, to identify the programs to be funded, and then to generate the necessary proposal to submit to these agencies for funding.

Nongovernmental sources

The last category of funding is that of nongovernmental sources. These encompass the following:

1. Foundations
2. Professional groups
3. Business
4. Industry
5. Unions
6. Colleges
7. Research institutions
8. Institutes
9. Other school districts
10. Private grantors

Each of these nongovernmental organizations provides funds to the specific programs they offer to sponsor. In every case, these programs provide in-service opportunities for teachers to become more proficient in carrying out the guidelines of the programs that are being funded. The following is a listing of the funding groups in each of the ten categories mentioned above.

1. *Foundations.* The most popular and well-known foundations are Ford, Rockefeller, Sloan, and Du Pont. Many of the major manufacturing and industrial corporations have as separate and distinct parts of their operations foundations that provide support to school districts in specific areas. Some of these industrial corporations are Westinghouse, General Electric, and Rohm & Haas. These foundations are a good source of funding and often can be persuaded to fund a worthwhile activity that a school district has identified.

2. *Professional groups.* Many professional groups, in an effort to advance the instructional program related to their particular area, provide inservice opportunities for teachers. An example is the American Chemical Society, which provides annual grants to teachers to enable them to upgrade their instructional program in the operation of a chemical laboratory training program.

3. *Business.* Many food chains offer grants to upgrade the instructional program in a particular area. An example is Acme Markets, which offers a grant for the establishment of a Consumer Affairs Teacher Training Center. This center is available to teachers for the examination of materials, for seminars, and for meetings with community people. In addition, the funds are used to purchase materials, equipment, and carpeting for a center.

4. *Industry.* Some of the local industries, in an effort to provide permanent placements for graduating seniors and summer job placements for sophomores and juniors, offer special grants to upgrade the coordination of job development services for students at high schools.

5. *Unions.* Programs are sometimes established between school districts and unions to continue the regular union apprenticeship program during the summer months.

6. *Colleges.* Often colleges are given specific grants to develop widespread programs in different school districts. One example is the University of Connecticut and its effort to provide a mainstreaming program. The funds are used to support comprehensive staff development activities for administrators, regular staff members, and special education teachers in selected secondary schools of a school district. The philosophy of the many faceted program is to integrate mildly retarded students into regular classes at the secondary level.

7. *Research institutions.* Many times research institutions, under cooperative arrangements with colleges and school districts, have established programs that are of mutual benefit to all three organizations. A typical example is the establishment of a competency-based training program for Child Development Associates, established between Research for Better

Schools, the Community College of Philadelphia, and the School District of Philadelphia. This program is an individualized, modularized, field-based training program used to train about twenty-five persons already employed as aides or teacher assistants in the district's early childhood programs. Funds from the grant provide the salary for a trainer-developer from the school district, who is developing a training program including these concepts:

a. Framework for viewing child development

b. Knowledge of instructional techniques

c. Skills in staff development

d. Ability to relate a child's home experiences to school programs

8. *Institutes.* Private institutes with a particular thrust or function often provide funds to enable school districts to implement their own particular programs.

9. *Other school districts.* Sometimes a particular school district is given a grant to develop certain kinds of curricula. One aspect of the grant is the dissemination of these materials when they have been developed. An example is the Spanish Curriculum Development Center in Florida's Dade County. A grant was provided to the School District of Philadelphia from the Dade County Public School District in Miami, Florida, to serve as a northeast dissemination center for the field-testing of the Spanish Curriculum Development Center and the Curriculum Adaptation Network for bilingual/bicultural educational materials. One component of the Spanish Curriculum Development Center program requires the services of resource personnel in different school districts to carry out field-testing. These people implement and critique materials and submit a field-review form to the coordinator of the Northeast Regional Dissemination Center.

10. *Private grants.* Private individuals often bequeath money to school districts to provide opportunities in specific areas.

In review, it would be difficult to visualize what shortcomings many school districts throughout the country would face if it were not for the varied funding sources that are made available to these school districts. It requires the efforts of many people to seek out these funding sources and to submit proposals to obtain money to support in-service education. In all these programs, one aspect of each program is that of evaluation, in terms of the desired outcome of a particular proposal. Therefore, it becomes necessary to come up with clear-cut objectives in relation to the particular program being carried out and to set up the necessary evaluative instruments to determine the effectiveness of a particular program. In these days of cost consciousness, it is imperative that every single dollar be spent in a wise and beneficial manner.

CHAPTER 7

The Roles and Responsibilities of Individuals and Institutions

SHIRLEY FRYE
LeROY C. DALTON

A MAJOR FACTOR in the successful outcome of any in-service program is the quality of the planning and organization. The planning and organization must involve personnel at all levels in the school system—and sometimes external to the school system—who assume roles and responsibilities that can be shared throughout the implementation and evaluation of the program. Because change is difficult to achieve, cooperation is required by all those who have a stake in in-service education. This chapter examines and recommends a cooperative in-service effort for people and institutions having different roles and responsibilities for the teaching of mathematics in the schools.

The chapter is divided into three major sections. The first section examines the roles and responsibilities of individuals such as the principal, the department chairman, and the mathematics coordinator in terms of their contributions to the in-service process. The second section examines the responsibility of teachers for in-service education and recognizes that in-service education is not something "to do" to teachers but instead requires of them a participatory role. Finally, in the third section institutions other than a local school system are analyzed in terms of their contributions to the in-service effort.

Spillane and Levenson (1976) aptly argue for in-service education in the *Phi Delta Kappan* (p. 439):

> The essential purpose of the public schools is to educate students to function in society. That skill can be taught only by teachers who are aware of the great and small changes within the immediate community and the wider world. Teacher training should be a continuing, never-ending process, closely related to the reality of the life of children and families.

A common goal for every person or group is the commitment to a program of continuing professional growth through in-service programs.

Pivotal School Personnel

A school system has many individuals who make decisions affecting the nature and quality of in-service education but who seldom participate directly in, or benefit from, the in-service program. Their understanding of the in-service needs, the program, and the program's outcomes is often the vital margin between a successful program and an unsuccessful one or no in-service program at all. They make the policy, administer the funds, and marshall the personnel resources that make an in-service program feasible. The successful carrying out of the roles and responsibilities of these key school personnel depend on their having adequate information for rational decision making. Their informational needs are examined in terms of the implications for the *manager of the in-service program.*

The design and implementation of an in-service program for mathematics teachers is usually the direct responsibility of at least one individual in a school system. The precise label or title for such individuals varies from one school system to another. The variation depends on the roles and responsibilities assumed in addition to the in-service education, the size of the school system, and the administrative organization and philosophy of that school system. Consequently, in this chapter "in-service program manager" will refer to the individual responsible for designing and implementing the program. For example, the "manager" could be the elementary school principal in a small school system or the mathematics coordinator or director of instruction in a large school system.

The likelihood of an effective in-service program is greater if the in-service program manager applies the guidelines for the design of in-service programs specified in chapter 4 and tailors the characteristics of the program to fit those described in chapter 5. Primary among these principles for design and implementation are—

1. using the long-range curricular plans in mathematics;
2. making comprehensive, thorough assessments of needs based on discrepancies between goals and performance;

3. involving teachers in decision making and participatory planning;
4. managing the resources of people, time, facilities, and money to make possible the realization of the in-service plan;
5. conducting an evaluation of the in-service program.

We assume that in-service program managers will employ these principles whatever their official titles.

The program manager must consider the decisions other school personnel can and should make that affect the course of the in-service education programs. The decision makers require information and judgment from the program manager if their decisions are to be rational instead of arbitrary and capricious. Moreover, this information and judgment not only allows the program manager to specify actions and responsibilities but also serves to explicate the roles and responsibilities of these decision-making personnel.

The superintendent

What should the in-service program manager expect of the superintendent? What should the superintendent expect of the program manager? The answers to these questions are found in the role of superintendents and the responsibilities of their position. The superintendent plays a key role in determining the success of the mathematics in-service program. But the actions of the superintendent must respect and serve all interest groups in the school community—for instance, reading and vocational education as well as mathematics education, and elementary school teachers as well as those in the senior high school. Thus, a major responsibility for the program manager is to provide evidence, information, and guidance to the superintendent that aids in the determination of priorities and in the balancing of the legitimate claims on funds and personnel for the many facets of the school program for which the superintendent is responsible.

The program manager often does not work directly with the superintendent but through an intermediary in the superintendent's office. Many school systems have individuals whose delegated responsibilities encompass in-service education, curriculum, and instruction. The program manager needs to recognize that these intermediary, fellow administrators have the same types of informational needs as the superintendent.

Determining priorities is clearly easier and can be done more rationally if the superintendent, working with the school board and fellow administrators, has created a supportive atmosphere for in-service education. It is significantly easier to maintain a spirit of growth in a staff than to have to begin anew with each idea for an in-service program. Policy that allows the redirecting of in-service energy and resources is more efficient in meeting the needs of the curricular and instructional program than policy that demands initial start-up energy and resources for each new in-service idea. Thus, the in-service program manager should expect the superintendent to maintain an atmosphere within the school system that honors the primary components of the systemic approach to in-service education advocated in chapter 4. He or she should expect the superintendent to reinforce the characteristics of successful programs highlighted in chapter 5.

A given principle for the design of an effective in-service program is that the program be related to long-range curricular planning. Thus, a superintendent must maintain policies that promote such planning. Simply announcing, "We will have long-range planning," is not sufficient. Teachers and other school staff must have the policy and resources available to consider and develop alternatives to test and use in the classroom.

The principle that in-service education be closely related to long-range curricular planning assumes that this planning is being accomplished. Curricular plans are not fixed or static in this age of complex school programs, the myriad of changing forces operating on children and youth, and the criticisms being leveled at the schools by outside interest groups. Rather, curricular plans are dynamic and evolving. A superintendent must guide the board of education and fellow administrators in the formulation of policy that reflects this evolving nature of curriculum in mathematics. The policy, and its implementation, should be designed to reward those segments of the in-service program that have a sound basis in curricular planning.

A major problem in in-service education at the school system level is that it has been reactive. When a new instructional problem arises—such as the hand calculator—the in-service program must gear up to react to the new crisis; when a different text series is adopted, the school system reacts by instituting an in-service program. But if the school system has a policy and process for long-term curricular planning, it will allow an in-service program to adapt more easily to the problems posed by the new or the unexpected. Thus, the principle of relating in-service education to curricular planning defines administrative policy for the superintendent's office and imposes a condition on the in-service program. This is necessary if in-service education is to be elevated beyond periodically coping with crises to become a continuous mechanism for the improvement of the school mathematics program.

The superintendent has the responsibility of working with the board of education to obtain an in-service budget adequate to support the in-service needs of the entire staff. Dollars for the schools are limited, and both the in-service program manager and the superintendent must recognize that most claims on the budget of a school system are legitimate. In-service education is but one of the many investments of school system monies that are important. Before a superintendent can recommend investing in in-service education, the arguments and rationale for the in-service program must be elevated beyond the motherhood-and-apple-pie level of discourse. Need must be demonstrated. Specific plans that allow for the prediction of outcomes and that indicate the wisdom of the investment must be available for consideration. The potential of the plan for serving teachers and students must be clear.

Superintendents cannot serve this function of assuring funds for in-service education unless the in-service program managers provide them information and planning with which to work. The role and responsibility of the superintendent in assuring adequate support for in-service education in most schools depends on his or her staff's providing facts and arguments to work with the decision-making bodies in the school system. Superintendents who go to boards of education without sufficient information and rationales for an in-service program have a notably poor track record in maintaining support for in-service education. They are forced into a crisis-oriented, reactive mode of in-service education programmed to "put out brushfire" problems when they develop.

There are several implications for the superintendent and school policy that result from this. First, the superintendent must have the support of a competent professional staff. Teachers, because of their fundamental responsibility for instruction, seldom are in a position to have the time or the perspective necessary for collecting the information and formulating the plans needed for the superintendent's use. In many school systems, teachers do not have access to the type of information required. Thus, the superintendent must have a cadre of principles, department chairmen, directors of instruction, and curriculum specialists who can formulate plans and give guidance for the support of in-service education. Given the importance of mathematics for children and youth in future learning and in coping with the realities of life beyond school, it is most important that some of this leadership group on whom the superintendent must depend be specialists in the learning and teaching of mathematics.

A second implication is that the superintendent must operate on a basis of needs assessment data. This is best formulated on the discrepancy model in chapter 4 but must incorporate the considered professional judgments of teachers and administrators at all levels. It should be observed that needs assessment should be based in part on the performance of teachers and students in meeting the mathematical objectives of the school program. This use of information is fundamental and extends beyond accountability to the definition of needs. Ultimately, it is the basis for demonstrating the effectiveness of the in-service program. It is easier for a superintendent to maintain an adequate level of support for in-service education if evidence of past program effectiveness is available. As a corollary, it should be noted that goals of in-service programs must be accomplishable and evidence of needs must be collected if this is to be a component of the superintendent's request for in-service funds.

A third implication for the superintendent's responsibility for in-service education is that the superintendent must resist the trade-off of resources that make the teacher more effective—such as in-service education—for the salary and other welfare issues of teachers. The survey of supervisors indicates that in-service education is a negotiable item in budgetary bargaining with teachers' groups in many school systems. This is unfortunate but is a fact of the educational enterprise. Thus, an in-service program not only requires justification and support at the policy-determining and decision-making level of the school board and the school administration, it also requires justification and realistic evidence of its effectiveness to the larger school community and to the teachers in particular. That is, the needs and the successes of the in-service education program must be publicized.

Fourth, the marshalling of resources for in-service education requires the superintendent to consider time as well as dollars. Many in-service programs fail because teachers simply are too busy to participate. Release time is a major problem for the superintendent to consider in formulating policy that makes in-service education possible.

The fundamental problem of superintendents remains: How do they guide the decision makers in a realistic assessment of priorities for in-service education? Given D dollars for in-service education for all facets of the school program, on what basis is the distribution determined? For instance, how are the mathematical in-service needs to be balanced with those for the science program? The in-service program manager in mathematics has the responsibility of representing the mathematical needs of the school program to the superintendent. The surveys of teachers indicate that although some general in-service education on topics of concern to all teachers (such as discipline) is important, respondents wanted at least some in-service education specific to the teaching of mathematics. For many teachers, the provision of only a general in-service education was equivalent to a cop-out from the responsibility for providing more specific in-service education.

The decisions on priority require the same kind of information as the decision of whether or not to have in-service education. The decisions are ultimately the questions of value that demand turning for guidance to students, parents, and the community at large as well as to the teachers. An in-service program manager needs to recognize and accept that there is an informational aspect of the problem of determining priorities. Individuals and groups other than teachers must be educated by the program manager about the goals of mathematics education if the goals of mathematics in-service programs are to be accepted and their relative importance understood.

In addition to policy that supports in-service education, most superintendents have found that several factors contribute to an atmosphere conducive to in-service education. One important component is the incentive system used to encourage teacher participation and leadership. Evidence from the survey indicates that teachers regard many of the financial arrangements, such as extra pay for participating in in-service programs, release time, salary scale advancement, and the like, as a reward for participation. But these features of encouraging teacher participation can contribute significantly to the expense of an in-service program. Moreover, they indicate to the teaching staff the support and enthusiasm—as well as the value—of in-service education possessed by the school system and the administration. The superintendent has a responsibility for providing tangible evidence of this support—as well as the more ineffable matter of demonstrating a positive attitude—through the publicity, promotion, and recognition of in-service programs and teachers' participation.

Some school systems have found that a curriculum center creates an atmosphere supportive of in-service education. Superintendents who work with their boards of education and administrative staff to see that teachers have ready access to the resource materials of a good curriculum center are building and maintaining an atmosphere for curricular decision making by teachers. Not only are they providing the teachers with an opportunity to use their professional judgment in considering instructional alternatives, but the curriculum center usually can serve as a setting for the in-service education.

A curriculum center is of limited value without an adequate staff to help teachers. Teachers' time is too limited and valuable for them to be in a center without a responsible individual who knows where materials are and how they are to be used. The staff should be responsible for assuring that the center is well stocked with appropriate current materials that are useful and stimulating to teachers. Supervisors, principals, and teachers all have the responsibility of identifying and suggesting materials for the center.

A critical characteristic of the curriculum center is the easy access of teachers to the center. If it is not convenient, teachers will resent the imposition on their limited time. If the school system covers a large area or if complicated traffic is a problem, smaller resource centers in local schools may be worth establishing. For some small systems, the curriculum center could be run in cooperation with neighboring school districts. If release time for use of the center is not feasible, then the curriculum center must have hours of access different from the normal school hours.

The curriculum center can provide a setting for extending teachers' consciousness about instructional and curricular alternatives and for exhibiting to teachers a school system's genuine interest in their continuing professional growth. It is an aid to in-service education and can provide a backdrop for long-term curricular planning.

The mathematics supervisor

Many school systems enjoy the services of a specialist in mathematics curriculum and instruction. The evidence of the teacher surveys indicates that the supervisor does make a difference whether teachers participate in in-service education in mathematics, whether it is available, and whether teachers regard the participation as worthwhile. For those schools having a supervisor, he or she is in a position to be the most effective cog in the in-service wheel. The *Handbook for the Mathematics Supervisor,* prepared and used in the Oakland County Schools, Pontiac, Michigan (1968), states, "Inservice education of mathematics teachers within a school system is a major responsibility of the mathematics supervisor" (p. 9). Often the supervisor is the in-service program manager with the primary responsibility of representing the interests and needs of mathematics students and teachers to the superintendent, the school board, and fellow administrators. Thus, the implications drawn from the superintendent's roles and responsibilities for the in-service program manager are of fundamental importance. The mathematics supervisor must provide the superintendent and other administrators a base from which they can work. We need not elaborate further on these implied responsibilities.

The supervisor's roles and responsibilities are a function of the administrative philosophy, policy, and procedures of the school system. Some schools give supervisors considerable nomothetic power; they can, for instance, recommend the termination of a teacher's employment. Others prefer the supervisors to work from a more cooperative base, building their power on earned recognition of their worth, judgment, and contribution. Frequently, mathematics specialists in the latter arrangement are called coordinators to reflect the cooperative base from which they work. Ideally, most supervisors prefer the cooperative base. We believe the roles and responsibilities stipulated in this section are of sufficient significance that they transcend the administrative organization of the school system.

The supervisor typically is employed by a school system large enough or with a sufficient resource base to involve other administrative personnel with the in-service process and planning. In many situations, the supervisor will have to work with the superintendent indirectly through an intermediate-level administrator, such as an instructional coordinator or associate superintendent for instruction. The role and responsibilities of the supervisor are relatively invariant if such intermediary personnel exist. And for the schools that regrettably do not have the services of a specialist in mathmatics education at the supervisor's level, the responsibilities must be assumed by, and partitioned among, central administrative staff and professionals at the local school level.

The roles of the mathematics supervisor include the following:

1. Creating an attitude among principals, department heads, and teachers that will make them desirous of professional growth and improved instruction

2. Identifying content and pedagogical needs of teachers through supervision, observation, discussions, surveys, and other means

When observing teachers, a mathematics supervisor should assess their content and pedagogical needs. These needs can be judged in relation to the teacher's ability to affect students' learning and growth and in terms of the correctness and appropriateness of lessons. Teachers' needs can be determined through means other than supervision, such as by noting low student performances on local as well as national tests of mathematical achievement, by observing a teacher's remarks and actions in group discussions on classroom-related topics, and by noting comments made by other teachers and parents. This responsibility can expand to making teachers aware of their needs through individual conferences and to suggesting books to read, courses to take, and other activities to satisfy these needs.

3. Informing the director of instruction, the superintendent, or the principals of the in-service needs of staff as they are observed, as well as writing a report to the director of instruction prior to the preparation of budget

The *Handbook for the Mathematics Supervisor* (1968, p. 10) relates, "An effective approach for the supervisor is to develop a climate in which faculty members, and administration, see the need without being directly informed by the supervisor." This is a worthy goal, and the supervisor should strive to accomplish it. However, where necessary, reports of the in-service needs of teachers should be made to the administration. These reports help insure that administrators are aware of needs so that they may take appropriate action to deal with them.

4. Submitting to the director of instruction or superintendent an estimate of the cost of in-service programs needed for the coming year, along with possible sources of help that might be obtained outside the district

The supervisor should be familiar with sources of financial aid outside the district budget—such as state and federal funds and funds available through agencies, foundations, and industry—and know how to apply for these funds.

5. Organizing in-service planning committees of teachers and principals and working with these committees in planning for in-service programs based on the principles of systemic planning advocated in chapter 4

6. Being in charge of and conducting some in-service programs or delegating these responsibilities to a capable staff member

7. Maintaining contact with the NCTM, the state mathematics council, the state department of education, the state mathematics consultant, and local colleges and universities concerning in-service opportunities.

The supervisor should encourage the staff to join professional organizations such as the NCTM and the state mathematics council, to read journals, to attend meetings, and to exercise leadership in the activities of these organizations.

8. Identifying, training, and using teachers with special talents to lead in-service programs

The mathematics supervisor should share knowledge, resources, and expertise in working with and helping teachers, with the aid of some of the more capable teachers in the system. These teachers can begin to lead in-service programs at workshops or at institutes. The mathematics supervisor should build leadership in the schools to act in this instructor role. This creates a valuable multiplier effect for in-service education.

9. Building an adequate base of curricular planning and development to serve as a foundation for in-service planning

The surveys of teachers indicate that if in-service education in mathematics is perceived to be related to long-range curriculum plans, teachers view the in-service education as more valuable than if it is not. Clearly for the mathematics supervisor, curricular planning and development should be a major portion of job responsibility irrespective of in-service education. The positive results of tying the in-service program design and implementation to the curricular planning and development make the curricular responsibilities even more important. The supervisor survey indicated that doubts about the sufficiency of teachers' knowledge of curriculum for in-service planning were common among supervisors. If a base of curricular planning and development is necessary, then the supervisor must address directly the problem of including teachers in the curricular planning and development process.

Part of the supervisors' responsibility in this area is assuring that teachers have adequate knowledge by keeping the district teachers informed about new curricular and instructional ideas and materials. Newsletters, announcements, and special, short-term awareness programs are strategies many supervisors have used effectively. Making sure that materials are available in curriculum centers can give teachers an opportunity to explore the materials directly. Encouraging a few teachers to try out new materials in their classrooms can provide a field test for informing other teachers about the materials. The supervisor should also work with librarians and other school media personnel to assure that each building has appropriate mathematics education journals. Each teacher should have ready access to other resources such as filmstrips, projectuals, tapes, and films, and the supervisor may find it effective to have some teachers review and evaluate these materials.

The planning and development of the curriculum require the knowledge of teachers and an atmosphere of searching through that knowledge base for the practical and useful. The supervisor can merely serve as a conduit for information, such as selectively informing teachers and other concerned individuals of research results by summarizing and interpreting the results for them. However, it is more effective—for the purposes of curricular planning and development—for the supervisor to establish a spirit of using those research results and conducting field tests or action research based on them.

Each of the suggestions above addresses the problem of building an adequate base of knowledge and an atmosphere for curricular planning and development but fails to meet the guidelines for participatory planning advocated in chapter 5. Each one focuses on knowledge from external sources and a somewhat passive receptivity to the ideas even though the use of materials and results is suggested. For effective in-service education, curricular planning and development must be more directly concerned with the local school curriculum and oriented toward action. Participatory planning cannot happen without adequate data concerning what is happening at the school level. By implication, the supervisor must work to keep teachers informed of how well their mathematics program is succeeding. This examination of student performance should not stop at a superficial examination of standardized test results but should approach the specific consideration of performance in terms of the goals of the mathematics curriculum. In addition, teachers, students, parents, and community members should examine carefully from time to time the goals that the curriculum is directed toward achieving. These two elements of the curricular development and planning process should culminate in curriculum guides adequate to serve as a base for the design of in-service programs.

The description of roles and responsibilities for the mathematics supervisor given above apply whether or not the supervisor is the in-service program manager. It is important to consider the nature of supervisors' responsibilities and roles when they are *not* the in-service program managers. The typical supervisor often must depend on other leaders in the mathematics program to conduct in-service programs because of the multiplicity of his or her responsibilities and the number of schools and teachers to be served. In many respects, supervisors have the same expectation of an in-service program manager as the superintendent. This is because they are the intermediaries between the superintendent and the program manager and will have the role of communicating the program manager's proposal—intent, rationale, needs assessment, and plan—to the superintendent. Supervisors should realize that they are typically the only persons in the administrative hierarchy possessing the technical expertise to comment knowledgeably about the mathematics education aspects of the proposal. They should be sure to use this expertise. Supervisors should expect complete and thorough follow-up evaluation of in-service program managers or, alternatively, design and conduct the evaluation themselves.

The principal

The principal's role in in-service programs is personal in nature because of his or her close association with teachers. It can be briefly outlined as follows:

1. To work with teachers to identify needs and to convince the mathematics supervisor or other administrative personnel including the superintendent of the need for in-service education to satisfy these needs

2. To encourage active participation in in-service education and to provide support throughout the in-service program

3. To help structure the in-service program and to use in the program teachers having special talents

4. To help evaluate the effectiveness of the in-service program

The supervising principal, through the evaluation of teachers, is in a position to identify some of their in-service needs in areas such as motivation, discipline, and classroom management. This can be done partially through classroom visitations with follow-up conferences. The principal should give the teacher the opportunity in these conferences to express desire for in-service education. In the elementary and early middle school, principals should also be able to identify the needs of their teachers in terms of the understanding of the mathematics they are teaching and the methods they are employing. The same is not always true for grades 9 through 12. Here the principal may have difficulty identifying subject matter and pedagogical needs of mathematics teachers. The mathematics supervisor can help in this situation. If the district does not have a mathematics supervisor, the mathematics department chairman may assist in the evaluation of a teacher. In addition to being evaluated by the principal, each mathematics teacher in a district deserves the right to be evaluated by a person well trained in mathematics and mathematics education.

The principal should be aware of the role of faculty meetings in in-service education. According to the *Handbook of Educational Supervision* (p. 223):

> A faculty meeting offers many opportunities in a program of in-service education because usually it is the major means of communication within a school. Despite its many advantages, evidence indicates that these meetings usually are not popular with the teachers. If properly planned and executed, staff meetings can create an atmosphere of working relationships and improve the quality of education within the school.

In particular, the elementary principal should give teachers an opportunity at faculty meetings—either before the entire group or in smaller groups—to express their in-service needs and desires. And teachers do need information about the achievement of goals if their judgment of need is to be professional. They should then be allowed time to determine their most urgent needs and to plan in-service programs that will satisfy those needs.

Once principals ascertain the in-service needs of teachers, then they have the responsibility of informing appropriate administrative personnel of these needs. They must realize, however, that the needs of teachers are only part of the information required in the needs assessment process. Cognizance of the goals of the program and success in achieving these goals are also important. This is to say, a major responsibility of the principal—particularly at the elementary level—is to provide information for the needs assessment process.

The principal can create a positive atmosphere among teachers for in-service education by demonstrating a supportive attitude toward in-service education and toward self-improvement in general. A positive atmosphere can be partially generated through the principal's involvement in in-service work designed for principals as well as in some of the in-service programs for teachers.

We argue that the nature of the totality of responsibilities of elementary school principals suggests the appropriateness of their being active participants in mathematics in-service programs. Because of the nature of the elementary school, elementary principals have a substantially larger role in instructional leadership than their counterparts at the high school level where there are department leaders in the subject areas.

The principal can encourage each teacher to participate in in-service education by other means. Teachers can be encouraged to join professional organizations and to attend conferences that deal with the subject matter they are teaching and with trends in teaching and curriculum planning.

The principal should provide support to teachers in their in-service endeavors, by offering words of encouragement, advice, help when needed, and by attempting to provide tangible rewards for their in-service endeavors from the school district.

The principal should provide leadership in involving teachers in structuring and planning needed in-service programs. For many situations, this means guiding cooperation with the in-service program manager. It might be best if the committee resulting from these actions is led by a teacher. The principal and the in-service program manager may act in an advisory role as members of the committee. The teachers might then see that they are playing a major role in determining the characteristics of the in-service program and would undoubtedly give the program more support.

The principal should have a productive enough relationship with teachers to be able to evaluate the effectiveness of the in-service program and should work cooperatively with the program manager, the mathematics supervisor, or the department chairman in this evaluation. By visiting classes taught by teachers who have participated in the in-service program, the principal can assess some of the outcomes of the program.

The fundamental responsibility of the principal to program manager is to maintain a cooperative, helpful attitude toward the program. In most schools, the principal has administrative flexibility to facilitate the participation of teachers in the in-service program. Through judicious staff assignments, the principal can provide release time for teachers to participate. He or she can provide the facilities for an in-service program. But sad tales abound of the lack of administrative cooperation compromising the efforts of in-service program managers. The basic problem is failure to recognize the need for administrative action enabling teachers to participate in the in-service program.

The department chairman

Many junior and senior high schools have a department chairman for mathematics. The roles and responsibilities of chairmen duplicate those of the mathematics supervisor; indeed, if the department chairmen operate in a school system without a mathematics supervisor, then they will have to assume the functions of a supervisor outlined in the previous section. That section identified roles and responsibilities that stem from the primary difference between a mathematics supervisor's job and the department chairman's. That difference is the "closeness" of the chairman to his or her peers on the teaching staff. The chairman typically has a day-to-day association with fellow mathematics teachers that is not possible for the mathematics supervisor. For most school systems, department chairmen do not have direct responsibility for classroom supervision or the concomitant authority for making decisions; they must operate more from a basis of peer respect than the typical supervisor. For the successful chairman, the lack in official authority is typically compensated for by the chairman's closeness and involvement in the daily challenges of teaching and learning. Following are some of the roles that the department chairman should assume:

1. To aid the principal and mathematics supervisor in identifying the needs of the staff and then to help convince the principal, mathematics supervisor, and superintendent's office of the need for in-service programs to satisfy these needs

Whether or not department chairmen are delegated the job of supervising the staff, they are still in a position for talking with teachers informally and regularly on topics of mathematical content and pedagogy. This affords an opportunity to spot the strengths and the weaknesses in the backgrounds of individual staff members. These strengths and weaknesses may not be readily observable to a supervisor who may see the teacher only once or twice a year. The chairman can pass on these observations to the mathematics supervisor, principal, or director of instruction, depending on the understood patterns for communications within the staff.

2. To make teachers aware of their individual needs through conferences and to suggest books to read, courses to take, and other activities to satisfy these needs

If the department chairman is assigned the task of supervising the mathematics staff, the observed in-service needs of the staff can be described to them through individual conferences and in-service activities identified to satisfy these needs. If supervision is not assigned, the task of informing individual staff members of observed in-service needs requires tactful diplomacy.

3. To work cooperatively with the mathematics supervisor, principal, and teachers in the planning and structuring of the in-service program and courses

It is important that classroom teachers have a voice in the planning and structuring of their in-service programs and courses. That they are asking for that "voice" is substantiated by their answers to an open-ended question asked on the pilot survey, "Do you feel that there is a need for in-service efforts to be restructured?"

-   "Teachers should be more involved in the planning."
-   "Too often it is planned by administration and not by teachers."
-   "Involvement of the teacher in choosing a topic of interest and topics that show methods would be of more value to me."

If teachers contribute to the planning of an in-service program, they are more apt to participate in the program. A major function of the department chairman is to facilitate the cooperative participation of teachers in planning in-service education and to transmit the teachers' desires to the administration. For districts with no supervisor of mathematics, this is a critical factor in assuring that in-service education does respect the mathematical needs of the program and the staff.

4. To recruit participants for the in-service course

One of the best ways for chairmen to recruit participants for an in-service program is to exhibit enthusiasm for the program themselves and advertise that they are going to enroll in the program. Department chairmen should actively participate in each in-service program that they are not conducting themselves, not only to set an example for the rest of the staff but also to improve their own background.

5. To maintain continuing departmental attention on the curriculum

In-service education needs to be related to long-range curricular planning if its effectiveness is to be maximized. Thus, curricular plans must exist. But given the forces impinging on the school mathematics programs and the consequent changing, evolving nature of the curriculum, the school mathematics staff needs to give continuing attention to the in-service planning. The department chairman is the natural person to assume leadership for this important work.

These five major functions are important for the good health of an in-service program. In addition, the chairman must assume or extend the roles and responsibilities identified for mathematics supervisors and elementary principals that were identified previously.

We conclude the section on the department chairman by identifying it as a major problem area. Some schools are not organized, and policy is not formulated, to use the leadership of department chairmen effectively. Most department chairmen would prefer that it were otherwise. The title *department chairman* in too many schools is relatively honorific and means that the individual is the ultimate mail drop for "Dear Department Chairman" correspondence. It is a means of paying off the senior teacher for length of service by providing an extra planning period and may involve some trivial, routine work in handling departmental data and a minuscule audiovisual budget. We feel that the department chairmanship can be much more than this.

The job description given immediately above for department chairmen is a sad commentary on the curricular and instructional leadership found in many secondary schools today. We hasten to add that this job description is grossly inaccurate for many school systems. Mathematics supervisors tend, however, to label in-service education for secondary teachers a major problem area. Cited are problems of attitude, lack of cooperation, failure to recognize instructional and curricular problems, reliance only on the traditional, and a belief that the answers are already possessed by the teacher. However, the secondary teachers' survey indicates a strong feeling of need for in-service education. *We assert that the primary problem is one of lack of leadership in mathematics education at the local school level.* The problem has evolved because the administration of many schools *does not let* leaders in the schools use their abilities and interests to the advantage of the school's mathematics program either by not giving them sufficient responsibility and authority or by not giving them sufficient time to provide leadership.

Using the department chairmanship is one of the most obvious means for improving the leadership vacuum in a secondary school. The principles of systemic planning enunciated in chapter 4 spell out the basic procedures needed for the design of in-service education and for the general leadership within a department. Thus, responsibilities and roles for the chairmanship are defined.

Often principals have not used the leadership capabilities found within their faculty and, hence, are not able to hold chairmen accountable for leadership. Principals in most high schools and junior high schools even twenty years ago were able to accept the responsibility for instructional leadership because of the small size of the typical school. But school consolidation and the attendent complexity of the school programs have meant that principals in most schools can no longer directly assume this instructional leadership responsibility. Thus, the principal should—in the interest of building a healthy mathematics program—make more use of the professional expertise found at the departmental level.

The responsibilities and roles of the department chairman for in-service education hinge on representing the interests of mathematics and mathematics teachers to the in-service program manager and the administration of the school system. The chairman collects information, participates in planning and implementation, and helps with follow-up and evaluation. For some domains of the curriculum, the mathematics department will have too few teachers to be able to afford its own in-service program. For example, if in-service education is needed for senior level, college-preparatory mathematics, most chairmen will have only a limited number of teachers with this responsibility. Thus, the department chairman has a responsibility to have a working relationship with chairmen in other neighboring schools for the purpose of cooperative planning and design of in-service opportunities for teachers.

In summary, the roles and responsibilities of several key and pivotal school staff members have been examined. We have posited an in-service program manager. This may be one of the key individuals identified above, in which case the guidelines for program design and implementation apply directly. Or, alternatively, the key individual may have to work with the program manager, in which case cooperation, information, and support are of the essence. In the latter case, the individual needs to be aware of the principles espoused in chapters 4 and 5 in order to use his or her unique responsibilities productively. The responsibilities discussed in this section have tended to be of two general types: (1) those providing an atmosphere and setting supportive of in-service education and (2) those specific to an in-service program in that they focus on long-range curricular planning and needs assessment. Worthy of particular note is the task of providing information to administrators responsible to all teachers and schools that will help them in determining priorities, since they must recognize that all teachers have legitimate claims for in-service education. The discussion of department chairmen at the secondary school levels identifies the problem of the granting and building of professional leadership responsibilities for the chairman as a major need of the secondary schools.

The Teacher

The teacher's position in the structure of a school system is one of the most critical in the educational process. Daily personal contact with the student provides the teacher the opportunity to motivate, guide, and direct the student in the learning process; or in essence, it provides the teacher the opportunity to give effective instruction to the student.

The teacher should search for ways of improving instruction. One way in which the teacher might enhance the probability for improving instruction is by implementing concepts, strategies, attitudes, and the like acquired in a sound in-service program. Sound in-service programs do not just happen. They occur through careful planning, planning in which those persons who stand to profit the most from the program—namely, teachers—are actively involved. It is the professional responsibility of the teacher to participate actively in the in-service planning. It is also the professional responsibility of the teacher to participate in an in-service program once it gets under way. The teacher acting in each of these two roles of "planner" and "participant" gives increased assurance that a sound in-service program has been planned and that someone has gained something of value from the program.

Considerable discussion describing the teacher's roles of "planner" and "participant" will be included in this part of the chapter. The role of teachers in controlling the destiny of in-service programs in their districts will be discussed briefly. The last major role of teachers in in-service education discussed will be that of directing their own self-study as a form of in-service education.

Providing the rationale for these four in-service roles of the teacher is the personal payoff or value that the teacher may obtain from this involvement and that it is natural for a teacher to want. Payoff for the teacher assumes one of the following forms:

1. Increased professional power
2. Increased self-confidence
3. Improved image with colleagues
4. Improved image with administration
5. Improved instruction

With these benefits from in-service education, it behooves the teacher to be enthusiastic and aggressive in accepting each of the four roles discussed below.

The teacher's role in planning in-service education

The planning of in-service education includes three major categories: (1) needs assessment, (2) topic identification, and (3) in-service program planning. Teachers should be actively involved in each of these.

In-service assessment of needs is closely related to curriculum planning. Teachers should be able to say, for example, "Our curriculum plan identifies that student performance in applications of mathematics is important. The evidence we have at hand indicates many students are not achieving this objective. Therefore, we need in-service training concerned with teaching applications of mathematics."

The in-service needs of a department cannot be assessed without the knowledge of which curricular objectives are and are not being satisfied. In assessing the in-service needs of a department, teachers must first know the curricular objectives of the department. To be knowledgeable about the curricular objectives, the teacher should be involved actively in their determination. (A department might need some in-service training in the area of how to determine objectives.) Most teachers gain appreciation for the objectives through involved study in the determination of the objectives. They become better acquainted with the total school curriculum in mathematics and are better able to teach to achieve the objectives.

It is equally important that the teachers have knowledge of the performance of the students relative to these objectives. Teachers have difficulty making logical, calculated decisions if they do not have information about the discrepancies between the ideals for their students' performance in the program expounded in the objectives and the actuality of the students' performance. In the supervisor's survey, there was an indication that many supervisors do not share with teachers information that would allow the teachers to behave in a professionally responsible fashion. If teachers are given data on student performance and sufficient time to analyze it in relation to the curricular objectives, most of them will be able to determine intelligently the in-service needs related to this comparison.

The Conference Board of the Mathematical Sciences' National Advisory Committee on Mathematical Education (NACOME), in its *Over-*

view and Analysis of School Mathematics, Grades K-12 (1975), considers teacher judgment on curricular matters important enough to make the recommendation that teacher education place emphasis on the "development of teacher judgmental abilities to make intelligent decisions about curricular issues in the face of growing outside pressure for fads and uninformed policy" (p. 141).

The additonal emphasis on training quoted above is desirable, but probably even more important is the element of "time." Teachers need more scheduled time to reflect, ponder, and study curricular objectives and their relationship to student performance. They also need more time for long-range planning. The heavy schedules of most teachers leave little if any time for them to do this kind of thinking. With class sizes increased because of slashed budgets, the situation is becoming more acute. With heavy loads, it is natural for teachers to think more about tomorrow than the distant future. This perhaps is why 44 percent of the supervisors on their survey indicated that they believe "teachers are so inclined to the practical, what-can-I-use-tomorrow attitude that in-service education loses its effectiveness."

Teachers should be aggressive in their demands for reasonable work loads. They should see that their negotiation units bargain for these things. They should provide the supervisor or in-service program manager with the evidence and support needed to generate and maintain the funding of the in-service program. This means taking the long view on curricular planning and its relation to in-service education, and it means not allowing in-service education funds to be bargained away in salary negotiations. They need to be aggressive in protecting any scheduled in-service time that they have, as well as in bargaining for more.

In the interest of improving instruction in the classroom, the teacher should—in addition to being aggressive in the determination of in-service needs—be receptive and cooperate with the principal, department chairman, mathematics supervisor, or in-service program manager when any one of them attempts to identify in-service needs. The teacher should also aid them in determining the in-service needs of his or her colleagues.

Once the needs have been assessed, the teacher should cooperate in determining the in-service topic or topics that will best relate to these determined needs. The teacher should be involved in the assessment of priorities in topic identification with respect to the choice of the topic that might address the most urgent in-service need or needs. Teachers should work as a team with the department chairman, principal, mathematics supervisor, or in-service manager in the topic identification.

Closely tied to needs assessment and topic identification is the planning of the actual in-service program, which involves determining the site, instructor or instructors, type of program (e.g., lecture, workshop, field trips, institute, or a combination of two or more of these), and amplification of what should be covered under the chosen topic.

The choice of the type of program will be influenced by the nature of the topic chosen. For example, if "motivation" is the topic, a workshop or a combination of lecture and workshop formats might be the most logical choice.

After the topic has been identified, the teacher should insist that one or both of the following two procedures be adhered to prior to beginning the program:

1. The planning team that has identified the in-service topic should prepare an outline for the in-service instructor, indicating goals it wishes to have the instructor address in the program.

2. The in-service instructor chosen for the course should prepare an outline of what will be covered in the in-service program and submit it to the planning team for approval.

If these procedures are followed, increased assurance is given that there will be no misunderstandings of what is desired and that the instructor will have spent time well in preparing for the in-service program.

The teacher's role as a participant in in-service education

Several possible participant roles in in-service education that can be assumed by a teacher are to serve as an instructor, a building leader, an active participant, or an aide.

A teacher with an unusual amount of training in both content and methods might volunteer as an in-service instructor if he or she has had classroom teaching experience at that level and if the teachers at that level feel that this teacher has the expertise necessary for teaching them about the topic. For example, a qualified senior high school teacher might volunteer as a junior high school in-service instructor. Probably the most significant qualification that this teacher should have beyond knowledge in content and methods at the junior high school level and expertise on the in-service topic is classroom teaching experience at the junior high school level.

One of the major dissatisfactions concerning in-service education— listed by the teachers both on the pilot survey and the project survey—was that the leaders did not have experience with classes or students like their own. Many of these incidents have occurred when high school teachers have made assumptions about the nature of the elementary or junior high school student or the program that are authoritative but inconsistent with the participant teachers' experiences.

It does give cause for concern that few institutions offer programs to help classroom teachers acquire the leadership qualifications to be in-service instructors. School districts could pay for such training and then reduce the teachers' load to enable them to teach in-service courses.

In the pilot survey, some teachers complained that the instructor went too fast and did not get around to them often enough in their workshop activities to show them what to do. They suggested that the number of in-service personnel be increased so that each participant might get the necessary help. The instructor might alleviate this type of problem by training teachers in that system to be instructor's aides. The in-service manager, principal, supervisor, or department chairman might suggest teachers who could be trained as such a person. This would also be a position for which teachers might wish to volunteer.

A school system large enough to employ a mathematics supervisor generally provides a great deal of responsibility for the supervisor other than the work related to in-service education. To make an in-service program successful, the supervisor needs leadership at the school level; that is, an in-service leader in each building on which to depend. This leader may be the department chairman or any other mathematics teacher in the building. The building leader can coordinate the in-service assessment of needs and the participatory planning.

The supervisor must exercise management skills and be willing and able to delegate responsibility to these building in-service leaders. By orienting the building leaders to the mode of operation and prescribing what is expected of them in the mechanics of the in-service operation, the supervisor will enable the building leader to have a better chance of succeeding. Such a leadership program in the schools can permit an in-service program generated and implemented by the leaders to spread through the schools with a multiplier effect. This plan will develop the leadership potential in the schools.

The supervisor's survey indicates a lack of complete satisfaction with the present in-service education processes. Only 37.6 percent of the supervisors indicated that needs assessment was based on achievement data of students in their schools, whereas 72.5 percent responded to the Ought portion of the question that it should be. A building in-service leader could improve this situation by aiding the supervisor. Achievement data from students in the particular building can be acquired and the supervisor can be helped to determine in-service needs based on these data.

The building in-service leader should try ideas encountered in in-service programs in his or her classes and encourage colleagues to do the same. By doing this, the leader could collect results that might indicate how well the ideas worked in actual application. Teacher input through the building in-service leader can improve the in-service process and the effectiveness of the in-service program in general. Teachers like to be professional and help control their own professional future. Having a building in-service leader is a step in that direction.

The in-service survey results indicate that elementary and secondary teachers want local in-service leadership. On the elementary teacher survey, 32.4 percent agreed with the item "There is an individual in my building or in my school system responsible for inservice education in mathematics," whereas 82.9 percent agreed that there ought to be. Respective percentage responses on the secondary teacher survey were 29.0 and 83.6.

Among the nine purposes listed for in-service education on the elementary and secondary in-service surveys, the purpose "Providing opportunity to share ideas with other mathematics teachers" was checked by 96 percent of the respondents as what ought to be, making it tie for first among the purposes listed in the survey. One role of the participant, then, seems to be that of being a good listener and being sure to have something worthwhile to share. One way for a teacher to have something to share is to be innovative in teaching and to try out new ideas and methods in the classroom.

The apathetic, self-satisfied, complacent attitude that some teachers project when asked to participate in in-service programs is a form of what might be called "peer boredom." These teachers would rather be bored with their jobs than try to improve in their work by taking an in-service course. The teacher can act in several roles as an ordinary in-service participant. One of the most important is to attempt to reduce this peer boredom by serving as a catalyst in getting colleagues to participate in an in-service program planned by the district. In this role the teacher enthusiastically enrolls in the program early and spends time promoting the program by talking positively about the program and its rationale, such as how the in-service program fits into the long- and short-range curricular plans, how it relates to the needs assessment, and how both the teacher and the student might benefit from the program.

There is considerable interest in making in-service education mandatory, but voluntary participation will delay any such action. The teacher could point out how supervisors feel about this matter by the fact that 86 percent of those answering the in-service questionnaire responded affirmatively to the survey question "Should in-service education be required of all who teach mathematics?" Then compare this with the percentage of elementary teachers (61.7) and secondary teachers (59.2) answering the same question in the affirmative.

The secondary teacher trying to get his or her colleagues to enroll in an in-service program might point out the fact that 54.6 percent of the secondary teachers answered no to the question "Are students as excited about learning mathematics as they ever were?" Many factors in the environment of a mathematics student today compete for attention; they need not be elaborated. The challenge to a teacher is great in this competition. A teacher should seek ways of increasing student interest in mathematics. Rosenberg (1970) discusses six potential generators of student interest in mathematics:

1. Goals of instruction
2. Enrichment content
3. Methodology of instruction
4. Instructional resources
5. The evaluation of learning
6. Qualifications of the mathematics teacher

Each of these items is a "live" topic for in-service education. The teacher should point out to colleagues the need for in-service programs in these areas to help each of them generate more interest in mathematics.

In answer to the survey item "The topics for inservice education in mathematics that receive emphasis in my school are," the three topics receiving the greatest number of checks on what ought to be for both the elementary and secondary teachers were "motivation," "applications of mathematics," and "improving student attitudes about mathematics." Over 93 percent of the teachers surveyed agreed that the three topics ought to receive emphasis in their schools. From these responses, teachers seem to be asking for in-service courses in these three areas. If such courses are offered by the district, the teacher participant has good reasons to encourage colleagues to enroll. Teachers have every right to be aggressive in this way and thus demonstrate their professionalism.

Another form of the peer boredom problem that appears once the in-service course has begun is evidenced by 27.4 percent of the elementary teachers and 33.8 percent of the secondary teachers answering that "my fellow participants were so bored and uninterested that it discouraged me." We shall refer to this problem as the "peer boredom gripe." Many teachers, including some new teachers, can easily become discouraged in the environment of colleagues displaying attitudes of disinterest and boredom. Their complaint is natural. It is strongly related statistically to whether the teachers found in-service experience satisfying and whether they have had a positive experience with in-service education in the past.

Further analysis of the surveys of elementary and secondary teachers revealed that the teachers are less likely to have the peer boredom gripe if—

1. the content of the in-service program is related to classroom needs;

2. the participants helped select the topics;
3. the leader has familiarity with classes like those of the participants;
4. planning and organization are evident;
5. the course is specifically planned for mathematics teaching rather
   than being too general;
6. there is a balance of mathematics content and methodology.

Results of the secondary teacher survey also showed that secondary
teachers who read the *Mathematics Teacher* are less likely to find peer
boredom discouraging. The probability that a teacher would identify peer
boredom as a major gripe decreased with experience. This might be interpreted that the younger teacher has a stronger expectation for payoff
for in-service participation, whereas the more experienced teacher is likely
to be jaded and disappointed by past experiences. It is possible that the
older teachers may simply feel that it is unrealistic to tie their appreciation
for in-service education and its effect to other people's reactions, that in-
service education is a personal thing destined to affect what they do in
their own classroom.

Teachers can reduce the peer boredom gripe by examining their own
attitudes about in-service education and how these attitudes are displayed.
Teachers should have a positive attitude on in-service education and work
aggressively in in-service planning to eliminate any of the factors that
might generate negative feelings. The surveys revealed that if elementary or
secondary teachers perceived students as being excited about learning
mathematics, then they tended not to have some of the complaints. The
answer to relieving peer boredom and the peer boredom gripe is for each
teacher (1) to think positively about students and their desire to learn and
(2) to work hard to improve the quality and kinds of in-service education
in an attempt to improve instruction in the classroom.

An experienced teacher can play an important in-service role in helping the new teacher. The following paragraph from the *Handbook of Educational Supervision* indicates what is at stake:

> The beginning teacher will continue to feel insecure when the students are
> not cooperative and lessons do not run smoothly. In such a situation teachers'
> suggestions often are more effective and acceptable to the beginning teacher
> than is the principal's help, for the teacher may feel too uncomfortable about
> difficulties to be frank with the principal. When the beginning teacher feels
> more at home in the new environment he should be encouraged to visit, volun-
> tarily, an experienced teacher's room for observation purposes. [Oakland
> County Schools 1968]

The question "Are new teachers generally well prepared to teach
mathematics?" was asked on the supervisor's survey. The percentage of

supervisors answering no to this question was 53.9. The intent of the supervisors is probably not so much to criticize preservice programs in mathematics education as to give a message to new teachers and those with whom they work that teacher education is a continuing process of growth and that teaching and learning mathematics is so complex that preservice mathematics education alone cannot be expected to be sufficient.

New teachers are constantly seeking answers to questions. It is hoped that they will find an experienced colleague who will serve as an in-service aide. In fact, in many schools the principal will assign an experienced teacher to serve in this role. This is a recommended procedure.

Since new teachers are seeking answers to questions of a pedagogical nature, it seems that their enrolling in in-service courses where questions of this type are discussed and ideas shared would be a natural thing to do. In-service courses of a content nature are generally also valuable for the new teacher. The rationale is that the preservice mathematics training is often very structured and time is not always given to the content items more directly related to school mathematics, which can be found in in-service courses. The following reveals the importance that supervisors give to in-service education for new teachers. In response to the question "New teachers expect to participate in inservice education throughout their professional life," 41.8 percent of the supervisors agreed that this is "what is," but 91.6 percent agreed that this is "what ought to be."

It would be good for the new teacher if participation in in-service activities were required for them for at least a certain period of time. However, this is unlikely to happen, since it is difficult to make in-service programs mandatory for the experienced teachers. It is hoped that the new teacher's sense of professionalism will encourage participation.

Self-directed, self-study programs

Probably the most efficient and effective type of in-service education is the personal, self-directed study program. This individually styled type of in-service education has a chance of being the most efficient and effective form of in-service education. It can provide what teachers want, when they want it. This is possible if the teachers are able to find the material when needed. There are a number of sources for the teachers' self-study.

The National Council of Teachers of Mathematics provides one of the best and most extensive sources of publications that a teacher can use for in-service self-study. Its yearbooks, monographs, books, booklets on special topics, and journals (the *Mathematics Teacher, Arithmetic Teacher, Journal for Research in Mathematics Education,* and *Mathematics Student*) all provide invaluable material that can help a teacher improve instruction (see NCTM's brochure of current publications). Other sources of material for self-study are publications of the School Science and Mathematics Association, the Mathematical Association of America, state and regional mathematics organizations, and the professional libraries and curriculum centers of institutions preparing mathematics teachers.

Being a member of professional organizations can be a significant aid to the teacher who wishes to obtain in-service education through self-study. The organizations provide information on upcoming conventions, workshops, institutes, and publications. And each of these areas provides the teacher with an opportunity for self-directed in-service study.

The mathematics teacher should selectively build a collection of mathematics books and booklets so that the materials are readily accessible. Also, the teacher should help build a mathematics library for each mathematics department or curriculum center. This provides the next most accessible source of materials at, of course, a lesser cost to the teacher. However, the teacher will make better use of the books if they are in a personal library. A compromise is for the teacher to have both a personal library and access to a departmental library. Thus, the personal cost can be reduced, and the teacher can be more selective in building a personal collection of books. The library or curriculum center of an institution as a source for materials has the distinct advantage, usually, of being more complete and offering the expertise of someone who may be more experienced in finding the needed materials.

In self-directed study, the teacher should read more than one source on a particular topic and not feel restricted to one author, especially in the areas of methodology or pedagogy. The teacher should obtain different points of view on any issue and then adapt the preferred ideas acquired from reading to improve instruction.

Another form of self-study is by observing others teach. Working out a plan for the intervisitation of classes in the department is an effective means to accomplish this. Ideas are sometimes gained from a real-life classroom situation that are difficult if not impossible to gain from mere reading.

The self-directed study plan is another form of in-service education that is indicative of the professionalism of a teacher.

Institutional Participants in the In-Service Process

The previous sections of this chapter have focused on the roles and responsibilities of individuals within the local school system. But a variety of institutions other than those indigenous to the local school system have formal and quasi-formal participatory roles and responsibilities for the in-service education of teachers. Critical among these are area service agencies, state departments of education, colleges and universities, and professional organizations. The functioning of each of these institutions is analyzed in this section.

Area agencies

In some counties or states, the concerns of a group of small school districts or those within a prescribed boundary are shared by an agency that serves as a coordinating system for the educational, financial, and material resources of all the districts. The services are more adequately handled for many schools where there is centralization, and the benefits of leadership in curriculum areas have more potential where there is an area mathematics specialist or area supervisor of the subject.

These intermediate school districts, or boards of cooperative services, often have the capability of providing in-service programs that local districts are not able to sponsor and of supporting the efforts with financial commitments. Initially they must assist districts in identifying needs and designing programs. Because the computer services are often handled by an area agency, data and information for any one district, for all the districts, or for any combination of them can be gathered and interpreted.

The area mathematics supervisor should coordinate the assessment of the in-service needs of the region and plan for the programs to satisfy the needs. The school districts must relate the in-service education to the long-range curricular planning on a systematic basis. Because the success of a regional program depends to a greater extent on the leadership involvement from the many districts, an area planning committee with wide representation should be organized by the supervisor. The committee should assume responsibility for the publicity, schedule, content or topics, physical arrangements, recruitment, and evaluation of the in-service program. The area specialist will have to ascertain that all these facets of the program are actually implemented or carried out and will usually also teach the course.

The agency will be most effective in the area of curriculum if the mathematics supervisor is also given these responsibilities:

1. To train teachers to teach peers—that is, to prepare a cadre of capable in-service instructors

In widespread geographic areas, the use of teachers with special talents to teach others is a great asset. It is necessary to use a training scheme with a multiplier effect in order to reach those teachers who are not near colleges, universities, or even other districts.

2. To develop films or videotapes of model in-service programs or to use prepared commercial ones for showing in remote districts

3. To provide suitable in-service models that small districts or single schools can replicate
4. To be a resource of information for classroom materials, professional literature, and audiovisual aids
5. To establish teacher-learning centers—permanent or mobile—for workshops and training sites

State department of education and state mathematics consultant

A state department of education provides a strong support and framework for in-service education by recognizing and accepting credit for in-service work toward certification or accreditation. The general responsibilities for in-service education in all curriculum areas assumed by the state department are—

1. to establish guidelines for in-service programs within the state;
2. to organize a procedure for sharing services of other districts and for using the state leadership when districts cannot provide their own programs;
3. to inform local districts of state and federal grants that are available.

The state department can also participate in writing proposals and requesting grants for statewide projects. A good example is the Right to Read projects under state sponsorships. These projects provide in-service education throughout the state by training local leaders.

Assistance should be given to individual supervisors as they write proposals for their local districts.

Within the state departments, the specific responsibilities relating to each curriculum area are delegated to the state consultant or supervisor for that subject. The tasks of the supervisor range from personal contributions in writing a designated column in the state mathematics journal or department newsletter to speaking at district meetings on pertinent mathematics topics or pedagogy to joint efforts in influencing state and national legislation.

Much of the work of the state mathematics consultant is directly or indirectly related to the in-service education of mathematics teachers. This office offers some roles in in-service education that are unique. For example, if a state adoption procedure is required for the acquisition of textbooks and materials, an organized program of training should be offered by the state supervisor to the evaluators and decision makers in the selection process.

Allendoerfer (1962) clearly recognizes that a state mathematics supervisor must be one who can organize or arrange in-service education. He summarizes the roles in this way (p. 4):

The state supervisor of mathematics should be:
- a missionary who exudes inspiration
- an organizer who can arrange inservice education
- a counselor who influences his constituents through persuasion rather than by authority.

The leadership potential of the state mathematics supervisor is clearly evident in this list of important responsibilities for in-service:

1. To counsel school districts on in-service education. Through counseling, the state mathematics consultant can help a district—

   a) to identify its in-service needs through visiting classes and conferring with teachers, principals, and the mathematics supervisor;

   b) to organize programs such as in-service courses, workshops, or institutes to satisfy its in-service needs;

   c) to acquire competent in-service instructors;

   d) to find scheduled in-service programs in the region, state, or nation, such as extension courses or conferences sponsored by national, state, or regional mathematics organizations that the teachers might attend;

   e) to find ideas for in-service programs in professional journals and elsewhere and advertise them to teachers and administrators.

2. To keep school administrators informed of in-service opportunities for their teachers

This can be accomplished by writing articles for the administrators' journals, by speaking at their conventions, and by making personal contacts when visiting their schools.

3. To work closely as an advisor to the state mathematics association in the planning and sponsoring of mathematics conferences focused on in-service education

4. To convince school superintendents and directors of instruction of the real need for a substantial annual budget for the in-service education of their mathematics teachers and administrative staff and the need for scheduling release time in the teachers' contracts without the loss of instructional time

5. To suggest to colleges and universities—including the state university extension division—types of in-service courses that are needed in the state for mathematics teachers

6. To evaluate new instructional media being used for in-service education in other areas of the country and suggest that the

proved media be used by the state universities and university extension or by the school district itself

For example, if the state mathematics consultant finds that a medium such as the telewriter is being used successfully for in-service courses by a university extension in some state, he or she might suggest that it be tried in his or her own state.

7. To organize state committees or task forces to generate state curriculum guides and various kinds of tests to be studied and used as models by school districts

The models should encourage local districts to construct their own mathematics curriculum guides and various kinds of tests to meet their community needs. This provides not only in-service training for those teachers and administrators who work on these committees but also a form of training for the many teachers who will read the published guides and tests. In-service education tends to be a by-product of the research and thought involved in the preparation of curriculum guides.

8. To influence legislation that supports in-service programs

The state mathematics consultant should meet with organizations such as the state education organization and the state school board organization to suggest and support legislation that will promote increased budgets for in-service education for mathematics teachers—budgets that include an adequate amount of mathematics in-service time built into the teacher's contract.

9. To provide model programs of in-service education

The state mathematics consultant should be aware of in-service programs that have been successful in other districts in the state and those that have been successful enough in other states to be written up in journals or passed on through other state mathematics consultants. The consultant should share this information with districts in the state and should also be knowledgeable about materials and ideas to use in the classroom, such as motivational materials, enrichment materials, new methods of teaching concepts, and so on. Again, these ideas should be shared with districts in the state.

10. To be an advisor for kinds of classroom instructional materials

In order to gain some of the needed information to be knowledgeable in this area, the consultant can organize state surveys on what instructional materials are being used in the classrooms of the state, such as textbooks, modules, films, filmstrips, physical models, calculators, computers, and so on. The consultant can analyze and disseminate this information together with any information in this area that might have been gleaned from sources such as publishers, college and university resource centers, commercial displays at conventions, and so on.

11. To encourage the use of live or filmed demonstration teaching as one means of in-service education at state and regional conferences

12. To work closely with state certification authorities to raise standards for the certification of mathematics teachers

The state mathematics consultant should recommend to state certification authorities what coursework requirements are sufficient to change the certification standards to improve the mathematics preparation of prospective teachers.

13. To encourage research in mathematics education in schools in the state, to act as consultant for such research, and to evaluate the research and disseminate the findings to the districts in the state

Although many groups are interested in controlling teacher training, both preservice and in-service, a balance must be maintained to guarantee an ongoing and productive program. Spillane and Levenson suggest a reasonable solution (1976, p. 438):

> Undoubtedly state education departments and the colleges will continue to play a useful role in teacher education, if only to counteract a too-rabid provincialism on the part of school districts. But instead of the present two-way control which has not produced effective teacher training systems, we may be able to develop a four-way partnership of state education departments, colleges, school districts, and teacher organizations which will design a respected and satisfying form of teacher training.

Colleges and universities

Colleges and universities have an opportunity to share their expertise with public schools by conducting on-campus and extension classes organized around content appropriate to local needs. The college departments that grant status to the goal of open communication with public schools and teachers should be lauded for their cooperative efforts. Dialogue with educators in the public schools is the first step in improving the articulation of their joint educational programs.

Because in-service education is a needed postcollegiate experience, the colleges and universities have a captive group of teachers ready for more of their offerings and services. Here are some roles and responsibilities that could be undertaken by the education or mathematics departments in a cooperative venture with the public schools:

1. To provide the staff that could serve as in-service instructors

2. To offer degree programs to teachers and curriculum specialists who are potential leaders in the area of in-service education

3. To assist in the design and curriculum content of in-service programs and courses

A survey described by Sherrill (1971) found that in a given school system the elementary teachers—

a) preferred in-service courses over summer courses;

b) preferred an integration of mathematics content and method, with an equal distribution of emphasis;

c) preferred joint planning by school personnel and university personnel;

d) preferred organization across schools in the system, but by grade-level groupings.

4. To provide tuition-free in-service courses to train cooperating teachers who supervise and counsel the college's student teachers

5. To develop evaluation tools for continual improvement of in-service courses

The evaluation component of any project is vital to the decision to continue or terminate it. The design of a good instrument should be part of early planning so that it is an integral part of the total plan. The expert advice of the university personnel could assist in the selection or development of the appropriate evaluative instrument.

6. To assist districts in maintaining a proper balance of content-related and methods-related topics in the course offered

7. To prepare their own staffs to distinguish among the varying needs of preservice and in-service education.

The need for such introspection is pointed out in *In-Service Education* by Harris and Bessent (1969, p. 3):

> Through the years college personnel have been very much involved and are increasingly so in leading in-service activities for elementary and secondary staff members, but they have steadfastly avoided anything approximating in-service education for themselves. There have been noteworthy exceptions to this generalization, however, for example, the University Council for Educational Administrations' career development seminars for professors of educational administration and supervision. Generally, however, in-service education in any formal organized sense is relatively unknown at the college level.

8. To offer in-service courses for administrators and supervisors that would focus on their roles in local and cooperative programs

The responsibility of the colleges for teacher training beyond preservice work is highlighted in the NACOME report (1975, p. 139): "Colleges of education. . . . together with local school boards and organizations representative of teachers must continually facilitate the maintenance of teachers' awareness of and input to current programs and issues."

9. To help local system personnel be aware of trends and programs that may improve curriculum or instruction and that may call for in-service education

10. To contract specific services, other than degree-oriented programs, with districts that have special educational needs; for example, the retraining of tenured staff who have new assignments for which they have limited background or preparation

11. To "work a miracle" and find methods of registration that can be be accomplished on campus with ease rather than perpetuating a time-consuming, nonproductive activity that frustrates the registrants

The reciprocal programs that are established between school districts and colleges or universities are investments in the total improvement or professional growth of educators. The university professor of education has a most important role in the continuing education through in-service education of the student teachers that the department has prepared and sent to the public schools. The changes in content, community expectations for schools, pedagogical techniques, and physical settings are all reasons for offering courses to the teaching staffs of the schools.

The professor should be willing to teach either on- or off-campus in-service programs requested by the schools or to recommend another qualified colleague for a particular course. Visits to different types of schools in a district to assess the needs of their mathematics teachers would tend to enhance the effectiveness of the in-service program. The school visits should include classroom visitations; conferences with principals, teachers, department chairmen, and the mathematics supervisor; and should be followed by general cooperative planning sessions with key people.

Because of the great number of school districts that draw on the expertise of college departments, ways must be found to promote more cooperative programs and more independent or in-house programs. University personnel should be invaluable in establishing a course that would teach the school personnel, teachers, and administrators the techniques of organizing, developing, and conducting successful in-service programs to suit the individual needs of that district.

Professional organizations

The National Council of Teachers of Mathematics, the School

Science and Mathematics Association, the Mathematical Association of America, and state mathematics associations have the leadership potential to improve the quality and quantity of in-service programs. Their responsibilities begin with the sharing of the results of research that support the need for programs that encourage continuing professional growth related to the topics identified by teachers and curriculum specialists.

The specific roles of these groups are—

1. to sponsor meetings, "focus conferences," minicourses, lecture series, and workshops having credit-earning opportunities for participants;

2. to publish in their journals and newsletters descriptions and evaluations of successful in-service models and designs;

3. to offer special help to teachers who are newly assigned to the teaching of mathematics with a bibliography of materials, articles, texts, and aids;

4. to formulate position statements that advocate in-service programs that present specified topics relative to content and methodology and that would prepare teachers for the changing focus in curriculum;

5. to use publications to disseminate innovative procedures, novel presentations of mathematical concepts, successful teaching strategies, and similar ideas that might be incorporated into local programs offered to teachers;

6. to develop a set of guidelines or a handbook for organizing an effective in-service program;

7. to seek out and identify leaders in the field of mathematics and mathematics education who could serve areas without a mathematics specialist;

8. to apprise state departments of education, state legislatures, and other agencies of local and state in-service needs;

9. to continue to sponsor a commission to study in-service, as well as preservice, needs of teachers;

10. to foster the development of local resource centers or teacher centers that are organized to meet the particular needs of the area.

In the NACOME report, the role is summarized succinctly (1975, p. 139): "That professional organizations continue to update and publish the profession's view of the educational needs of mathematics teachers and that professional organizations take an active and aggressive role in apprising decision-makers in teacher education, certification, and accreditation of these views."

The National Education Association, the American Federation of Teachers, and their affiliated state and local organizations exhibit their interest in quality education by urging their memberships to grow professionally through in-service participation. They are most effective in convincing boards of education of their responsibility and cooperation with them—

1. to provide in-service programs for the staff just as industry and business do for their employees;

2. to negotiate into the contracts scheduled days for in-service opportunities and school visitations without decreasing the number of teaching days (in this way teachers would receive remuneration for time spent in professional growth activities that would not encroach on the instructional time);

3. to emphasize that an important use of evaluation is to analyze teacher performance in order to overcome the weaknesses through in-service participation.

Professional organizations and unions can be instrumental in promoting this role of in-service education that builds on the capabilities of individuals and strengthens their pedagogical skills. Robert Luke, in his article "Collective Bargaining and In-Service Education," said (1976, p. 469): "If we are to practice what we preach about the importance of involving those affected by a decision in helping make that decision, it is imperative that teachers, *as members of their professional associations,* find the means to involve themselves in the formulation of policies related to in-service education. Collective bargaining is the means by which this is done." With a decreasing number of available teaching positions and a reallocation of assignments to tenured teachers, the training of teachers on the job is a major challenge. This is a view of Spillane and Levenson (1976, p. 437): "Teachers' organizations have been effective in upgrading salaries, improving working conditions, and protecting the jobs of their members. The time has come for them to tackle the two problems of training and numbers."

Conclusion

A quote from *Elementary School Mathematics: A Guide to Current Research* summarizes the intricacies involved as roles and responsibilities are assumed in the in-service implementation and planning (Glennon and Callahan 1975, p. 106):

It seems fair to say that mid-career education of teachers is crucial if change in education is to be achieved. Such organizational variables as cooperative planning, grade-level classes for teachers, duration of the program, and type of instructor may affect the results of the program. It would seem important to keep in mind that the complexity of educational change, including teacher change, is often underestimated.

Teacher education institutions are no longer in total control of the training of teachers, and many groups and individuals are now influencing both preservice and in-service programs. According to the NACOME report, "the Commission (on the Education of Teachers of Mathematics) rightfully calls attention to the trend toward teacher demands to participate in the design of teacher education programs, teacher certification, and program accreditation and the trend toward school district reliance on their own resources . . . in the design and implementation of in-service education" (1975, p. 92). It is imperative that, as stated in the introduction, a cooperative effort be required by all those who share an interest in improving instruction.

CHAPTER 8

In-Service Education and Its Relation to Higher Education

EDWARD DAVIS

GENE MAIER

BARRY MITZMAN

THIS CHAPTER begins by describing what has been the traditional role of colleges and universities in the in-service education of mathematics teachers. Then, the relationships and arrangements currently being used in in-service programs are considered. Although many traditional relationships still remain, there are reasons for the emergence of new ones, which will be the focus of the third portion of this chapter. Next, recommendations and projections for the future will be made. Finally, suggestions will be offered for predisposing preservice teachers toward expecting and designing in-service education in their future.

The Role of Colleges and Universities in the In-Service Education of Mathematics Teachers

Colleges and universities—through their faculties and course offerings—have been involved in the in-service education of mathematics teachers for a long time. The first methods text for teaching secondary school mathematics was published by a college professor in 1850 (NCTM 1970, p. 29). Teacher institutes were begun in the middle 1800s; the first summer institute for teachers of mathematics was held at Duke University in 1941 (NCTM 1970, p. 316). In-service education was a requirement for recertification for many teachers by the 1920s, and according to Gibb,

167

Karnes, and Wren (1970, p. 316) in the Thirty-second Yearbook of the National Council of Teachers of Mathematics (NCTM), the principal methods of in-service education in the 1920s included college course work, personal conferences with supervisors, classroom observation by supervisors, and supervisory bulletins. Sueltz's study, *The Status of Teachers of Secondary Mathematics in the United States,* reports teachers studying both content and methods courses in in-service training (1933). Sueltz noted that courses in mathematics and courses in general education were offered on a much larger scale than courses in teaching mathematics. Further evidence of the interest of colleges in the in-service training of mathematics teachers is found in a 1935 Mathematical Association of America (MAA) commission publication, "Report on the Training of Teachers of Mathematics."

As interesting as a history of the in-service education of mathematics teachers may be to some, it is not the focus of this chapter. Here we shall primarily consider the role of colleges and universities in in-service education in the second half of the twentieth century. In regard to this, the Thirty-second Yearbook of the NCTM, *A History of Mathematics Education in the United States and Canada,* contains the following statement (NCTM 1970, pp. 329–30):

> The second half of the twentieth century has seen an unprecedented series of forces directing the attention of educators to the need for improving the background and effectiveness of in-service teachers. . . . The most important programs in teacher education have been those supported by the National Science Foundation (NSF) since it was established by Congress in 1950. NSF activities have taken the form of summer institutes, in-service institutes, academic year institutes, fellowships, and cooperative programs between colleges or universities and school districts or systems.

This same yearbook notes that the first National Science Foundation (NSF) summer institute for high school mathematics teachers was at the University of Washington in 1954 (p. 330). In the summer of 1968 there were 458 institutes in science and mathematics—the high-water mark for this type of activity. The yearbook goes on to point out other pertinent facts (pp. 330–31). Summer institutes for elementary school teachers of mathematics began in 1959 at the University of Michigan and at Rutgers University. The year 1965 saw thirty-nine institutes for elementary school teachers. All told, NSF-sponsored college summer institutes have involved approximately 117 000 mathematics teachers, supervisors, and principals, and academic-year institutes enrolled approximately another 19 000 teachers of mathematics in full-time, on-campus work. NSF-sponsored college in-service institutes for local school districts began in 1957 and have involved more than 80 000 teachers in after-school or evening meetings.

By the middle 1970s, virtually all NSF-sponsored college institutes had been discontinued. The reasons for the termination of these institutes are varied and complex. They include policy changes at NSF, budgetary considerations, and a series of political developments. The latter are perhaps best summarized and referenced in a open letter from Walter L. Gillespie, director of the Division of Science Education Resources Improvement of the National Science Foundation. The letter included the following paragraphs (1975):

> The HUD-Independent Agencies Appropriation Act for fiscal year 1976 (Public Law 94-116), which includes appropriations for the National Science Foundation, was signed into law on October 17, 1975. This law specifically states: "no funds shall be used . . . for Instructional Improvement Implementation budgeted for in Elementary and Secondary School Programs of the Science Education Improvement activity." Therefore, no awards will be made during this fiscal year (through September 30, 1976) for these activities. No guidelines for preparing proposals for implementation activities also will be issued. Directories announcing teacher training opportunities also will not be published.
>
> Further background information regarding the concerns expressed about the Foundation's pre-college curriculum development and implementation activities and the status of the reviews of these activities is summarized in the following articles published in *Science:*
>
> Volume 188, May 2, 1975, pp. 426–428;
>
> Volume 189, July 4, 1975, pp. 26–28;
>
> Volume 190, November 14, 1975, pp. 644–646.

The magnitude of the involvement of mathematics teachers in institutes should not cause us to ignore other avenues of in-service education that continued during the 1950s and 1960s. The May 1954 "Bulletin of the National Association of Secondary School Principals" had as its topic "mathematics in secondary schools today." Its chapter on in-service education discusses the following forms of in-service education: school system workshops, local organizations of mathematics teachers, classroom visitations and conferences, professional conventions and publications of the NCTM, and college-sponsored institutes.

As noted, NSF sponsorship during the past fifteen to twenty years has resulted in colleges and universities playing a major role in the in-service education of mathematics teachers. With some modification in format, it is likely that colleges and universities will continue as one major resource for in-service education in the next decade. Teachers' beliefs on this point are reflected in items 18, 19, 26, and 55 on the survey (see chap. 2) of elementary and secondary teachers, and items 11, 12, 13, 92, and 93 on the supervisors' questionnaire (see chap. 3). In particular, item 55 on both the elementary and the secondary surveys shows approximately 50 percent of the teachers reporting that colleges and universities are currently providing the majority of opportunities for in-service education and that this ought to be the case.

Colleges and universities have, to a large extent, packaged their in-service offerings in the form of credit courses. Teachers have frequently used college credits to obtain advanced degrees, partly because certification policies and salary schedules have encouraged them to do so. Since degree programs, in some sense, belong to the institution offering the degree, the content of courses frequently taken by practicing mathematics teachers has largely been selected by college personnel to fit the needs of teachers as seen by professional groups and by national commissions and conferences. In training teachers, college personnel have also been influenced by their perceptions of the needs of the nation and of the subject itself—mathematics.

However, in the past few years, faculties of colleges and universities have begun to change their offerings and sometimes their beliefs on how the needs of teachers are best determined. Many readers have firsthand knowledge of the changing position of individuals in higher education as it relates to the in-service education of mathematics teachers. But before discussing these changes in the following section, we turn to a national conference called in 1960 to study the question of the in-service education of high school mathematics teachers. We do this to help portray the changes in offerings and beliefs of university personnel in regard to in-service education.

In March 1960, a conference on the in-service education of high school mathematics teachers was held in Washington, D.C., under the joint auspices of the U.S. Department of Health, Education, and Welfare (HEW) and the NCTM. When parts of the conference report, "Inservice Education of High School Mathematics Teachers," are considered, some evidence is found of the causes for current in-service programs and the concerns of college teachers and school administrators about in-service education (USOE 1961). The opening address included these remarks on the prominent position mathematics had come to hold in society (p. 1):

> Space Missiles are only symbols of the great explosion of scientific knowledge of the 20th century. One of the most important factors contributing to this explosion is the revolutionary advance in both the development and the use of mathematics.
>
> Not only are new requirements being placed on mathematics in the fields of physics, chemistry, and engineering; but in other fields mathematics is being put to new and even more astonishing uses.
>
> The demands of society require a thorough revision of our present secondary school mathematics curriculum.

Curriculum revision posed a problem for teachers, as noted by the dean of the College of Arts and Sciences of the University of Virginia (USOE 1961, p. 11):

> Despite their willingness to work, our school mathematics teachers do not have enough mathematical power to adapt to the demands of a new curriculum.

At the time of the HEW conference, colleges and universities, as well as state departments of education and local school systems, were offering a large number of in-service courses to mathematics teachers—at elementary and secondary levels (1961, pp. 18–35). These courses, often housed in what we have identified as institutes, were predominantly mathematical in nature. Methods of teaching played a minor role. Methods for the most part were considered to be ways of presenting particular mathematical topics and portraying in some sense the spirit in which a mathematics class was to be conducted—a spirit of inquiry. At this conference, "methods" referred more to the way the college instructor taught than to teachers' actions in school classrooms. This is exemplified by the position taken by another invited speaker (p. 36):

> There are a few college people who have the right combination of interest and background in both content and methods to be able to appeal to the teachers. Using poor instructors has hurt inservice education programs in the past. Teachers who choose to take classes not required for every teacher in the system must be motivated to the hard intellectual activity involved. Not only their natural human inertia, but also their traditional practical viewpoint, must be overcome. Teachers must realize that although inservice education may be of no immediate application in the classroom, it may still be very valuable. . . . The supervision of inservice education must be in the hands of a person trained in mathematics.

The emphasis for in-service education was on the study of mathematics. Why? Henry Van Engen, also invited to address the conference, states a position widely held at that time (p. 39):

> In view of the problems confronting our sociey, there can be no excuse for teaching mathematics in the schools unless it encourages our youth to think like mathematicians. Of course, a similar statement could be made about art, music, social science, science, and any other subject taught in the schools. Schools do have their utilitarian objectives, but above all they are working with the intellect of the young people and this intellect must be so developed as to enable today's youth to understand tomorrow's mathematics. This is a primary function of the schools.

Van Engen goes on to advocate that courses for college credit should be content oriented and that methods lie in the domain of the school system (p. 41):

> Courses offered by collegiate institutions for credit toward an advanced

degree are beyond the control of the school system, as they should be, and their basic purpose is to advance the knowledge of the teacher in his specialty.

Courses sponsored by the school itself are quite another matter. They should be highly practical in nature—practical in the sense that they discuss mathematical ideas that have their roots in the courses being taught to the children.

Concerning the state of affairs of elementary school mathematics, Van Engen reflects what was a widely held opinion of college personnel (pp. 41-42):

> There is no greater need in the educational system than the need to provide an adequate mathematical background for the elementary teacher. The colleges have been seriously negligent in this matter. . . . To remedy this situation, the elementary teacher must be introduced to modern arithmetic, certain fundamental ideas of geometry, number theory, and algebra. For the present, the schools must do this, and it must be done through inservice courses.

Van Engen identifies what was a serious problem in the early 1960s—the lack of college teachers having elementary or secondary school teaching experience (p. 42):

> The problem of staffing inservice courses can be difficult. In some cases nearby college staffs can be used. However, the college instructors who can teach the kind of practical course described in this paper are few and far between. It is difficult for anyone to teach a good course for teachers without having had considerable experience teaching school mathematics.

Why all this emphasis on mathematics in the in-service education of mathematics teachers? The prevailing opinion was that to teach a subject effectively, one must be engaged in learning that subject. This was noted by Van Engen with this remark (p. 46):

> Most certainly, the good teacher and the good teaching staff will never cease learning; in particular, they will never cease learning mathematics. It cannot be otherwise, for how can a teacher instill the love of learning if the teacher does not know what it means to love learning sufficiently to pursue it constantly?

It should be emphasized that the needs one perceives are a function of the situation as one sees it. In the late 1950s and early 1960s the United States was engaged in a contest for technological supremacy in space. Undoubtedly this contributed to an overemphasis by the schools to produce engineers, scientists, and mathematicians—and the eager acceptance of solutions of how to produce these professionals. To their credit, educators at elementary, secondary, and college levels began to work collectively in responding to what was believed to be the nation's need to increase the mathematical knowledge of students. It is not surprising that college scholars first dominated this partnership and that curriculum reforms were created to upgrade the mathematical competence of students. The way was led by the National Science Foundation's sponsoring the School Mathematics Study Group. After all, colleges had the responsibility for the final products of the system, and their perceptions of necessary curriculum reforms and accompanying in-service programs held the prospect of quickly producing the desired product—more capable mathematics students.

That the nation's economy did not continue to demand increasingly large numbers of engineers, scientists, physicists, and mathematicians and that the urgency to produce large numbers of people in all fields highly trained in mathematics has somewhat abated should not mask the fact that demands for reform in education are always a result of economic and social pressure as well as academic influence. Current demands on the educational system should be viewed as a function of societal needs. Programs and policies touted today as meeting paramount national needs will give way to others as society and the economy change. Today's programs and policies will become as dated as those of the late 1950s and early 1960s. As long as demands on the schools change, a need for in-service education will exist.

Colleges and universities can provide a buttress against two inherent dangers in the evolving in-service education of teachers—namely, the teacher's cynicism that can arise as new programs and their prophets appear, and the tendency to accept new programs too quickly and to abandon—prematurely—incompletely developed or successful older programs. Cogan speaks to this point in the National Society for the Study of Education (NSSE) yearbook on teacher education (1975, p. 273):

> In-service programs may also, in a sort of "suicidal" pattern, drain off and exhaust the very energies they are supposed to nurture. This strange phenomenon occurs most often in the school systems most energetic in mounting in-service programs. One characteristic of these efforts is that they tend to occur in cyclical fashion in response to educational innovations. The tragedy of the cyclical process is that both the fads and the promising innovations suffer almost exactly the same fate.

Institutions of higher education should be a testing arena for new ideas and provide leadership to see that new programs are implemented properly, carried to fruition, and evaluated. It is possible that colleges and universities can perform these functions in a more objective way than school systems or local school leaders consumed in the day-to-day administration of programs to which their ego is often attached.

Some additional observations should be made before considering the current relationships between colleges and the in-service education of mathematics teachers. First, the need to train teachers in methods other than those pertaining to the presentation of specific mathematical topics has been advocated by some mathematics educators at the college level for some time. Methods associated with the laboratory approach to teaching mathematics; applications as a way of teaching mathematics; problem-solving experiences; and the use of manipulative materials—all certainly predate the sputnik era. The message of master teachers and creative professors, such as George Polya and Kenneth Kidd, was transmitted in efforts toward the in-service education of mathematics teachers before the 1960s. Polya's *How to Solve It* was first published in 1945. Kenneth Kidd had developed scores of mathematics-laboratory activities by 1954 when he wrote the following (p. 400):

> Yet still another test of how meaningfully mathematics has been taught is the success that students have in *relating* mathematical ideas to specific and significant phases of their experience.
>
> It is a very sobering experience for a mathematics teacher to talk with teachers who teach his students in shop, home economics, chemistry, or physics. Do his students relate class work with fractions to the use of a ruler in marking of 2-3/4" on a board? Do they recognize that finding 1/2 of a recipe which calls for 3/4 cup of an ingredient involves finding 1/2 × 3/4? Do they apply their skill in solving equations effectively to the proportions of chemistry or the formulas of physics which do not appear in the same form as those on which they have practiced?

Perhaps it took the pressures of the sputnik era to get programs for *specialized* in-service education for mathematics teachers under way on a considerable scale. Such programs are expensive, and government and foundation funds are often earmarked to meet specific needs deemed critical at given times.

Finally, whereas some may be quick to criticize colleges and universities for overemphasizing mathematics in the in-service education of mathematics teachers during the last twenty years, it should be noted that mathematics-dominated in-service programs had considerable impact on the production of many specialists in mathematics education and on the creation of programs to produce mathematics educators. Specialists in mathematics education now exist in considerable numbers and are leaders (teachers, supervisors, and professors) in many educational contexts. To a large extent, these are the leaders who are attuned to the needs of mathematics teachers today and who have been changing the form and content of in-service education in the past few years.

The Changing Role: New Offerings and New Relationships

Today a host of in-service activities are being conducted by colleges and universities. Although some of these offerings and relationships were present in small numbers in the early 1960s, all have now become commonplace. From almost an exclusive emphasis on college courses in mathematics, many current programs focus on pedagogical concerns in teaching mathematics. Mathematics courses still exist, and rightfully so, but they no longer completely dominate college-supported in-service programs. Methods courses now comprise a significant portion of in-service offerings, and it is likely they will do so in the near future.

What do teachers mean when they use the term *methods*? In the preceding section, methods referred to a spirit of inquiry and ways to present specific mathematical topics. To many teachers, methods refers to anything that helps them in the classroom. One way to depict what teachers mean by this term is to reproduce part of the report of the 1974 NCTM survey on in-service education conducted by the Commission on the Education of Teachers of Mathematics (NCTM 1975).

Approximately four hundred NCTM members were asked to list three topics for which they felt the greatest need for in-service work. Later in the form, they were asked to check in-service topics that they felt would be most beneficial. In both question formats, teachers gave a higher priority to topics other than mathematical content. Topics relating to motivation received particular emphasis. Following are the preferences of the 266 teachers responding to the survey, with the number given of teachers checking each topic.

Motivation	148	Consumer math	95	Behavioral	
Metrication	139	Creativity	87	objectives	50
Laboratory		Audio visual	88	Transformational	
learning	137	Discovery learning	87	geometry	49
Slow learners	135	Evaluation	86	Teaching	
Learning styles of		Psychology of		computation	48
students	127	learning	81	Cultural charac-	
Mathematical		Testing	79	teristics of students	44
games	125	Computer		The math I am	
Development of		languages	78	teaching	41
instructional		Geometry	76	Reading	40
materials	124	Career education	70	Background on	
Problem solving	112	Open education	66	math I am	
Classroom use of		Discipline	64	teaching	39
computers	112	Probability	61	Algebra	37
Applications	102	Topology	56	Measurement	35
Gifted learners	100	Problems in		AP Calculus	31
Enrichment	99	mathematics	53	Proof	24
Individual		Statistics	51	Calculus	23
differences	96			Combinatorics	20

Mathematics teachers still feel a need for mathematical content in in-service work. However, their perception of their needs includes more than mathematical knowledge. More importantly, they want to identify topics for in-service work, and they want these topics to be practical. (See items

88, 89, and 90 in both teacher surveys and items 32 and 33 in the supervisors' survey.)

Consider elementary and secondary teachers' responses to items 65–77 in the present survey. On all items but one, for each form, a sizeable majority of teachers agreed on what should be studied in in-service programs and agreed these topics were not receiving enough emphasis at the present. A check of the supervisors' responses in items 69–81 shows agreement with the teachers. Of the thirteen topics in items 65–77 (and 69–81), only four are basically mathematical (items 67, 68, 69, and 74 on teachers' forms). The others reflect concerns for methods in teaching mathematics.

Elementary and secondary teachers also agree with supervisors on another point. Consider the responses to items 93–98 on the teachers' surveys and items 50–55 on the supervisors' form. Instead of requiring teachers to pay in order to participate in in-service programs, some arrangements pay the participants. College programs not leading to degrees (many teachers seem to want such programs) seek to attract teachers by being accessible and, on the surface, highly relevant to the day-to-day problems of classroom teachers. Other programs "pay" teachers with system credits toward tenure or salary increments or both, or result in meeting state certification requirements. Some locally run staff development (in-service) programs can be used in lieu of college courses to meet certification requirements. Pennsylvania and Minnesota currently allow nonuniversity master's equivalency credit toward recertification for participation in locally designed in-service programs.

Inducements to participate in in-service programs were formerly centered in either the teacher's commitment to continue professional development or in state regulations for recertification—usually accompanied by salary increments. Newer in-service arrangements contain two other threads. The survey (items 93–95) indicates that teachers feel it is the duty of the system to provide not only the program but the *time* to attend (release time) in-service meetings. If teachers attend on their own time, they expect to be paid. In other cases, teachers are motivated to attend by the relevance of the program. In *all* cases, teachers view in-service participation as a way of becoming better equipped to perform professionally. This is a legitimate interest. Notice items 78–86 and 91–92 on the teachers' surveys. Student achievement is important, but it is not the only reason teachers want in-service training. Teachers feel that they have a right to better their working conditions through increasing their professional competence. In-service programs are seen as a way to obtain a better environment in which to work. As teachers become better organized, this demand becomes a part of contract negotiations. Teachers will strongly resist being held accountable for student achievement when it is known that there are other significant factors influencing that achievement in addition to the classroom teacher. It is reasonable to believe that teachers will be more willing to be accountable for using correct or appropriate teaching practices—when these have been shown to be effective or accepted by the profession.

What forms have been developed by colleges and school systems in in-service ventures? Many in-service programs are a combination of one or more of the following:

Short courses and workshops
Contracted training of teachers and production of materials
Private in-service agencies staffed by college personnel
Consultant work
Conference credits
Cooperative grants to the school systems and universities
Programs from external institutions

Short courses and workshops—perhaps patterned after extension programs in agriculture—are offered in a variety of locations, usually at the convenience of teachers. Local facilities have been used after school, weekends, and on days when students have been dismissed so that teachers can participate. Colleges and universities have used state and regional meetings of mathematics teachers to offer one- or two-hour credit courses as options for those in attendance. Participants attend either a series of meetings or one continuous meeting over the span of two or three days. Short courses and workshops are almost always targeted on one specific topic, such as problems in reading mathematics, diagnosing and treating students with arithmetic difficulties, paper folding in nonmetric geometry, or using hand calculators in teaching advanced high school mathematics.

Not all short courses and workshops are conducted on a credit basis. Sometimes school systems contract with a college or with an individual college teacher to offer the program. At state and regional meetings of mathematics teachers, college instructors (as well as classroom teachers and supervisors) frequently offer their services as a professional contribution.

In addition to short courses and workshops that are conducted over a span of a few days or weeks, colleges and universities offer courses over more extended periods of time. Courses meeting weekly, on or off campus, are commonly found. The University of Georgia offers in-service courses on a drive-in basis one weekend a month—participants drive in to attend sessions on Friday evening and Saturday. Lodging is arranged for teachers at their request.

Many school systems contract with colleges or universities to offer in-service programs. Often participants can attend free of charge and receive credit from their school system or pay a matriculation fee and also receive college credit. In contracted arrangements, the school system frequently has considerable input into the topics being offered and the kinds of services they receive. Contracts include visits to classrooms by college personnel for consultation with teachers or demonstration teaching, the production and revision of curriculum guides or sets of objectives, and leadership in creating, purchasing, and using manipulative aids. Contracts have also included summer course work for teachers to either precede or follow school-based programs during the academic year.

School systems also contract with colleges and universities to assess needs and for help in obtaining and carrying out grants from governmental and private foundations. Often it is advantageous to both the school system and the university to work cooperatively in seeking outside sources of funding for compensatory, enrichment, or innovative programs. Granting agencies are thus assured that needs have been identified and that implementation plans and agreements have been made.

A variation of the cooperative arrangement described above is for one college or university to contract with a number of school systems to provide an in-service program. In such cases, the school systems may be small or spread out over a large geographic area and not have resources to provide specialized in-service programs. Small school systems can also be at a disadvantage when it comes to obtaining outside funds because they do not have personnel skilled in applying for such funds and because the number of people affected by the proposed program will be small. Cooperating with other school systems allows a small system to share the cost of specialists and also to capitalize on increased purchasing power.

Cooperative and contracted programs are also constructed by school systems, publishing houses, and private individuals at a university or college. Private in-service agencies staffed by college personnel are active in many localities and offer short courses and workshops throughout the year. Their emphasis is usually on practical matters in teaching mathematics. It is not uncommon for teachers attending privately sponsored workshops to pay an additional matriculation fee to a cooperating college and receive graduate credit.

Colleges and universities have been both agressive and cooperative in offering in-service courses to teachers. Some colleges offer credit courses far outside their geographic location—for example, teachers in the Midwest have been known to take off-campus courses from colleges located on the West Coast. Courses are conducted by adjunct professors of the absentee institution. Adjunct professors can be on the staff of some other institution, a retired professor, or simply a monitor administering assignments sent from the absentee institution. Sometimes local colleges and state agencies refuse to accept transfer credit from teachers having credits from absentee institutions, the feeling being that such in-service offerings are conducted for the primary purpose of generating income for the institutions, are inadequately supervised, and do not result in the professional development of a teacher.

At the other extreme are cooperative credit programs. In Georgia, for example, many state colleges and universities—and a number of private institutions—cooperatively offer and staff a variety of graduate courses for teachers. This permits teachers to take a limited number of courses on a graduate program from a local institution and be assured of the right to transfer credit to another school in the state.

One of the potential sources of difficulty for colleges and universities in offering in-service education to mathematics teachers is in the area of graduate credit. As the kinds of in-service offerings depart from the curriculum of traditional college courses in order to focus on practical matters, administrators of graduate schools can become reluctant to award credit. This problem is becoming serious at some institutions where graduate school decisions are made by those who hold a traditional view of the nature of the subject matter appropriate in graduate level courses. This problem of credit is exacerbated when one realizes that all mathematics teachers are in need of in-service training and that the undergraduate records of some teachers do not meet the requirements for admission to a given graduate school. Some institutions resolve this difficulty by providing two kinds of credit—academic and institutional. Institutional credit does not apply toward a degree, but if institutional credit is recognized by school systems and state recertification agencies for salary and licensing, much of the tension is relieved. To the extent that universities, state agencies, and school systems have not resolved this issue, the problem remains a serious one. It seems that reasonable accommodations by all parties must be made. Those institutions, state agencies, and school systems that cannot resolve these difficulties lose the opportunity to improve the quality of teachers and may find themselves involved in legal confrontations with teachers denied opportunity to improve their professional and financial standing.

Reasons for the Changing Role

There are at least two external forces and one internal force causing colleges and universities to change some of their approaches to in-service education. One external force is the legitimate desire on the part of local and state school officials to have a voice in the form and substance of in-service programs. When school officials provide financial support for programs, it should not be a surprise when they wish to have some control over the offerings or when they want to know what happens as a result of their expenditures. School officials have always taken an interest in in-service training because of their desire to improve their educational program. More recently, school officials have been faced with pressures from the second external force causing colleges and universities to change some of their in-service offerings: teachers' organizations.

Where teachers' organizations have grown in strength in recent years, local control of in-service education has increased. Teachers are seeking the initiative in developing and planning their in-service experiences. National and local teachers' organizations have demanded greater teacher control of in-service programs in collective bargaining. It is urgent that teachers, through their professional organizations, involve themselves in the formulation of policies related to in-service education, argues Robert A. Luke, professional associate for instruction and professional development, National Education Association (NEA). "University personnel and other representatives of the intellectual community are a resource, a part of the team that help make in-service happen. Teachers are not now content to let the college faculty either implicitly or explicitly make the needs assessment and determine the teaching methodology. Those who are to be the object of the in-service activity demand a voice in what those needs are and in helping design the delivery system" (Luke 1976, p. 469).

Because the teacher surplus has brought a decline in preservice enrollments, many colleges are concerned by the trend toward local control of in-service programs. Teachers today are better educated, many already having master's degrees. Fewer have need of substantial course work or degrees in order to maintain their credentials or gain salary increases. In addition, some public and private agencies are now competing with colleges by offering in-service work. Lower enrollments in colleges of education may soon no longer justify large faculties.

What has been the response of college-based teacher educators when teachers want to have substantial control of their in-service program? Some have sought to cooperate; others have seemed to resist the change. Edward C. Pomeroy, executive director of the American Association of Colleges for Teacher Education (AACTE), a spokesman for college-based teacher educators, feels that teacher organizations and local school districts will soon outpoint colleges in designing and controlling in-service programs. Pomeroy believes colleges and universities should give leadership to in-service education to insure that it is professionally sound as well as politically viable. He argues that although teachers know what is needed to update their specific skills, knowing *what* they need and knowing *how* to design and deliver programs for professional upgrading are separate matters and that the responsibility for designing and delivering continuing education programs belongs to teacher educators, working cooperatively with others (Pomeroy 1975, pp. 196–201).

Morris Cogan argues in the Seventy-fourth NSSE Yearbook that "professors are needed in the school sites to offer instruction in the relationships of theory, research, and practice" (Cogan 1975, p. 217). He feels that college professors must be involved daily in the schools in order to become familiar with teachers' needs and feelings and to establish credibility by teaching children. Professors teaching in field-centered preservice courses are in a good position to translate theory into practice and to help in designing in-service programs.

There are those who feel that colleges and universities, particularly professors of education, have failed to give adequate preservice programs and often argue that these institutions and professors are incapable of providing worthwhile in-service programs. Certification requirements are seen as having provided education faculties a degree of protection from competition, guaranteeing them a certain demand for their course offerings. The results, writes Charles E. Silberman (1970), have been useless or ineffectual courses, and although there are exceptions, the intellectual level of most education courses and programs is almost scandalous. Teachers' organizations, voicing the feelings of their members, have also claimed that most college education courses are irrelevant to the reality of the classroom.

Those who contribute to diatribes against teacher education and blame colleges and universities for monopolizing it—through accreditation and certification requirements—often overlook three significant issues. First, they lump all education courses and professors together. They do not separate general education courses and faculties from those concerned with subject matter areas. The second is that many institutions of higher education have changed, and are continuing to change, their programs to provide classroom experience prior to—and in some cases, after—student teaching. Many colleges are seeking ways to structure their programs to provide a transition between theory and practice. The ERIC publication *Promising Practices in Mathematics Teacher Education* (Higgins 1972) contains over thirty descriptions of field-based training programs. Clearly, many collegiate educators are involved with redesigning methods courses to make them more relevant.

A third, and more important, oversight of some critics of teacher education is a failure to consider the overwhelming complexity and difficulty of the assignments of most classroom teachers. Frequently, a new teacher is given an abundance of students that are often extremely difficult to teach because of their limitations, handicaps, and attitudes. Perhaps *no* preservice (or in-service) program will be able to train teachers adequately for the responsibilities and working conditions many teachers presently face. It has been noted earlier that improved working conditions are one of the primary reasons teachers want and demand in-service education. Critics of education should consider directing some of their efforts and invectives at those who provide and control teachers' working conditions. Colleges and universities and professors of education have a modest amount of responsibility in this area.

Instead of castigating schools, preservice and in-service training, and classroom teachers, education critics—many of whom are college personnel—should consider crusading for working conditions that would permit or encourage teachers to practice the theory they already know. The average high school mathematics teacher is often fortunate to be assigned one dutyfree planning period each day. Divided among five teaching assignments (classes), this amounts to approximately ten minutes of planning time for each class. This, of course, is more planning time than many elementary school teachers receive. Time still has to be found for grading, conferences with students, parents, and other faculty; and supervisory and clerical duties. If the foregoing sounds too familiar, perhaps it is because too many college educators, teachers, and administrators have come to accept the unprofessional working conditions that many teachers face. The demands of teachers' organizations for professional working conditions should be supported by college faculties. Such conditions hold promise for college and university training programs to increase their impact on practice. The American Federation of Teachers (p. 7) takes the following position on professional working conditions:

20/20 Vision for Teachers

Goal: Modern, properly equipped classrooms; limitation of maximum class sizes to no more than 20 pupils (and fewer in special and "difficult" classes); no more than 20 classroom periods a week; and complete relief from nonteaching chores such as keeping clerical records, supervising buses, lunchrooms, and playgrounds.

Good teaching conditions are good learning conditions. Makeshift, poorly equipped, and crowded classrooms; onerous, often unnecessary, paper work; distracting nonteaching assignments; and full classroom schedules rob students of their chance to learn and prevent teachers from achieving full professional status. When teachers, . . . insist on proper teaching conditions, improvements soon are evident, and students, as well as teachers, benefit.

The internal force causing institutions of higher education to change some of their in-service offerings is the beliefs and expertise of many of their faculty members. As mentioned earlier in this chapter, programs such as the National Science Foundation's institutes have helped create a pool of resource people for the in-service education of mathematics teachers. Many of those given advanced training in mathematics education now hold college positions and are responsible for, or interested in, training mathematics teachers. Many came from classroom teaching and have not forgotten its challenges. These professors are receptive to making in-service education relevant and have a teaching background disposing them to visit classrooms and to be critical of theory not conducive to viable classroom practice.

Projections and Recommendations

Teacher professionalism, teacher unionism, and local funding of in-service education have all grown in recent years. With them has come a trend toward local control of in-service education. One vehicle being used by both teacher organizations and local school systems in planning and conducting their in-service experiences has been the "teachers' center." We project that teachers' centers will play an increasing role in in-service education in the near future.

Teachers' centers

"Teachers' center" refers to a wide variety of locally controlled organizations seeking to help teachers find and create resources and solve common problems. Teachers' centers appear to have been influenced from similar institutions found in Great Britain and have been defined as "a place where teachers share teaching experiences, have access to a wide range of instructional resources, and are trained in specific instructional competencies" (Schmieder and Yarger 1974, p. 62). At present, teachers' centers receive financial backing from a variety of sources, including school districts, private foundations, commercial publishers, teachers' organizations, and the federal government. The amount of autonomy of each center's staff and members varies as much as the sources of financial support. A recent estimate places the number of existing centers at about forty-five hundred and growing (Schmieder and Yarger 1974, p. 6). Thomas O'Brien (1975, p. 43) describes the assumptions behind two centers in the St. Louis area:

> We very strongly believe teachers should be agents rather than patients. That is, it has too often been the case in American education that teachers have to settle for pre-packaged, instant-success, 'Teacher proof' programmes parachuted from on high by curriculum reform groups, universities, school administrators and publishers, and far too often mathematics education for them consists of isolated and disarticulated activities, games and gimmicks, without any consideration of the purpose those activities purport to serve. We think that such a situation need not be the case.
>
> We think that the professional obligation of teachers is to develop their own *point of view* with respect to education, not to allow others to foist disarticulated tricks upon them.

Some would incorporate teachers' centers within existing institutional arrangements for teacher education. One HEW-sponsored task force, representing higher education, endorsed teachers' centers, though preferring to call them "personnel development centers." The higher education task force, however, complained that in the U.S. Office of Education's plans for such centers, too little importance was attached to the role of colleges and universities in the process. Many college and university personnel, the task force said, found it disturbing that university involvement in centers should be dependent largely on a local school system's inclination to turn to them for help. The task force recommended that colleges and universities be represented on policy governing any personnel development centers (American Association for Colleges of Teacher Education 1974).

Other HEW-sponsored task forces representing chief state school officers, community members, and administrators and supervisors also reported their views on the continuing professional development of teachers. Each report manifests a certain tension between the desire to collaborate with other parties and the desire to maintain the power and status of one's own group. It is not yet clear what new realignments of influence and control will emerge.

A teachers' center is a place, but it is also an approach to in-service education. The approach might be called "peer teaching"—teachers helping teachers. And the approach can be adopted without establishing any particular place called a teachers' center.

During the past four years, teachers throughout the state of Oregon have collaborated in developing a statewide program of in-service training in mathematics, called the Oregon System in Mathematics Education (OSME). Supported by the National Science Foundation, the program has enabled elementary and secondary teachers to provide in-service experiences for more than four thousand of their peers.

The OSME staff has acted as in-service brokers. They visit with groups of teachers and administrators in nearly every town and city in the state, identifying locally perceived needs in mathematics and seeking to provide support for local teachers to organize a project to meet those needs.

These local projects, each with its own local project director and planning committee, have taken a variety of forms. Many involve a series of credit workshops on elementary mathematics focusing on active-learning or discovery-teaching methods, a subject of particular interest to many teachers. Generally, workshops are taught by practicing classroom teachers.

Developing leadership among teachers is a slow process. The planning committees for each project provide a useful framework for identifying and encouraging teachers who are potential "mathematics enthusiasts"—teachers who enjoy mathematics and who are willing to help others teach mathematics. Members of project planning committees are encouraged to lead workshops. Those experienced in leading workshops in their own districts may be asked to help lead workshops elsewhere. They are invited to participate in conferences and other leadership activities conducted by OSME and by the state affiliate of the National Council of Teachers of Mathematics. They are gradually brought into a community of mathematically oriented teachers around the state, and membership in this informal community provides support and recognition for their efforts to improve the mathematics program of their own school or district.

This peer-teaching model is especially appropriate for mathematics workshops because many elementary teachers regard mathematics as dull and difficult. Teachers leading workshops bring a special informality and sensitivity to other teachers' needs and feelings. They enjoy a unique credibility with other teachers if they are able to say, "I tried this with my kids the other day, and this is what happened. . . ."

The role of higher education

Teachers' centers and peer teaching might appear to exclude colleges and college faculty from in-service education. One research study indicates that outside "experts" are not the most effective leaders of school districts' in-service programs. The Rand Corporation's study of 293 federally supported projects for educational change found that the most successful projects—which employed outside consultants as trainers—dropped them after the first year (Mann 1976, p. 331). Teachers in the projects felt that most visiting consultants could not relate to the particular problems they were experiencing in their classrooms, or that their advice was too abstract to be helpful. "It was unusual for outside consultants to have either the time or the inclination to provide assistance in other than a lecture format" (McLaughlin 1976, p. 345).

But this need not be the case. Teaching and research conducted by higher-education institutions can make an important contribution to the improvement of both K–12 education and teacher education—if that teaching research is made meaningful to teachers and available to them in forms usable in the classroom. A recent study, "Governance of Teacher Centers," describes the operations of four centers in Rhode Island, San Francisco, Atlanta, and Des Moines; universities collaborate in the governance of two of the four (Dambruch et al. 1975).

Patricia Orrange and Mike Van Ryn (1975) discuss roles and responsibilities of the various participants in continuing education for teachers. They point out that institutions of higher education need to modify or redesign the services they now provide and that although they should continue to offer advanced degree programs for those who wish to pursue them, it is important for universities and colleges to focus their programs on the job-related needs of practicing teachers.

Douglas Powell (1975) cites a Northwestern University survey of colleges of education that found a "modest yet significant" trend among universities to develop programs that focus on the professional needs of teachers in the school setting. Nearly all the colleges surveyed anticipate greater involvement in in-service education in the future. But Powell suggests such involvement may not come easily. Professors may have to assume roles unlike those traditionally found in the university. Universities may have to provide greater rewards for faculty involvement in in-service education as well as in teaching and research. Classroom teachers should be given some control to decide the content of university-based in-service programs.

The preceding section attempted to point out some of the ways institutions of higher education were responding to the concerns voiced above by Orrange, Ryn, and Powell. Higher education can continue to have a major role in mathematics in-service education to the extent that it continues to respond to the needs and desires of teachers' organizations, including teachers' centers and local and state agencies responsible for administering education. These groups are demanding a larger and larger role in controlling in-service education and have matured to the point where they no longer need or want federal agencies or institutions of higher education to prescribe and administer in-service programs.

Recommendations

We recommend that the resources and personnel of colleges and universities continue to be available for the in-service education of mathematics teachers. We urge these institutions to make their resources accessible and useful to those involved in public education and to be open to changing the form and nature of their offerings as needs and desires of teachers, administrators, and local boards of education evolve. We also urge colleges and universities to exercise leadership in influencing the needs and desires of educators and public officials by conducting research, using existing knowledge in identifying problems and proposing solutions, and conducting teacher training programs.

To facilitate the implementation of these recommendations, we pointedly recommend that universities and colleges—

1. expedite, simplify, and make less rigid the registration and admission procedures for in-service programs;
2. reduce costs of registration where students are not availed of all the usual university services and facilities;

3. arrange for participants in in-service programs to receive institutional credit (credit recognized by certification agencies) for successfully completing specially designed in-service programs when these participants cannot gain acceptance into the regular graduate program;

4. design post-master's graduate programs for teachers and for training managers of in-service programs;

5. recognize the creative and outstanding accomplishments of faculty members working in in-service capacities to the same degree that they are supposed to in on-campus undergraduate and graduate programs;

6. sponsor research in areas of concern to managers of in-service education, such as needs assessments, design, conduction, assessment of in-service programs, and working conditions and teacher competence;

7. be receptive to the needs and desires of school system personnel in designing special courses and modifying existing course offerings.

We advocate that local boards of education and teachers' organizations seek out the expertise and resources of colleges and universities in assessing needs and in designing, conducting, and assessing in-service programs for mathematics teachers. We support the emerging practice of contractual arrangements for in-service programs between school systems and colleges and universities where those receiving in-service programs have a voice in determining the content and form of the program.

Preparing Preservice Teachers for In-Service Education

Colleges and universities can make a significant contribution to the future in-service education of preservice teachers. Although we do not have data indicating how concerted an effort colleges presently make in this regard, we surmise that efforts in preparing undergraduates for continued professional education or growth are modest. Undoubtedly many students receive an acquaintance with professional organizations and perhaps often are oriented on the form and mechanics of obtaining an advanced degree. But undergraduate programs can, and in some cases do, accomplish more than acquainting students with organizations and degree programs. They can engender expectation and a positive attitude toward continued professional growth. How? We shall describe one approach.

Undergraduate programs can be designed and conducted to convey the problem-solving approach to teaching. A teacher is constantly confronted with problems. Some problems are perennial; others arise unexpectedly. Some are interpersonal in nature; others are content oriented. Regardless of the problem's nature or source, teachers need to identify the difficulty, to conjecture causes, to gather relevant information, and to propose and try out solutions. As a result of engaging in such problem solving, a teacher's knowledge of mathematics and pedagogy increases— the teacher grows professionally.

Problem solving as a dimension of teaching mathematics can be a theme in methods courses and in student teaching. Problems of management and of content presentation can be posed in methods classes. Problems in student teaching do not have to be posed—they are there. Methods instructors and teaching supervisors can deal with problems in teaching as part of the content of the course.

Where is the in-service education in the problem situations above? In-service education can appear in the places and ways students look for information and possible solutions to problems in teaching. Journals, publications, meetings of professional organizations, additional coursework, interactions with colleagues, systemwide workshops, and every other vehicle of in-service education can be *used* by the methods instructor or student-teacher supervisor in dealing with problems in teaching. In short, preservice teachers can be involved with (not just exposed to) in-service education in solving problems in course work and student teaching.

There are numerous benefits to involving preservice teachers in in-service education. They gain knowledge of, and expectations for, in-service opportunities. But more than this, students will enter teaching with first-hand knowledge that although problems occur for all teachers, one need not face these problems alone. Help is available! Perhaps this realization can help overcome feelings of despair that often overwhelm first-year teachers; or what is far worse, a belief that one is alone and faced with problems for which there is no solution. Such feelings may be behind comments such as "Oh, you can't do anything about that anyway" or "Those kids will never do anything; so why knock yourself out trying?"

One mechanism teacher education programs could use in concert with a problem-solving approach to teaching is an occasional newsletter to their graduates. A newsletter would be a place to advertise in-service programs and inform teachers of professional meetings and publications of interest. A newsletter could also include teaching tips (perhaps in a question-and-answer section), placement information, ideas for mathematics clubs, a section on challenging problems, and possibly the coordination of meetings among groups having common interests. Contributions from readers could engender a feeling of comradeship. The newsletter itself would be a small in-service effort in its own right.

There is no reason to believe that methods instructors are reluctant to counsel and advise their former students. A newsletter can be one mechanism to foster continuing professional relationships. Teachers and college instructors have much to gain from continued interactions.

CHAPTER 9

Evaluating Programs of Mathematics In-Service Education

DAVID W. WELLS
MARY MONTGOMERY LINDQUIST

PROGRAMS of in-service education that are planned in accordance with the guidelines given in previous chapters of this handbook are based on the results of an assessment of needs designed to identify differences between what the mathematics program is at the time of assessment and what the mathematics program ought to be in the future. The plan for such an in-service program identifies (1) the goals and objectives (product) selected for that program, (2) a step-by-step description of the in-service process to be implemented, and (3) a definition of the evaluation activities to be constructed. The evaluation of the in-service program will be designed to determine the adequacy of the plan for the program, the value of the in-service process, and whether the goals and objectives of the program were achieved. This chapter will discuss what to evaluate about the plan for the programs, the in-service process, and the product of the program. Some suggestions will be offered on how to evaluate each of these elements. First, however, a brief discussion of some of the political considerations to be taken into account in planning and implementing the evaluation of in-service programs will be undertaken.

Some Political Considerations

The manager of mathematics in-service education for a school system has the responsibility of planning and implementing effective and satisfying programs. Each program should be evaluated to provide adequate information for improving subsequent programs. However, there are other important political purposes to be served by evaluating in-service programs. Among these purposes are—

1. to help justify the use of school resources to the decision makers of the school district;
2. to increase the probability that school resources will continue to be available for in-service education;
3. to provide appropriate information about the quality of in-service education to selected audiences.

If the results of an evaluation are to be used to achieve these purposes, the competent manager of in-service education realizes the advantages of establishing a record of producing successful programs and for reporting the results of evaluations in a useful and honest fashion. To establish. such a record, it is necessary that the programs selected for implementation have a high probability of success.

A program designed in accordance with the guidelines given in this handbook is based on the identified needs of the participants and is planned and implemented with their commitment to making it successful. Furthermore, the results of the in-service survey indicate that teachers assign a high value to in-service programs directly related to their teaching assignment. Therefore, a competent manager of in-service education recognizes the political advantages of giving a high priority to programs that are defined by an assessment of needs, are planned cooperatively with the participants, and are related directly to the assignments of the participants. It should also be pointed out that an in-service manager with such a record is likely to get approval and support for in-service programs designed to satisfy some identified needs of the mathematics program that are not necessarily directly related to the immediate teaching assignment of the participants.

The value of an in-service program is often determined by the product it produces. However, experienced managers know that it is not uncommon for many decision makers of a school district to decide whether an in-service education program is valuable during the in-service process and prior to the achievement of the product. Therefore, a politically astute manager will make sure that the process is well planned and evaluated during the implementation and that the evaluation provides the type of information that can be used by those decision makers to arrive at a decision based on the best information available. An in-service manager who does not follow this practice is likely to find that decision makers will obtain information from other sources during the process and reach a decision about the value of the program prior to the achievement of the product. In the event that their decision is negative and is based on bad information, it will certainly be used by the adversaries of in-service education to support their point of view. Consequently, the evaluation must provide for a systematic way of providing accurate information to the decision makers of the district during all phases of the process.

In many of the school systems with a collective bargaining agreement in effect, the teachers' organizations are attempting to exercise considerable control over in-service education. In some instances the organizations want to be a strong force in determining the type of in-service to be offered, the schedule for implementing programs, and the resources allocated to support in-service education. However, competent managers recognize that most of the individual members of the organizations are more interested in participating in successful in-service programs than in controlling all such programs. Consequently, these managers will plan and implement programs that are based on the results of an assessment of needs and implemented according to a plan that has the support of the participants. By the extent to which the manager is successful in using this strategy, the participants will benefit from programs of high quality, and the force of the demands by the organization for control of in-service education will be diminished.

A competent manager will disseminate the results of an evaluation to several different audiences. Included are the decision makers of the district, the board of education through the superintendent, the planners of the program, the participants, the others directly related to the program, and the groups who have a right to know. Since the needs of the various audiences for information concerning the results will differ, the report furnished each one will include the factual information necessary to satisfy its needs. For example, after reviewing the report of a major in-service education project, one board of education member was heard to say during a meeting, "I have read all this statistical data about means, differences that were significant or not significant, but I am still not sure whether the in-service program did what it was supposed to. Why can't these reports be written in clear simple language?" Compare the attitude of this board member with the attitude of one who received a report of a program that listed the objectives and described the extent to which each one had been achieved. This report was then supplemented by a well-prepared oral report by selected enthusiastic participants in the program.

The competent manager realizes that the things most remembered and used by the members will be from the oral report.

There is little doubt that the evaluation of in-service education programs is to some extent a political activity. The results of each evaluation will provide useful information that can be used by the adversaries or supporters of in-service education. However, the most important decision that in-service education managers can make is to guarantee that all concerned persons get an honest and forthright description of the results of an evaluation; for they know full well that colleagues and constituents will tolerate an occasional program that does not achieve all the objectives listed in the plan but that they will not tolerate or permit the covering up of such results by any means whatsoever.

What to Evaluate

For in-service programs designed in accordance with guidelines given in previous chapters of this handbook, it seems appropriate to evaluate the plan for the program, the in-service process used, and the product produced by the program.

- The plan should be evaluated to determine whether it produced an in-service process that resulted in the expected product.
- The extent to which the objectives were achieved by the participants (product) should be evaluated. The value of the program will be determined by the product it produces.
- The in-service process that produces the product should be monitored and evaluated as it progresses. The information derived from this activity can be helpful in deciding how to modify the plan and the in-service process for this and subsequent programs.

The nature of the design of the evaluation will be influenced by the way the results of the evaluation are to be used. It is expected that the results will be used by the in-service education manager to improve subsequent programs. However, if the manager believes that the results of the evaluation will be used by the decision makers in his or her school district or other funding agencies to justify a position on the expenditure of funds for in-service education, in the negotiation of the in-service provisions of a collective bargaining agreement, or in some other way that will have a long-term impact on in-service education in the school system, it is necessary that this information be considered in designing the evaluation.

The plan

The plan for an in-service program is a blueprint for satisfying the needs of the participants that were identified by the assessment of needs and for evaluating the in-service process and the product of the program. It specifies in precise terms the goals and objectives to be achieved by the participants and describes an in-service process that will enable the participants to achieve these objectives and consequently the goals.

The primary purpose of evaluating the plan is to determine whether the participants are likely to achieve the goals of the program. To accomplish this, it is necessary that the evaluation of the plan first determine whether—

1. the goals are consistent with the results of the needs assessment;
2. the goals have been translated into a set of operational objectives;
3. the achievement of the objectives implies the achievement of the goals;
4. the in-service process described will enable teachers to achieve the objectives;
5. the evaluation activities are adequately defined and described.

After it has been determined that the plan defines the goals and objectives, other factors are to be considered. The evaluation should then determine whether the plan—

1. is consistent with existing policies of the school district and with the provision of the collective bargaining agreement then in effect;
2. can be carried out in an effective manner with the resources available;
3. describes a cost-effective program;
4. should be implemented in the current political environment;
5. describes a program that is likely to be well received by the participants.

These are, in effect, permission points to proceed with the plan.

The depth of this initial evaluation depends on the extent of the proposed in-service program and the need to justify the plan. However, the evaluation of the plan should not require more time, money, and effort than its creation and development.

Since the plan for the in-service education was developed by the program manager, the evaluator, and a subset of the program participants, it seems reasonable to conclude that their adoption of the plan is equivalent to a satisfactory evaluation. However, in some instances it might be desirable from an instructional or political point of view to obtain assistance from one or more outside consultants. For example, suppose that the in-service education was necessary to install a program that was mandated by action of the state legislature, and the probability of success was not as great as for other in-service education activities usually operated in the district. The use of outside consultants could increase the probability of acceptance of the plan by the decision makers. Also, if the in-service program was to be based on a model developed by another school district, consultants for that district could be of help in evaluating the plan. However, in any event the initial evaluation of the plan should be completed prior to beginning the in-service process.

On completion of the in-service process, a further evaluation of the plan should be considered for the following reasons:

1. To determine whether the plan encouraged appropriate communication among planners, participants, and presenters or leaders during the in-service process

2. To determine how the plan might be modified for future programs

3. To determine whether the plan was flexible enough to permit necessary changes during the process of in-service education

4. To determine whether the plan encouraged or discouraged the achievement of important goals or objectives not included in the plan

5. To help explain identified strengths and weaknesses of the process of in-service education

6. To help explain any differences between actual and anticipated outcomes

7. To assure that if the plan is used again, the results will be similar

The process

In order to evaluate the in-service process, it is necessary to determine the extent to which the program is being implemented according to the plan and the extent to which the teachers are progressing toward the achievement of the objectives of the program.

The evaluation of the in-service process might very well be the most important part of the total evaluation of the program. The competent manager realizes that the product of the in-service process has been defined in terms of identified needs of the participants. Consequently, they recognize the value of the product. However, the quality of the process will determine the extent to which the objectives are achieved and the value of the process as a model for future in-service programs.

To maximize the probability of the process's producing the expected outcomes, the planners need information to identify or predict any flaws in the implementation of the process and to determine whether the predicted progress toward producing the product is occurring. With adequate information available, the planners will be able to make the necessary modifications so that the process will be as productive as possible. To obtain this information, it is necessary that a set of appraisal and observation instruments be developed and used to monitor the process.

The evaluation of the process is important for in-service programs of short duration. However, if one considers the cost in human and financial resources of planning and implementing an in-service process that extends over a long period of time and the high probability of having to make adjustments in the process during the in-service program, it can be seen that a careful evaluation of the process is critical to the success of such programs.

Evaluating the product

In order to evaluate the product of an in-service education program, it is necessary to determine to what extent the objectives specified in the plan were achieved by the participants. It is desirable to determine whether any other important outcomes occurred that were not expected.

If the achievement of the objectives requires that participants acquire new knowledge, develop new skills, or modify their attitudes, the objectives must be defined in terms of the participants' performance at the end of the process. Then the objectives can be used to select or develop appropriate instruments of appraisal or observation and collect and analyze the data generated by use of the instruments. The information derived from the analysis of the data must provide sufficient evidence for competent program managers and evaluators to judge whether the objectives, and consequently the goals, of the program have been achieved. Also, if the participants fail to achieve one or more of the objectives, the analysis of the data can serve as a basis for diagnosing why they were not achieved and to suggest ways to modify subsequent programs to make them more effective.

If the achievement of the objectives of the program are defined in terms of an identified instructional or curricular problem to be solved, the evaluation of the product must determine whether an acceptable solution resulted from the in-service process. The evaluation begins by defining essential parts of the problem in such a way that the achievement of each part implies that an acceptable solution to the problem has been determined. For example, the identified problem of a school system might be the lack of any systematic procedures for selecting textbook materials for an elementary mathematics program. To accomplish this task, the problem might begin by developing a set of criteria for use in evaluating each series of textbooks under consideration for the program. Some of the essential elements of a textbook program to be considered are—

1. mathematical content;
2. methods of presentation;
3. testing and maintenance activities;
4. provisions for individual differences;
5. a teacher's edition.

Although it is likely that each of these areas will be separated into their essential parts, it seems reasonable that the solution to the original problem is implied by establishing a set of criteria for evaluating each of the essential parts of the elementary mathematics programs available.

The objectives of the in-service program may be defined in terms of knowledge, skills, and attitudes, or in terms of an instructional problem that is important to the school system. In each case, however, it is necessary to determine whether the objectives of the program have been achieved in order to evaluate the product.

The objectives of a program may be defined in terms of the performance of the teacher or in terms of the performance of the students of the teacher. For example, the goals of an in-service program might be to increase the computational skills with whole numbers and decimals for students in the middle school. This goal can be translated into a set of objectives that define precisely the computational skills to be acquired by the students, and then an in-service process can be designed for the mathematics teachers in the school to achieve these objectives. To determine whether the objectives have been achieved requires that the students' performance be the source of the data collected and analyzed.

The goal of an in-service education program might be to increase the teachers' knowledge about measurement. In this instance, the objectives will be defined in terms of the teachers' performance. The source of the data collected and analyzed will be the performance of the teachers. It is not always true that the achievement of the objectives by the teachers in the program will be reflected in the immediate achievement of their students. In fact, the risk is great enough to require a competent in-service program manager to avoid trying to establish a connection between student achievement and teacher achievement of the goals of an in-service program.

The NCTM in-service survey indicates that two out of three elementary and secondary teachers of mathematics believe that achievement data of students should be used to evaluate the effectiveness of in-service programs. However, in spite of this endorsement, politically astute program managers will limit their efforts to connect student achievement to teacher achievement in in-service programs to those instances where they have a high probability of success. For example, if a school system that has offered little or no instruction in the metric system of measurement implements an intensive in-service program for teachers prior to installing such an instructional sequence, the students of the teachers are very likely to show substantial increase in their knowledge and use of the system as a consequence of participating in the instructional sequence. However, an in-service program designed to improve immediately the ability of students to use mathematics to solve problems does not have a high probability of success.

How to Evaluate

There is no simple design, no standard procedure, no routine that is the answer on how to evaluate in-service education. It is a complex task to evaluate anything with uncontrollable variables, and in-service education certainly has many of these. However, there are techniques within the reach of every in-service manager, and there are evaluators available to assist with extensive evaluation.

In planning the evaluation of an in-service program, one should keep in mind the purpose of the evaluation as well as the strengths and limitations of the staff and other resources. One may easily fall into the folly of spending more time, effort, and money on evaluation than on the creation and implementation of the in-service program. On the other hand, one should not dismiss the responsibility of evaluating.

Remember that the purpose of in-service education is to improve education. One of the benefits from evaluation may be illuminating—that is, the evaluation may shed light on problems, issues, or significant features (Parlett and Hamilton 1972).

Several techniques and suggestions are discussed in this section on how to evaluate the plan, the process, and the product of in-service education. A full treatment of the techniques is not given because this would require an entire book. References are included for those who wish more in-depth knowledge.

The plan

Evaluating the in-service plan is primarily a question of determining its validity and practicality. Therefore, it is mainly a task of making professional judgments by those involved in the planning as well as by others whose expertise may assist in this determination.

This professional judgment can be tapped in several ways: group discussions, written reactions, individual analysis, and panel ratings. Following are some suggestions how each of these ways can assist in some parts of the evaluation of the original plan.

Group discussion. Group discussion is often an illuminating way to evaluate certain parts of a plan, since it may also assist in solving any problems. When group discussion is used as a technique of evaluation, there needs to be a clear-cut method for making the decisions. This could be by consensus of the group or by the in-service manager. To discuss and then reach no decision will not accomplish the evaluation.

A group may have designed the in-service plan and, in so doing, engaged in much discussion. It may be well to have this group look at its plan and determine whether the goals are consistent with the assessment of needs, whether the in-service process will enable the participants to achieve the objectives, and so on. However, there is a danger in using this same group. It is much like asking children to solve an addition problem by using counters and then asking them to validate their answers by using counters. They are likely to make the same mistake and, more importantly, not understand why they are being asked to validate. Likewise with the committee; they were given the task of planning an in-service program that met the goals, and to reanalyze it may be futile. Thus, it may be better to have another group evaluate the program. Realize that if this is done, then the likelihood of replanning is great unless the task of evaluating is made clear.

Certainly, if one person has done the planning, then reactions from a group may be invaluable not only for the critique but also for eliciting their involvement.

Written reactions. There are times when written reactions to an in-service plan may be beneficial. For example, in determining whether the plan is consistent with the existing policies of the school district or the collective bargaining agency, one may be wise to have written input from both of these groups. Not only can they point out where discrepancies exist or omissions are made, but also they are involved and more likely to be supportive.

If the in-service program is conducted by a group from outside the school system, a memorandum of agreement that specifies the roles of both parties often eliminates problems at a further date.

The written reactions may also take the place of an agreement group discussion. Key personnel may be unable to attend a group discussion but may have valuable input. Even if the in-service program is a short, one-time session, it may be worthwhile to get reactions from key people. For example, if the in-service program is for a high school's mathematics teachers, it may be well to get a reaction—either written or oral—from the chairman.

Individual analysis. Often the questions of practicality can best be evaluated by individual analysis. For example, the manager is probably in the best position to analyze and determine the availability of resources. The cost effectiveness can be documented by the manager or his or her staff, although final judgment may need to come from others, such as school administrators or the school board.

Ratings by panels. One of the best uses of this technique would be to determine whether the in-service program will enable participants to reach the objectives. In particular, a panel of experts might rate the content of the program. For example, suppose the program is to assist teachers in selecting problems that lead to creative problem solving. After an initial selection of problems had been made, a panel of mathematicians, mathematics educators, and teachers could rank the problems as shown in the chart in figure 9.1. From this ranking, the problems could be selected, assuring that there would be a mixture of suitable to nonsuitable problems that varied from highly creative to routine.

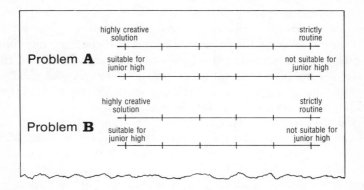

Fig. 9.1. Creative problem solving

Any of these formative evaluations may result in the plan being revised and further evaluated. For example, suppose that it is determined that the plan does address the concerns of the needs assessment, but the cost is too great for the expected effectiveness. Then the plan should be revised and reevaluated to see if it still meets the concerns of the needs assessment.

On completion of the in-service program, the plan should be further evaluated by those involved in the planning as well as by those involved in future planning. Probably group discussion and individual analysis are the most helpful techniques to use to determine whether the points set forth on page 193 are met.

The in-service process

There are two reasons to evaluate the in-service process: (1) to make changes either as the in-service program progresses or for future programs, or (2) to show that the in-service process reached expectations.

In order to evaluate the in-service process, information may need to be gathered before the beginning of the in-service program. This information may include the participants' knowledge of content or methods, their attitudes, their teaching behaviors, or other background data. This information can be used immediately in the in-service process. For example, suppose a prior assessment of needs shows the need for an in-service program on managing small groups for mathematics instruction in the elementary school. An initial survey of the participants indicates that a considerable number of them instructed small groups in science. It may be beneficial to separate these participants from the others or to use these participants' experiences with the entire group. The preassessment of the participants may also be necessary if change due to the in-service program is to be shown. Depending on the sophistication of the evaluation design, the same information gathered about participants may need to be gathered about nonparticipants.

One of the most neglected aspects of evaluation is during the in-service process. Even if the in-service program is a short, one-time program, evaluation is needed. This evaluation may consist only of the presenter's own subjective observation of the audience. As any good teacher knows, this observation may influence a decision to make immediate changes in the presentation or in future presentations.

If the in-service program is longer than one session, then periodic evaluations during the in-service process may serve general functions. First, these periodic checks give an indication of needed alterations in future sessions. Second, this record of progress may point to specific strengths and weaknesses of the in-service process that may assist in planning future in-service programs. For example, if after four sessions, 75 percent of the participants had mastered certain objectives, and after the remaining sessions, only 5 percent more have mastered these same objectives, then it may be well to consider reconstructing the seven sessions. If this information had been gathered only at the end, the need for change may have been overlooked. Third, these periodic checks may indicate what parts of the in-service process are responsible for particular changes in the final outcomes. For example, if the purpose of the in-service program is to increase the use of manipulatives in the teaching of mathematics, it may be noted that there were significantly more manipulatives being used after the eighth session.

On the completion of the in-service program, it may be necessary to evaluate. Gathering reactions from the participants or from the experts attending sessions provides information for future changes. To show that the program was effective, it may be necessary to gather information about the participants' knowledge of content or methods or their attitudes. This same type of information may also need to be gathered after the participants have had an opportunity to put their newly gained knowledge or ideas into classroom practice. Reaction to the program at this time could be different from that obtained immediately at the close. Also, the retention of knowledge or the stability of attitudes may be examined at a later date.

The techniques for gathering this information about the in-service process are similar to those used to evaluate the in-service product. Thus, before considering the techniques, the type of information needed to evaluate the product is described.

The in-service product

If an in-service objective is to change what happens in the classroom, then the in-service product should be evaluated. As with the evaluation of the in-service process, the evaluation of the product may either be of a formative nature that assists in decision making of changes in future programs or of a summative nature that helps to justify the program.

Even in evaluating the in-service product, one may need to collect data prior to the in-service program. This may be the same data about participants suggested for evaluating the in-service process. Baseline data on the students of participating teachers, as well as on students of nonparticipating teachers, may be needed if it is necessary to show change in student performance, attitude, or behavior.

The evaluation of the in-service product may begin any time after the beginning of the program and continue for any length of time thereafter. Periodic checks on classroom practices or outcomes may shed more light on the effectiveness of the program than one final evaluation. If long-term results are expected, the evaluation may occur at a time quite distant from the completion of the program.

Techniques to evaluate the in-service processes and products are similar. No matter what techniques are used, try to use multiple measurements when feasible (Webb et al. 1969). For example, instead of just using a questionnaire, also use an interview. Since many of the measurements could be made in natural settings—the in-service sessions or the classroom—consider using as many unobtrusive measures as possible (Webb et al. 1969), such as records of attendance at the sessions, of students' attendance at school, and of attendance at other in-service programs. For example, a significant increase in enrollment of a repeated in-service program could be a strong indication of the success of the first session.

Observation. Observational techniques can range from highly subjective (how one feels about a session) to highly objective (counting the number of times each student answers a mathematics question correctly). Objective observational ratings are not simple to devise; the interreliability of the raters needs to be considered, the cost may be prohibitive, the observers may be biased, and the observations may be interactive with the situation. Despite these seemingly overwhelming disadvantages, many of them can be overcome. For example, by training the observers, the interreliability can be increased; or by having the observers in the classroom serve more than one purpose (see McLeod [1972]), the interaction with the situation may be minimized. Observational techniques have many advantages. Observations are usually made in the natural situation, which eliminates many of the artificial factors of other techniques. Observation does not require verbalization about what is being observed. Thus, it is appropriate for young children or when it is not advantageous for those being observed to center on what is being observed. It is probably the technique that can assist in formulating more hypotheses or plausible explanations.

Observations should be used to evaluate the in-service process. The observation may be made to determine the reaction of the audience, the quality of the presentation or the content, or the interaction of the group. It may be the presenter's own subjective observation, or it may be of others. For example, suppose the in-service topic is on questioning techniques, in which sample lessons emphasizing questioning are presented. Those trained in observational techniques could evaluate the effectiveness of the presentation. This could serve two purposes: (1) as feedback for the presenters to use in modifying future sessions and (2) as an illustration to the participants of the amount of questioning or interaction. Other consultants, such as content, product, or media specialists, may also be appropriate observers. Do not overlook the possibility of having some of the participants serve as observers. Consider whether the observation should be open ended or whether a structured observation rating form should be devised.

Observational techniques may also be appropriate for evaluating the in-service product. It is particularly important if a description of what happens in the classroom—either the teachers' or the students' behavior—is needed. This may be needed either to show that the in-service objectives were met, to give alternative hypotheses of why certain objectives were or were not met, or to indicate needed changes for further in-service programs.

Interview. Another technique that is helpful to use along with observation is the interview. An interview will often substantiate or raise questions about observations. Of course, it may also be used without observations. In either case, the interview may be highly structured or more open, depending on its purpose. Usually when an in-service program is evaluated, the interview should have some structure but be open ended enough to obtain the feelings of the interviewee and to ascertain unexpected outcomes.

The interview technique may be used with any of the groups in which observation was appropriate. In addition, there may be other groups appropriate to interview that were not observable. For example, it may be appropriate to interview administrators, teachers who did not participate in the in-service program, or parents. For further information about interviewing, see chapter 8 of Wiersma's *Research Methods in Education: An Introduction* (1969).

Questionnaire. Another technique for collecting data is the questionnaire. Because of cost, questionnaires permit making larger samples than observational or interviewing techniques do. As with interviewing, they may be used with in-service participants, students, and others. The questionnaire may be structured to the point of yes-no or multiple-choice answers, or it may be open ended. If it is highly structured, it may force the respondents to a decision that is not completely reflective of their view. If it is entirely open ended, the data may be extremely difficult to analyze.

Designing questionnaires is not a trivial task, and as Oppenheim states, "Questionnaire design cannot be taught from books, every investigation presents new and different problems. A textbook can only hope to prevent some of the worst pitfalls and to give practical, do-it-yourself kind of information" (1966, p. vii). Because of the usefulness of questionnaires in many situations, it may be advisable to look at some practical suggestions, such as those found in Borich (1974) and in Oppenheim (1966).

Paper-and-pencil tests. Certainly, paper-and-pencil tests are a legitimate way to collect information both on achievement and attitude. Careful consideration should be given in evaluating achievement in whether a criterion-referenced test or a norm-referenced test is more appropriate. For the evaluation of many phases of an in-service program, criterion-referenced tests will permit judgment on whether the objectives are met.

Many textbooks contain valuable suggestions about constructing and using objective tests. For further information and references, see Lindquist (1951), Nunnally (1964), and the NCTM Twenty-sixth Yearbook (1961). Measures of attitude and other affective traits often present more of a problem. Many of the available tests are not appropriate for specific in-service programs. A good discussion of such testing can be found in Anastasi (1968). In terms of mathematics and the affective domain, see Aiken's article "Attitudes toward Mathematics" (1970).

Work samples. Another often overlooked but viable technique of obtaining data is by collecting work samples. This may be done during the in-service process from the participants or while evaluating the in-service product from the students and teachers. These work samples may include projects, papers, or other written assignments. They may include such things as teachers' records if one purpose of the in-service program is to implement a new management system. Or they may include a presentation, such as microteaching, made by a participant during the program. For many types of in-service programs, a work sample may be a more appropriate measure than an objective test.

In summary, whatever techniques that are used to evaluate the plan, process, or product should be a part of the in-service plan. The techniques will vary according to the type of in-service program, the need for evaluation, and the resources available. Making practical evaluation a part of the program should produce better programs in the future and a smoother path for obtaining funds, time, and the participants' support.

Summary

The primary purpose for evaluating a program of in-service education is to provide adequate information to the in-service manager, the planners of the program, and the decision makers in the district for their use in improving subsequent programs and in determining the value of the program. It is important that this purpose be kept firmly in mind while planning an evaluation. Planners of an evaluation are likely to generate many interesting questions for investigation. Consequently, they may be tempted to design an evaluation that is more characteristic of a research effort than an evaluation. Yielding to this temptation could increase the cost and not increase the value of the information derived from the evaluation. The evaluation design should be limited to collecting and analyzing only the data required to provide the manager, planners, and decision makers with the information necessary to satisfy their separate needs.

In the final analysis the most important evaluation of an in-service program is the one made by each participating staff member. If the individual staff members can honestly declare that the program upgraded their competence in a way that made them more effective in carrying out their responsibilities or solved an important instructional problem for them, all the other evaluations conducted to furnish information to persons other than the participants will have little impact on their behavior. Perhaps the way that has the highest probability of causing this type of evaluation by individuals to occur is to plan, implement, and evaluate in-service programs in accordance with the guidelines given in this handbook.

CHAPTER 10

The Future of In-Service Education

THE ADVISORY COMMITTEE

IN-SERVICE EDUCATION TODAY has been the subject of this handbook. Current perceptions of in-service education held by teachers and supervisors responding to the surveys were discussed and analyzed in chapters 2 and 3. Each of the other chapters reflects the current wisdom of professionals who deal with in-service education in mathematics on a continuing, day-to-day basis. The discussions and recommendations for the policies, the design, and the implementation of in-service education reflect this current experience and are designed to fit the current educational environment, focusing on the needs of the professionals who teach and function within today's schools.

The purpose of this chapter is to go beyond the present context for in-service education and to offer considered judgments about the future. Early in the course of the NCTM In-Service Project, the Advisory Committee was hopeful that new approaches to in-service education would be found, offering a significant promise for future in-service education. We looked forward to describing in this chapter promising practices and structures based on new knowledge and recently developed technologies. We had anticipated finding and recommending field-tested and evaluated techniques and mechanisms holding forth the potential of dramatically improving the nature and effect of in-service education.

Many programs worthy of consideration for adoption or adaption were found. However, we found no startlingly new and different in-service mechanisms that hold forth a potential for significant improvement in in-

205

service education. Further, we suggest that this conclusion is reasonable and understandable. The purposes and objectives of in-service education for teachers have remained constant across the years. If teachers in 1920 had responded to the in-service survey, they would have valued the same nine purposes found in the Ought parts of items 78–86 that teachers value today, although there might be some shifts in the relative standing of the purposes. The goals specified in chapter 1 are ideals that served in-service educators well in the past as well as today.

The conclusion that no bold new mechanisms for in-service education were found is appropriate and understandable for another reason. Wise and creative professionals have been working in the field of in-service education for years. They have "scrambled" to find ways of offering services to teachers and to locate means of improving the mathematics program. They have tried many ideas, sifting and sorting out those that are effective from those of lesser promise. One should expect that in-service educators would have discovered and are aware of the more fundamental and primary principles for effective in-service education but that we are not using what is already known about good in-service education. An examination of the 1957 yearbook of the National Society for the Study of Education, *In-Service Education for Teachers, Supervisors, and Administrators*, and its historical sections in particular, reveals many of the same basic principles enunciated in this handbook. However, careful analysis of the guidelines for in-service education found in the NSSE yearbook does reveal differences when compared to the guidelines that might be developed today. These differences are symptomatic of changes in the educational environment, society's goals for the schools, and teachers' professionalism. They are evidence of the small, incremental nature of changes to be expected in in-service education.

Three domains of constraint appear to limit progress in in-service education to small incremental steps. We label these domains of constraint with the words *tradition, resources,* and *lack of knowledge.* The domains of constraint interact to limit creative progress in in-service education. Any novel recommendations for improving in-service education must be made with a realization that these constraints are operant.

Tradition is a powerful force operating on in-service education, and schools are bound by it. The teaching profession not only operates within the confines of these school traditions but enjoys its own tradition-determined procedures and attitudes. The institutions of higher education that provide all the preservice education and a considerable portion of the in-service education for teachers are precedent-respecting institutions with strong traditions. On the one hand, precedent-determined traditions decrease the risk of error and protect against poor investment of resources. On the other hand, precedent-determined traditions are a constraint on creative ventures that might generate new ideas and mechanisms for in-service education. People's imaginations are severely limited by what they are currently doing and the paradigm of what they think they can do. Traditions create a momentum in teacher education that frequently requires considerable controlled force to offset if change is to be produced.

The second constraint, that of *resources,* establishes a boundary condition on the implementation of the possible and proved but, in addition, hampers the development of new ideas for in-service education. Most in-service educators are busy, responsible people doing the best job they can in serving the needs of teachers and schools. Given the myriad activities, their scope and nature, the typical professional has little time or energy for creative, reflective thought. Further, if the professional has a creative idea for in-service education, its initial implementation frequently requires start-up or seed money—another scarce resource.

Finally, the third constraint against creative developments in in-service education is the *lack of knowledge.* The NACOME report (1975) argues effectively about the state of knowledge concerning mathematics learning and teaching. The report makes several recommendations for needed research and needed information. Most of the lacunae of knowledge identified by the NACOME report directly affect our capabilities for improving in-service education. The present state of knowledge concerning learning and teaching makes significant the risk of designing and implementing good (and bad) in-service programs that treat the wrong problems. The knowledge of teaching practices or of what actually transpires in classrooms is sufficiently limited to warrant the conclusion that diagnostic assessment of needs is but a dream. And teacher education processes and content are seldom related to effects on the classroom performance of children in mathematics. Simply stated, the knowledge of learning and teaching mathematics is insufficient for the purposes of creating and designing in-service programs. An interesting additional product of this lack of knowledge is that it makes it difficult to recognize whether an in-service program *does* promote improved performance of teachers.

Each of these domains of constraint severely affects the future of in-service education for mathematics teachers. The Advisory Committee argues that the information collected in the surveys, in the program descriptions, and elsewhere in the course of the NCTM In-Service Project focuses attention on a number of forces, issues, and problems relative to these constraints. If in-service education is to be a significant factor in improving school mathematics programs and is to affect profoundly the professional capability of teachers, then these forces, issues, and problems need careful definition and explication. The magnitude of the steps toward future improvement of in-service education is a function of control and understanding of these forces, issues, and problems.

The Advisory Committee believes that several conclusions and recommendations are implicit in the evidence collected by the NCTM In-Service Project. The statements are offered for two purposes. First, they provide guidance for the control and understanding of the forces, issues, and problems affecting future improvements in mathematics education, and second, they are a summary of the contents of this handbook.

In-service education will assume significantly greater importance in the future than it enjoys now or has enjoyed in the immediate past.

This conclusion is supported by evidence of changes in the educational background of teachers, their inclination to stay in teaching longer, and their lack of inclination to interrupt their teaching (and to return to it later). The data from the survey are consistent with the data of other surveys. A greater percentage of teachers are getting master's degrees at an earlier age. Because of their investment of time and energy, they are inclined to stay in teaching longer. The advanced degree, even though it may not be related to mathematics education, is evidence of an increased professionalism. But a younger recipient of an advanced in-service degree means a greater probability of obsolescence of knowledge for and about teaching mathematics throughout the latter portion of a teacher's professional life.

The problem of obsolescence of knowledge for the teacher is exacerbated by the rate at which new knowledge and tools are being generated for classroom usage. The bibliography of research in mathematics education reported in 1975 alone contains more than four hundred entries (see Suydam and Weaver [1976]). Many more researchers are presently busy examining processes of teaching and learning mathematics than in 1960. The technical aspects of mathematics teaching have been dramatically reoriented by the computer, and we have only a glimmer of the effect of the hand calculator. New curricula are generated rapidly in response to changing societal pressures. We see no evidence that the rate of development of new knowledge and tools for teaching and learning mathematics will slow down in the foreseeable future; indeed, we expect the development to accelerate.

Given the longer professional life of teachers, the predicted expansion of knowledge about teaching and learning processes, and the new tools and curricula, we are forced to conclude that in-service education will assume even greater significance in the future.

Corollary: Desired, important changes in the school mathematics program are more likely from significant investment of energy and resources in planned in-service programs than in the examination and redesign of preservice teacher education.

Comparatively speaking, more is at stake in in-service than in preservice education. Of course, effective in-service education is difficult without a base of sound knowledge and positive attitudes established in preservice programs; the importance of preservice education is not being denied. However, there is compelling evidence that there is much more to learn about mathematics and mathematics teaching than is possible in the four or five short years of a preservice program. If this is questioned, examine a copy of "Guidelines for the Preparation of Teachers of Mathematics" (1973) prepared by the Commission on the Education of Teachers of Mathematics for the NCTM. The technical knowledge alone is in excess of what is possible for the large majority of undergraduate students. In addition, they must acquire a considerable amount of practical teaching skill. There is a limit to what can be accomplished in a preservice program simply because of time; however, if teachers work within a school system offering a continuing in-service program, then those teachers have the potential of learning throughout their professional lives.

We grant that it is critical to have sound and exciting preservice programs in order for the teachers to make a good beginning in the profession, but we quarrel with the NACOME report's undue emphasis on preservice education and correspondingly lightweight discussion of in-service education. Although supply-and-demand data are brittle because of the variability of forces affecting the choice of teaching as a career by students, the data concerning length of tenure in the profession and the increasing number of teachers who attain their second professional degree early indicate that in-service education represents the best investment of the limited resources of time, energy, and money.

The single change in in-service program design that would do the most in improving in-service education and have the greatest impact on students' understanding of, and performance in, mathematics is using systemic program design.

The survey data of the teachers were overwhelming in the evidence that they provided that curricular plans and instructional needs of the school mathematics program seldom were the direct concern of in-service education. The effect of not designing a program in terms of programmatic needs of school mathematics is to decrease significantly the probability of in-service education having impact on student performance. The additional strong conclusion entailed by the survey's data is that teachers' satisfaction with in-service education and their willingness to participate in it are functions of systemic planning.

Chapter 4, "Guidelines for Designing In-Service Programs," defines the factors that must be accounted for in program design and offers one systematic means of using these factors in planning. Two corollaries appear trivially obvious:

Corollary 1. Assessment of needs is an important component of any effective systemic approach to program planning.

Corollary 2. For the assessment of needs to be complete and to be useful in program planning, teachers must participate.

Needs assessment is currently a popular term; it means many things to different people. Traditionally, the meaning for many teachers and in-service educators is captured by the phrase "felt needs." For program-planning purposes, this is not sufficient. The "felt needs" phrase indicates an aura of personal need strongly tempered by attitudinal and emotional considerations. This value-laden determination of needs does not necessarily have much factual foundation. Systemic planning *requires* a different orientation to needs assessment.

The discrepancies between ideals of performance and actual performance are the important facts needed to extend needs assessment from the weak and ineffective "felt needs" basis to a productive and useful program of needs assessment. Teachers must be involved in the examination and definition of goals and objectives of the school mathematics program. This is one form of decision making that is at the essence of behaving as a professional. This is not to say that only teachers should determine goals and objectives; parents, the scientific community, and society generally have an important stake in the value-laden task of determining goals for the schools (Hershkowitz, Shami, and Rowan 1975). Teachers need to be aware of the total mathematics program in their school rather than confining their purview to their teaching level or only to the classes they teach.

To complete a realistic and useful program of needs assessment, teachers must have the performance data of their students and themselves relative to accomplishing the goals and objectives of the mathematics program. By examining the differences in ideals and performance, teachers can make considered professional judgments about what facets of their teaching are in need of in-service attention.

Two additional notes about a discrepancy basis for needs assessment must be mentioned. (1) Standardized test results *alone* are not a sufficient base for performance data; they are not specific enough to goals and objectives, since the tests are designed for other purposes. Needs assessment requires more comprehensive data collection. (2) The type of information required for a comprehensive ongoing program of needs assessment contains the types of information needed by school boards and administrators for a variety of other decision-making responsibilities in addition to in-service education. A sound assessment of needs is cost effective.

Corollary 3. The most appropriate locus for in-service education is the teacher's school system.

Systemic in-service program design requires a design based on the school mathematics program. Need we point out that the teacher's school system is privy to information needed for needs assessment that is not generally available? The school system controls many of the variables critical to in-service success and satisfaction, according to the surveys. The school system controls the variables that allow teachers to participate. Follow-up is more likely and feasible if the in-service program is located in the school. Certainly schools should use the wisdom and expertise of outside experts, but the evidence is compelling that teachers value the contribution of experts more if that contribution is directly related to the mathematics program of the local school.

In-service education should be based on a foundation of "protected" resources.

We assume that in-service education is a continuing, ongoing need of teachers. A surprising number of teachers wrote on their survey forms statements such as "What in-service?" or "We used to have an in-service program, but my school did away with it n years ago," where $n \in \{1,...,7\}$. Because in-service education does not have direct impact *observable* to taxpayers, it becomes a budget item that can be excised. Given the magnitude of in-service need, it should not be allowed to exist on a shaky, uncertain financial foundation. A firm financial base protected from shifts in the political climate is needed for in-service education.

An interesting effect of the 1957–1970 era of nationally funded programs for in-service education that we believe to be important was the creation of an expectation on the part of teachers and in-service educators that funds for in-service education would be available. Teachers and other mathematics educators are beginning to realize that national priorities are the resultant of vectors of political mood and reflect societal needs other than education. Dependence on national funding reduces the stability of resources for in-service education. If in-service education is to be provided on a regular, continuing basis, then funding sources need to be closer to the action. The vagaries of political priorities force in-service program design away from program-related planning and into a reactive mode of designing in-service programs to fit the latest emphasis of funding agencies.

This recommendation is probably farther from the realm of the possible than any other recommendation made by the Advisory Committee. Indeed, it will probably require years of concerted effort to make a protected financial base for in-service education a reality. An important component of that effort must be the calculated collection of evidence demonstrating the effect of in-service education on pupils and teachers. That evidence will not be available unless in-service education is conducted on a systemic basis that relates in-service teacher education closely to the curricular and instructional components of the school mathematics program. It is politically naive for the mathematics education community to expect funds to be granted for in-service education solely on the basis of statements of good intentions.

Funding agencies external to the school system should have policies that encourage school systems to relate in-service education programs to long-term curricular planning and effective needs assessment programs.

The Rand study of educational change reported by Berman and McLaughlin (1975) documents that the individuals submitting proposals for external funding of educational programs fall into two categories: (1) the entrepreneurs, who locate the conditions on funding and then design a program proposal to fit those conditions; and (2) the problem solvers, who, having identified a difficulty in their school, search out a source of funding that will provide resources to solve the problem. According to the study, the effectiveness and success of the programs generated on the latter basis is significantly better than those generated on an opportunistic, motivational base. The likelihood of impact on school programs extending beyond the period of funding is significantly increased if generated from the problem-solving basis. We argue that this is compelling evidence that external funding agencies need to encourage and to reward programs founded on principles of systemic planning as detailed in chapter 4.

A characteristic of the in-service education efforts in both the immediate past and the present is their faddish character. Career education became a catchword, and immediately a host of opportunists discovered long-ignored needs for mathematics in-service education related to career education. Thus, in-service education opportunists are like surfers looking for the large wave of interest to assure funding rather than making considered judgments based on the needs of children and teachers. The phaselike character introduces an unpredictability into planning in-service education that effectively builds the potential for disappointing both teachers and taxpayers.

Clearly, new priorities for school mathematics can evolve, and unforeseen problems can emerge that are significant. These priorities and problems may be so sudden in development that systemic planning introduces a lag in responsiveness of the in-service program. The rapidly expanding availability of hand calculators is an example of a new technology generating such an in-service need. The legislative action for metric measurement is another example of a rapid shift in priorities that caught many in-service educators without in-service programs and materials available for immediate use. The new awareness of the number of students with discalculia defines an emerging priority. We argue that although the mainline external funding policies should encourage and reward systemic planning, some of the funds should be reserved for the design and creation of in-service programs to respond to unforeseen, emergent new priorities.

We note two other funding responsibilities of external funding agencies. First, funding agencies have a responsibility to provide seed money for the pilot testing of risk ventures. Some new, creative ventures in in-service education are predictably of high risk because they involve untried ideas. For the school system with limited resources, it is hard to justify the expenditure of their own funds for the implementation of unproved programs without evaluative evidence. Second, some (but not all) of the research and evaluation needs for in-service education should extend significantly beyond the responsibilities of the school system. Hence, the external agencies need to provide funding for basic research and evaluation activity.

In summary, external agencies need to implement policy to damp the perturbation of in-service education resulting from educational fads by rewarding and encouraging in-service education based on systemic planning. But external agencies are in a special position to respond to the newly emergent in-service needs and to implement basic research and evaluation of creative ventures in in-service education. The latter responsibility is the appropriate setting for external agencies to influence future development in in-service education by prudently using the opportunistic, entrepreneurial motivation of many mathematics educators.

The design and implementation of training programs for supervisors or in-service program managers should be a matter of high national priority.

The teacher surveys provide weak evidence that the existence of school system supervisory personnel responsible for mathematics programs does make a difference in the in-service program. Thirty-seven percent of the supervisors responding to the survey indicated that their position was in jeopardy because of budgetary considerations. This may be symptomatic of supervisors not being sufficiently effective in demonstrating their worth to the teachers and to the school mathematics program. We argue that there are many skills to be learned in order to conduct an effective, ongoing in-service program. The teacher surveys present compelling evidence that most teachers want in-service programs in mathematics education from a specialist in the field. Parenthetically, we observe that many supervisors in mathematics in many school systems are being replaced by instructional generalists who are responsible for in-service education in all disciplines. In many states the requirements for supervision certificates are formulated with no specification of disciplinary knowledge, expertise, or interest.

The training of chairmen to serve secondary school mathematics departments also deserves careful attention. However, we must note that some school systems do not presently give department chairmen sufficient responsibility and authority to operate effectively. For many junior and senior high schools, cultivating the leadership skills of a good chairman is a sound investment in in-service education.

It should be noted that no refined, research-based guidelines for the supervision of mathematics programs in the schools exist. Evidence of what makes an effective supervisory specialist in in-service education has not been collected. A basic requirement appears to be skill as a teacher coupled with good judgment and common sense. Other projects similar to the NCTM In-Service Project are needed to collect evidence to guide the design of sound educational programs for supervisors of mathematics.

The people and institutions concerned with in-service education need to develop political awareness.

In-service education depends on resources, and the primary source of resources for in-service education is tax monies. Many societal needs other than education compete for the tax dollar. Within education there are many worthy ways of using resources. If in-service education for teachers of mathematics is important, then those concerned with it must help the power brokers and decision makers determine priorities.

We suggest that it is not only appropriate but necessary for organizations such as the NCTM (at the national, state, and local levels) to represent the interests of teachers of mathematics. This includes keeping decision makers in government informed of needs and problems; it means leaders working actively to keep the membership informed of decisions affecting the course of in-service education; it means that members of such organizations have a responsibility for political activism.

A significant aspect of the politics of in-service education is information and its use. In-service program managers need to face realistically the fact that an in-service program depends on the political vagaries of the time. Whimsy and unpredictability can be reduced by effective use of information. Advertise what the in-service program is doing and what its goals are. One of the important secondary reasons (some would argue that it is a primary reason) for evaluation is to demonstrate program effectiveness. That translates to "Mr. Decision Maker, you have been wise in investing funds in in-service education—see what a difference it has made." Then you add the kicker, "We have conducted a needs assessment. It shows. . . ." Requests for money are better received following closely on the heels of success. Whether the decision making about education priorities is rational or not, a major part of the political reality of establishing and maintaining an in-service program is the effective and judicious use of information.

It is important to recognize that the ultimate decision makers in education are the voters. The wise in-service program manager builds enthusiasm for the school mathematics program and the concomitant in-service effort on a broader political front than just his or her professional colleagues. Attention to involving or informing the public sector in some aspects of teacher in-service programs may help to develop informed and sympathetic voter support important to the ultimate success of the program.

Institutions of higher education should examine carefully their participation in in-service education.

A significant number of teachers have a degree beyond their initial professional degree; they are young enough for the Advisory Committee to suggest that institutions of higher education should design post-master's-level programs specifically for teachers. We note that teachers are more inclined to enroll in programs beyond the master's level if they live in states or work for school systems that offer pay and certification levels beyond the master's level. We doubt that programs beyond the master's will be sought by the majority of teachers without additional incentive.

We argue that if the surveys are construed as a market analysis for creating new master's-level professional degrees, then it is hard to justify the expenditure of resources to develop new programs. The teacher population simply is not there. It is more efficient to redesign old programs to have more appeal to prospective students. The days of large numbers of teachers participating in master's degree in-service programs are over for the immediate future. It would be unfortunate if, in the press for students, the academic standards of master's degrees were lowered. We hasten to add that the traditional in-service master's degree is still needed by the beginning teacher.

Institutions of higher education marketing in-service programs for teachers who have a master's degree need to consider how to treat several problems. Many teachers complain vehemently of the red tape and bother of registration procedures geared to full-time students. Many institutions do not recognize the special problems of students who are not seeking a degree. Many state university systems receive a smaller amount of money from tax sources for the nondegree student, but in-service education typically has expenses for each student that are more comparable to those seeking advanced degrees. This inconsistency in funding provides a major limitation on what institutions find possible by way of service to schools.

Many institutions of higher education are attempting to market nondegree in-service programs to specific local schools. This is laudable; in most instances, it is an attempt to tie in-service education more directly to teachers' needs and problems. However, most institutions of higher education do not have policies and procedures established to cope with this type of program. Few institutions know the real costs of such programs. The traditional reward system for the university professors does not recognize this type of service to schools and teachers.

We strongly endorse the efforts to improve the cooperative base for in-service education of the schools and the institutions of higher education. This is one of the major needs of in-service education. The frequency of teachers expressing dissatisfaction with in-service education because of a failure to relate the in-service program to needs assessment and the school mathematics program was a major element in the survey data. Clearly, improving the cooperation between schools and institutions of higher education is one of the best means of reducing the problem.

One of the major responsibilities of institutions of higher education is to extend the knowledge base. This academic tradition suggests that the researching and evaluation of the domain of in-service education is fitting and appropriate. Authors of the chapters in this handbook were continually frustrated by the paucity of research and evaluation evidence concerning in-service education. A major need is the study of what conditions yield an in-service program that translates into improvement in student performance. Guidelines for mathematics supervisors appear to be based primarily on good sense and judgment. We hope that a more analytic research base could be generated for their education.

In-service education programs should be designed to appeal to and extend the professionalism of teachers.

Two statements serve to summarize the teacher survey data:

1. Most teachers desire a voice in determining the nature of the in-service program in which they participate.

2. If teachers reported bad experiences with prior in-service education, typically they indicated that they had not shared in making decisions about that in-service program.

The Advisory Committee opines that this is compelling evidence in support of this recommendation. Although teachers recognize that they need help, they feel they are sufficiently wise and experienced to want to participate in the design and planning of their in-service program and to share in the responsibility of its effect. We believe this is the essence of professionalism.

The process orientation advocated in each of the chapters of this handbook provides a mechanism for involving the teacher in professional action and, hence, is appealing to this sense of professionalism. Clearly, some teachers are not very professional, but for the large majority of respondents to the survey, the personal commitment to behaving professionally was elemental to a successful experience with an in-service program in mathematics.

Sampling Processes and Materials for the Surveys

A SCHOOL was selected following the procedures outlined at the beginning of this Appendix. Then the principal was sent a letter requesting cooperation with the survey, along with a letter and survey form for the teacher. A complete packet of the materials sent to an elementary school principal follows. The principal's letter describes a process for the random selection of a teacher on the staff. Ten different letters were used for elementary principals to assure representativeness of selection across the school staff.

The secondary principal's letters were of parallel construction but are not contained in this Appendix. Only the secondary teacher's survey form is shown. A supervisor's letter and survey form are also exhibited.

The final entry of this Appendix is a map showing the number of responses for the elementary and secondary teachers and the supervisors on a state-by-state basis. A fifty-first category is shown reporting the number of forms returned without addresses.

Procedure for Selecting Schools for Sampling

1. The number of public elementary schools selected from each state (including the District of Columbia) was computed on the basis of the ratio of the state's total public school (elementary and secondary) enrollment. Thus:

$$n_{\text{state (E)}} = \frac{N_{\text{state (E)}}}{N_{\text{total (E)}}} \times N_E$$

where

$n_{state\ (E)}$ = number of public elementary schools sampled in the state

$N_{state\ (E)}$ = public school enrollment in the state

$N_{total\ (E)}$ = total U.S. public school enrollment

N_E = sample size (elementary) = 4000 public elementary schools

Example: State of Ohio

$N_{Ohio\ (E)}$ = public school enrollment in Ohio

$N_{total\ (E)}$ = U.S. public school enrollment

Hence:

$$N_{Ohio\ (E)} = \frac{2\ 382\ 315}{44\ 984\ 957} \times 4000$$

$$= 212 \text{ public elementary schools}$$

Thus, 212 public elementary schools were sampled from the population of public elementary schools in Ohio.

2. The unit population for each state and the District of Columbia was computed as follows:

$$\text{Unit population for state} = \frac{N_{state\ (E,S)}}{n_{state\ (E)}}$$

where $N_{state\ (E,S)}$ = school enrollment (elementary and secondary) for the state

Example: State of Ohio

$N_{Ohio\ (E,S)}$ = 2 382 315

$n_{Ohio\ (E)}$ = 212

Hence, the unit population for Ohio

$$= \frac{2\ 382\ 315}{212}$$

$$= 11\ 237 \text{ students per public elementary school sample unit}$$

3. School districts in each state were first grouped by county. The total school enrollment (elementary and secondary) of all school districts in a county was computed. This number was divided by the unit population for that state to determine the number of public elementary schools to be sampled from the county.

Example: Franklin County, Ohio

Total school enrollment in Franklin County = 183 362

Unit population for Ohio = 11 237

Number of public elementary schools sampled from the population of public elementary schools in Franklin

County, Ohio $= \dfrac{183\ 362}{11\ 237}$

$$= 16 \text{ (to nearest whole number)}$$

4. If the total school enrollment in a county was less than one-half that of the unit population, then the county was combined with one or more neighboring

county(ies) to give a combined school enrollment approximately equal to one, two, or more times the unit population. Then the number of public elementary schools to be sampled from this group of counties was determined by dividing the combined school enrollment by the unit population.

Example: Jackson and Meigs counties, Ohio

Total school enrollment in Jackson County = 6 889

Total school enrollment in Meigs County = 5 019

Combined school enrollment = 11 908

Number of public elementary schools to be sampled

$= \dfrac{11\,908}{11\,237} = 1$ (nearest whole number)

5. For large school districts within a county, the total school enrollment in each district is divided by the unit population to determine the number of public elementary schools sampled from each district.

    Example: Columbus Public School District, Franklin County, Ohio

    Total school enrollment in the Columbus Public School District
    = 102 623 students

    Number of elementary schools sampled from this school district

    $= \dfrac{102\,623}{11\,237} = 9$ (nearest whole number)

6. The individual public elementary schools were then randomly selected from an ordered listing of all public elementary schools in the particular school district (or county or combined counties). The schools were ordered by their arrangement in the state education directory.

Sample Elementary Principal's Letter

November, 1975

Dear Principal:

Enclosed is a questionnaire for a teacher in your school. It is part of a survey of teacher perceptions about inservice education related to teaching mathematics.

The goal of this NSF funded project is to produce a Handbook for Inservice Education. The Handbook will offer practical suggestions to those who conduct inservice education for teachers and give guidance to those responsible for policy decisions concerning inservice education. The National Council of Teachers of Mathematics believes that it would be inappropriate to create the Handbook without reflecting teachers' perceptions of inservice education. Thus, we ask your help and cooperation.

Only a few teachers are being surveyed in your state. We need your help to assure that your state is adequately represented in this national survey. Select a teacher according to the following scheme and give that teacher the enclosed materials.

A. Alphabetize the names of the teachers in your school but exclude from the list any teachers who do not teach mathematics if your school departmentalizes or has differentiated staffing. We are interested in those teachers K-8 who teach mathematics.

B. If there are 12 or more teachers on the list, give the form to the twelfth teacher.

B. If there are between 6 and 11 teachers on the list, give the form to the sixth teacher.

C. If there are less than 6 teachers on the list, give the form to the second teacher.

We think this is an important and potentially significant project. We do urge your cooperation. We appreciate your prompt attention to this questionnaire and thank you in advance for your help.

Respectfully,

Alan R. Osborne, Director
NCTM Inservice Project

Elementary Teacher's Letter

November, 1975

Dear Mathematics Teacher:

Your principal has just given you a questionnaire. It concerns inservice education for teachers of mathematics at the elementary and secondary school levels. We do hope that you will take the time to complete it and return it to us in the attached stamped envelope. We need your help.

The National Council of Teachers of Mathematics has received a grant from the National Science Foundation to study inservice education. The product of this study will be a Handbook for Inservice Education, a document useful to those responsible for inservice education. It will contain practical suggestions for improving inservice education for those who conduct inservice education for teachers and for those responsible for the policy decisions about inservice education. The National Council of Teachers of Mathematics believes that it would be inappropriate to make recommendations about inservice education without reflecting the experience and wisdom of you-- the teacher who participates in inservice programs.

We realize how valuable your time is. You have lessons to plan, tests to write and papers to grade. It will take time to complete the questionnaire. (The preliminary version of the questionnaire took people like yourself about thirty minutes to complete.) But you are one of a small sample of teachers in your state asked to participate in this national survey. We do need your response to reflect adequately the opinions and perceptions of teachers across the entire country and, more particularly, your own ideas.

Do feel free to answer with some candor. We promise to respect your privacy by maintaining confidentiality of the responses.

Enclosed is a questionnaire, a response sheet and a stamped envelope. Directions are given on the questionnaire. Return only the response sheet. You may feel that some of the questions warrant longer answers than the response form allows. If this is the case, turn the form over and write an extended response on the back if you are so inclined. Do note that part II of the questionnaire asks you to indicate both what is and what ought-to-be for inservice education.

We look forward to your response. Before the fact, we would like to thank you for this professional contribution.

Respectfully,

Alan R. Osborne, Director
NCTM Inservice Project

INSERVICE QUESTIONNAIRE
ELEMENTARY

O.M.B. no. 99 - S75010
Approval expires March, 1979

I.   General Information and Opinions

Blacken with a pencil the appropriate columns on the Questionnaire Response Form. If you want to write a more extended response to any questions, use the back of the response sheet.

1.   If you had the opportunity to start again, would you choose teaching as your profession?

2.   Are you satisfied with your present teaching position?

3.   Would you prefer to teach at a higher level than you are teaching presently?

4.   Are you generally satisfied with the inservice education you have had in the past?

What mathematics do you presently teach?

5.   Preschool or kindergarten
6.   Grade 1 or 2
7.   Grade 3 or 4
8.   Grade 5 or 6
9.   Other

10. Do you read the <u>Arithmetic Teacher</u> magazine?

Are you presently satisfied with the following facilities for teaching mathematics in your school?

11. Classroom
12. Textbooks
13. Library materials for students
14. Professional, personal use library
15. Calculators
16. Laboratory or activity learning materials

17. Do you feel a need to participate in mathematics inservice education?

18. Should each school system have an organized inservice education program available for all who teach mathematics?

19. Should inservice education be required of all who teach mathematics?

20. Are students as excited about learning mathematics as they ever were?

21. Do you have tenure?

22. Have you participated in any inservice program(s) since September 1, 1973?

If your answer to 22 was "yes", indicate the sponsoring agency(ies) who conducted the inservice program(s). If no, omit 23 through 28 and proceed to 29.

23. My school system
24. A state educational agency
25. A district or regional educational agency
26. A college or university
27. A private concern such as a publisher
28. A professional group such as the NEA or NCTM

29. On the whole, have your experiences with inservice education been positive?

My major gripes about inservice education in the past have been:

30. It has not fit my needs in the classroom.
31. I did not help select the topics.
32. The leaders have not taught classes like mine.
33. The program was poorly planned and disorganized.
34. The program was too theoretical.
35. Everything was old-hat; I had seen it all before.
36. It was inconvenient; too far and at the wrong time.
37. The program was so general it did not help in the teaching of math.
38. The only reward was the personal element of self-satisfaction.
39. The leaders had other things on their minds other than my problems.
40. Too much method and too little mathematics.
41. My fellow participants were so bored and uninterested that it discouraged me.
42. Materials used in the inservice were too expensive for practical classroom use.

43. The number of college mathematics content courses I have taken is:

   a) 0   b) 1   c) 2   d) 3   e) 4 or more

44. The number of college courses, exclusive of student teaching, that I have taken concerned with methods of teaching mathematics is:

    a) 0   b) 1   c) 2   d) 3   e) 4 or more

45. My salary is in the range (do not include summer school):

    a) less than $8,499   c) $10,000 - $12,499   e) More than $15,000
    b) $8,500 - $9,999   d) $12,500 - $14,999

46. My highest earned degree is:

    a) Bachelor's Degree   b) Master's Degree   c) Doctorate   d) Other

47. The average number of students in my mathematics class(es) is:

    a) 0 - 18   b) 19 - 25   c) 26 - 30   d) 31 - 35   e) More than 35

48. My school is:

    a) urban   b) suburban   c) rural

49. I have taught

    a) less than 5 years   c) 10 to 14 years   e) I'm an old pro; more than 20 years
    b) 5 to 9 years   d) 15 to 20 years

Inservice Education -- As it IS and as it OUGHT-TO-BE

Respond twice to each remaining question. First, on the left, describe your perception of what is the current state of inservice education in your school. Next, on the right, state what it should be like in your school. Note that on these second items you should state your opinions but do be realistic!

For both the what is and what ought-to-be questions:

    A = strongly agree   C = disagree
    B = agree   D = strongly disagree

Example:

    Most students like mathematics.

          IS   OUGHT-TO-BE

    A   B   Ⓒ   D   Ⓐ   B   C   D
         Disagree   Strongly
                                 Agree

50. My school system has an inservice program.

51. Inservice education is about teaching methods rather than mathematical content.

52. Inservice education is required to maintain certification.

53. Inservice education is required to maintain tenure.

54. Systematic follow-up in the classroom is provided after an inservice program.

55. My school district depends on neighboring colleges and universities to provide the majority of opportunities for inservice education.

56. Teachers complete inservice programs with materials for classroom use that they have made themselves.

57. There is an individual in my building or in my school system responsible for inservice education in mathematics.

58. Single-topic, all-day inservice programs are available five or six days during the school year.

59. I give some of each of my summers to inservice work.

60. Inservice education programs are conducted by personnel within my school system.

61. My school district has an inservice program designed specifically for teaching mathematics.

62. My school district has an inservice program but it is not designed for mathematics teaching specifically.

63. Inservice education programs are short and to-the-point.

64. Inservice education programs consist of several short, weekly meetings all organized around a single theme or topic.

The topics for inservice education in mathematics that receive emphasis in my school are:

65. Computational skill
66. Motivation
67. Applications of mathematics
68. Mathematical structures
69. Metrication
70. Use of calculators
71. Students with learning difficulties
72. Diagnosis
73. Evaluation
74. Transformational geometry
75. Transition between grade levels
76. Remediation
77. Improving student attitudes about mathematics

The purposes of inservice education reflected in my school include:

78. Keeping "alive" professionally.
79. Learning about new curricula.
80. Learning new mathematics.
81. Studying new methods of teaching mathematics.
82. Analyzing problems, such as discipline, faced by all teachers; not just teachers of mathematics.
83. Facilitating the use of a new text or text series.
84. Providing opportunity to share ideas with other mathematics teachers.
85. Building enthusiasm for teaching mathematics.
86. Describing new materials and information of direct use in my classroom.

87. Money is budgeted for inservice education by my school district.

88. I participate in identifying topics for inservice education.

89. I can use in my teaching most of the mathematics I learn in inservice.

90. I have been able to use in my teaching most of the methods demonstrated in inservice education.

91. Achievement data of students in my school are used to determine needs for inservice education.

92. Achievement data of students in my school are used to evaluate the effectiveness of inservice programs in my school.

My school encourages inservice education by:

93. Providing release time from classroom duties.
94. Paying expenses for inservice education offered by non-school agencies.
95. Paying me to participate in inservice education.
96. Giving credit toward acquiring tenure.
97. Giving credit toward promotion.
98. Participation in inservice education can result in being placed in a higher pay bracket.

Open-ended questions -- answer on the back of the form.

99. Identify three topics for which you feel the greatest need for inservice.

    a) _____
    b) _____
    c) _____

100. What suggestions would you make to improve inservice education?

101. Do you know of a good inservice program? If so, send us the name and address of someone we may contact about the program.

O.M.B. no. 99 - S75010
Approval expires March, 1979

General Information and Opinions

O.M.B. no. 99 - S75010
Approval expires March, 1979

Blacken with a pencil the appropriate columns on the Questionnaire Response Form. If you
want to write a more extended response to any questions, use the back of the response sheet.

1. If you had the opportunity to start again, would you choose teaching as your profession?

2. Are you satisfied with your present teaching position?

3. Would you prefer to teach at a higher level than you are teaching presently?

4. Are you generally satisfied with the inservice education you have had in the past?

What mathematics do you presently teach?

5. College preparatory; grades 7 through 9
6. College preparatory; grades 10 through 12
7. Non-college preparatory; grades 7 through 9
8. Non-college preparatory; grades 10 through 12
9. Other

10. Do you read the <u>Mathematics Teacher</u> magazine?

Are you presently satisfied with the following facilities for teaching mathematics in your
school?

11. Classroom
12. Textbooks
13. Library materials for students
14. Professional, personal use library
15. Calculators
16. Laboratory or activity learning materials

17. Do you feel a need to participate in mathematics inservice education?

18. Should each school system have an organized inservice education program available for all
who teach mathematics?

19. Should inservice education be required of all who teach mathematics?

20. Are students as excited about learning mathematics as they ever were?

21. Do you have tenure?

22. Have you participated in any inservice program(s) since September 1, 1973?

If your answer to 22 was "yes", indicate the sponsoring agency(ies) who conducted the inservice
program(s). If no, omit 23 through 28 and proceed to 29.

23. My school system
24. A state educational agency
25. A district or regional educational agency
26. A college or university
27. A private concern such as a publisher
28. A professional group such as the NEA or NCTM

29. On the whole, have your experiences with inservice education been positive?

My major gripes about inservice education in the past have been:

30. It has not fit my needs in the classroom.
31. I did not help select the topics.
32. The leaders have not taught classes like mine.
33. The program was poorly planned and disorganized.
34. The program was too theoretical.
35. Everything was old-hat; I had seen it all before.
36. It was inconvenient; too far and at the wrong time.
37. The program was so general it did not help in the teaching of math.
38. The only reward was the personal element of self-satisfaction.
39. The leaders had other things on their minds other than my problems.
40. Too much method and too little mathematics.
41. My fellow participants were so bored and uninterested that it discouraged me.
42. Materials used in the inservice were too expensive for practical classroom use.

> *Note: Questions 44-101
> are the same as those
> found on the elementary
> teacher's form; see
> pages 223-24.*

43. The number of mathematics courses I have taken <u>after calculus</u> is:

   a) 0 to 3   b) 4 to 7   c) 8 to 11   d) 12 to 15   e) more than 15

NAME _____

SCHOOL
ADDRESS _____

ZIP CODE _____

DO NOT MARK THIS AREA

Inservice Questionnair

Elementary   Secondar

INSTRUCTIONS

1. Use ordinary lead pencil - not ink or ballpoint.
2. Be sure each mark is black and fills the box.
3. If you change a response, erase the mark completely and mark your new response.

National Council of Teacher of Mathematics

	is	ought		is	ought
50			75		
51			76		
52			77		
53			78		
54			79		
55			80		
56			81		
57			82		
58			83		
59			84		
60			85		
61			86		
62			87		
63			88		
64			89		
65			90		
66			91		
67			92		
68			93		
69			94		
70			95		
71			96		
72			97		
73			98		
74					

YES NO
1
2
3
4
5
6
7
8
9
10
11
12
13
14
15
16
17
18
19
20
21

YES NO
22
23
24
25
26
27
28
29
30
31
32
33
34
35
36
37
38
39
40
41
42

43 A B C D E
44 A B C D E
45 A B C D E
46 A B C D E
47 A B C D E
48 A B C D E
49 A B C D E

OMB NO. 99-S 75010
Approval Expires 3/79

Supervisor's Letter

November 28, 1975

Dear Supervisor:

The National Council of Teachers of Mathematics is conducting a study of inservice education. This study, funded by the National Science Foundation, will have a Handbook of Inservice Education as a final product. The intent of the Inservice Project is to produce a product that is helpful to those responsible for inservice education.

We are collecting several kinds of information in preparing the Handbook. One of the important types of information the Project is seeking is the perceptions of supervisors and coordinators of mathematics. The enclosed questionnaire is directed to that end. We would appreciate your completing the enclosed questionnaire and returning the answer form in the enclosed stamped envelope at your earliest convenience.

We realize that you are busy but we do need your help. Your views of inservice education are unique. The Handbook would be incomplete without reflecting your experiences and insights. The questionnaire is designed to reflect your perceptions of the issues and problems of inservice education. It asks questions about the "what is" of inservice education as well as the "what ought to be."

We are quite aware of the fact that issues and problems of inservice education are changing. Sometimes a short-answer question will not fit your situation as closely as you would prefer. If this is the case, do feel free to elaborate on any question on the back of the answer form or on a separate cover letter. And you may feel that there is an issue or problem that is simply not covered by the questionnaire. If so, do let us know about it. Your responses will be used by the authors of the Handbook as they prepare their sections.

Do feel free to answer with some candor. We promise to respect your privacy by maintaining the confidentiality of the respondents.

We look forward to your response. Before the fact, we would like to thank you for this professional contribution.

Respectfully,

Alan R. Osborne, Director
NCTM Inservice Project

Project Advisory Board: Alan Hoffer, Richard Wilkes, Thomas Rowan, Edward Davis, Floyd Downs

I. General Information and Opinions

1. I enjoy supervisory work in mathematics education.

2. I am satisfied with my present responsibilities.

3. I feel that I am making a difference by helping teachers do a better job in the classroom.

4. Are you generally satisfied with the inservice education that you have been able to provide for teachers of mathematics?

With how many teachers do you work?
5. Less than 25
6. 25-50
7. 51-150
8. 151-500
9. More than 500

10. Are new teachers generally well-prepared to teach mathematics?

11. Do your schools have an organized, regularly scheduled inservice program for mathematics teachers at the elementary school level?

12. Do your schools have an organized, regularly scheduled inservice program for mathematics teachers at the secondary school level?

13. Should inservice education be required of all who teach mathematics?

14. Are students as excited about learning mathematics as they ever were.

15. Because of budgetary problems, is your school system considering doing away with supervisory personnel?

16. Did you have training and education beyond classroom experience to prepare you for your present responsibilities?

Do you find constraints on inservice education today because of:
17. budget;
18. lack of interest on the part of teachers;
19. poor facilities;
20. inability to provide teachers with release time;
21. lack of administrative cooperation at the individual school level.

22. Do your schools use an organized process of needs assessment to define and justify inservice program content?

23. Are your inservice offerings based upon long-term curricular plans?

24. Are teachers' perceptions of inservice program needs consistent with long-term curricular plans?

25. Do you provide classroom follow-up to teachers after an inservice education program?

26. Do teachers participate in long-term curriculum planning?

27. Most inservice education in my district sees the teacher participating as an unpaid volunteer.

28. Do teacher contracts with the school board provide a constraint against after-school inservice education?

29. If an evaluation of inservice education is required, must it include achievement data of the students of the teachers who participated?

30. Do you regularly have teacher-participants evaluate their inservice program?

31. Do you feel that secondary school teachers need a different type of inservice program than elementary school teachers?

32. Do you feel that content (as compared to methods) is the secondary school teachers' major need in inservice education?

33. Do you feel that content (as compared to methods) is the elementary school teachers' major need in inservice education?

34. Do you have control of discretionary funds that you can use to provide inservice education in mathematics ?

35. Do you have access to funds for inservice education that are generated from non-local school tax sources?

36. Do teachers help select the topics for inservice education in your system?

37. Do teachers help select the organization or administration of inservice education in your system?

38. Are there resource people, such as district or state personnel, that you can use for help with your inservice program?

39. If so, do you use them?

40. Local school administrators generally are helpful to me in setting up and implementing inservice programs for teachers in mathematics.

41. I find that most schools have one or more teachers whom I can depend on to assume leadership in inservice education.

42. Location (convenience) is a major factor determining teachers' willingness to participate in inservice education.

43. For what grade levels do you have responsibility?

   a) elementary   b) junior high or middle school   c) senior high   d) A, B and C   e) B, C

44. Estimate to the closest percentage how much of your time is given to administrative tasks? (ie. filling out forms, budget, meetings, paper shuffling,....)

   a) 10%   b) 20%   c) 40%   d) 55%   e) 70%

45. With how many schools do you work?

   a) less than 7   b) 7 to 20   c) 21 to 40   d) 41 to 75   e) more than 75

46. What percentage of your time do you estimate is given directly to inservice education?

   a) 10%   b) 20%   c) 40%   d) 55%   e) 70%

47. Exclusive of the salaries of supervisory personnel, I would estimate that my school invests the following for inservice education per year for each teacher:

   a) 0¢   b) 25¢   c) 50¢   d) $1.00 to $5.00   e) more than $5.00

48. The majority of schools with which I work are:

   a) Urban   b) Rural   c) Suburban

49. I serve
   a) several independent school systems out of a district office;   b) only part of the schools in my school system;   c) all of the schools in my school system

Inservice Education--As it IS and as it OUGHT-TO-BE

Respond twice to each question in this section. First, on the left, describe your perception of what is the current state of inservice education in your school. Next, on the right, state what it should be like in your school. Note that on these second items you should state your opinions but do be realistic!

For both the what is and the what ought-to-be questions:
   A = strongly agree   B = agree   C = disagree   D = strongly disagree
   Example:
   Most students like mathematics.

IS				OUGHT-TO-BE			
A	B	C	D	A	B	C	D
		disagree			Strongly		
					Agree		

My school system encourages inservice education by:
50. Providing teachers release time from classroom duties.
51. Paying expenses for inservice education offered by non-school agencies.
52. Paying teachers to participate in inservice education.
53. Giving credit toward acquiring tenure.
54. Giving credit toward promotion.
55. Participation in inservice education can result in teachers being placed in a higher pay bracket.

56. My state requires that a few days each year be given to reserve education as part of teachers' contract.

57. Inservice education is a point of negotiation when teacher groups bargain for a new contract with the school system.

58. The state provides protected money for inservice education that cannot be used in any other way.

59. The state department of education provides significant help in designing and conducting inservice programs.

The major purposes of inservice education reflected in my school system include:
60. Keeping "alive" professionally.
61. Learning about new curricula.
62. Learning new mathematics.
63. Studying new methods of teaching mathematics.
64. Analyzing problems, such as discipline, faced by all teachers; not just teachers of mathematics.
65. Facilitating the use of a new text or text series.
66. Providing opportunity for mathematics teachers to share ideas with other mathematics teachers.
67. Building enthusiasm for teaching mathematics
68. Describing new materials and information of direct use in my classroom.

The topics for inservice education in mathematics that currently receive primary emphasis in my school system are:

69. Computational skills
70. Motivation
71. Applications of mathematics
72. Mathematical structures
73. Metrication
74. Use of calculators
75. Students with learning difficulties
76. Diagnosis
77. Evaluation
78. Transformational geometry
79. Transition between grade levels
80. Remediation
81. Improving student attitudes about mathematics
82. My school system has a special inservice program above and beyond orientation for beginning teachers.
83. Inservice education programs are short and to-the-point.
84. Inservice education programs consist of several short, weekly meetings each organized around a single theme or topic.
85. Single-topic, all day inservice programs are available five or more days during the school year.
86. My school district has an inservice program but it is not designed for mathematics teaching specifically.
87. Inservice programs throughout the year are all related to a single theme or goal.
88. Achievement data of students in my school are used to determine needs for inservice education.
89. Achievement data of students in my school are used to evaluate the effectiveness of inservice programs in my school.
90. Inservice education is required to maintain certification.
91. Inservice education is required to maintain tenure.
92. My school district can depend on neighboring colleges and universities to provide inservice opportunities.
93. Teachers can receive college credit for participation in my school system's inservice program.
94. Teachers are so inclined to the practical, what-can-I-use-tomorrow attitude that inservice education loses its effectiveness.
95. Elementary teachers in my school district want inservice education for mathematics teaching.
96. Secondary teachers in my school district want inservice education.
97. I can require a particular teacher to attend an inservice program.
98. New teachers expect to participate in inservice education throughout their professional life.

III. Open Ended Questions - Respond on the reverse of the answer form

99. What is the biggest problem or difficulty that interfers with your inservice program?
100. What major trends seem apparent for inservice education in the future?
101. We need descriptions of effective inservice programs. Do you have a description of yours at hand? Would you send it to us please?

Thank you for your time!

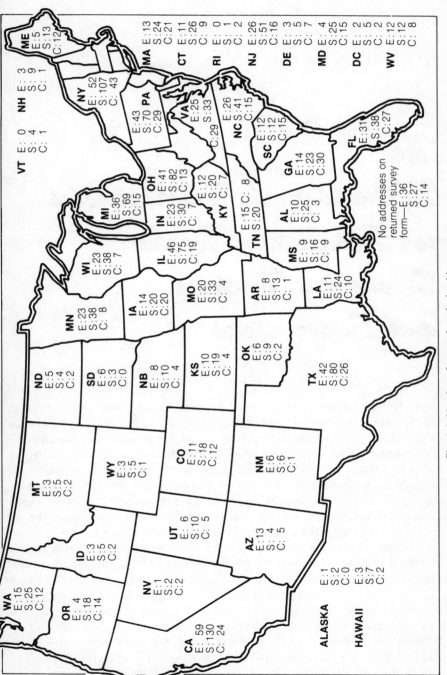

Fig. A.1. Number of respondents by level by state

E = Elementary, S = Secondary, C = Supervisors (members NCSM)

The Is/Ought-to-Be Discrepancies for Elementary Teachers, Secondary Teachers, and Supervisors

THE DISCREPANCY between the mean Is response and the mean Ought-to-Be response for each of the item-pairs 50 through 98 for each of the three populations is displayed below. Each item was scored on a zero-to-three scale, zero corresponding to "strongly agree" and three to "strongly disagree." The item-pair discrepancy for a given population is graphed as a segment on the interval (0,3) with the endpoints named by the mean responses. Thus, the length of the segment indicates the magnitude of the discrepancy between the Is and the Ought opinions of the respondents; the longer the segment, the greater the discrepancy.

If the populations responded to the same item, the discrepancies are exhibited together for purposes of comparison. The elementary teachers' mean responses are labeled with an "E," the secondary teachers' with an "S," and the supervisors' with a "C." Following the list of items common across the populations, the discrepancies for other items are given. The item numbers correspond to the item numbers on the teachers' survey forms until the pool of items common across the three populations is exhausted; then they correspond to item numbers on the supervisors' scale.

Nearly all the item-pair responses have the Is mean response more negative than, or graphed to the right of, the Ought mean response. In the few cases in which the Ought is graphed to the right of the Is, the reversal is noted by an "R" printed on the discrepancy segment. These R discrepancies need careful consideration since they are so atypical.

Hotelling's *t*-test statistic was used to test the hypothesis of equality of the means for the Is and Ought responses to each item pair for each population. A sufficiently large F value was obtained for each population to produce a probability level small enough ($p < .0005$) to allow examination of individual item-pairs. Each item-pair in which the hypothesis of equality of mean responses ($p < .01$) is not rejected is indicated by an asterisk. You will note that for the large majority of item-pairs, support for equality of mean responses was not found. That is, the discrepancy appears to be noteworthy.

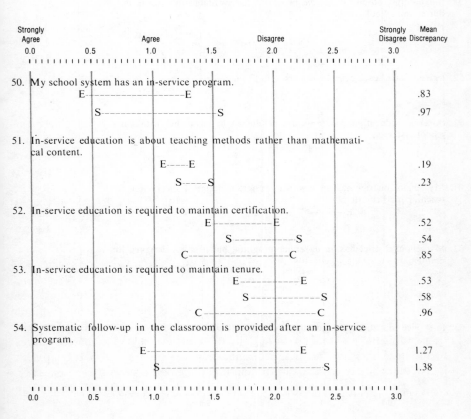

Strongly Agree 0.0	0.5	Agree 1.0	1.5	Disagree 2.0	2.5	Strongly Disagree 3.0	Mean Discrepancy

55. My school district depends on neighboring colleges and universities to provide the majority of opportunities for in-service education.

E——E .20

S S -.02

C————C .40

56. Teachers complete in-service programs with materials for classroom use that they have made themselves.

E———————E .68

S——————————S .82

57. There is an individual in my building or in my school system responsible for in-service education in mathematics.

E——————————E 1.07

S————————————S 1.13

58. Single-topic, all-day in-service programs are available five or six days during the school year.

E——————————————E 1.19

S————————————————S 1.23

C————————————C 1.00

59. I give some of each of my summers to in-service work.

E——E .27

S————S .41

60. In-service education programs are conducted by personnel within my school system.

E——E .21

S————S .37

61. My school district has an in-service program designed specifically for teaching mathematics.

E————————————————E 1.30

S——————————————————S 1.47

62. My school district has an in-service program, but it is not designed for mathematics teaching specifically.

E—E .10

S-S -.03

C-C .04

63. In-service education programs are short and to the point.

E———————————E 1.20

S——————————————S 1.25

C———C .44

0.0	0.5	1.0	1.5	2.0	2.5	3.0

Strongly Agree		Agree		Disagree		Strongly Disagree	Mean Discrepancy
0.0	0.5	1.0	1.5	2.0	2.5	3.0	

64. In-service education programs consist of several short, weekly meetings all organized around a single theme or topic.

```
                        E------------------E                    .73
                        S--------------------S                  .85
                        C--------------------C                  .76
```

The topics for in-service education in mathematics that receive emphasis in my school are (this question stem applies to questions 65–77):

65. Computational skill

```
              E-------------------------E                       .99
                 S--------------------------------S            1.18
                 C----C                                         .18
```

66. Motivation

```
                 E------------------E                          1.14
              S----------------------S                         1.21
              C-------------C                                   .72
```

67. Applications of mathematics

```
                 E------------------E                          1.15
              S---------------------------S                    1.45
              C-----------------C                               .95
```

68. Mathematical structures

```
                    E----------------E                          .88
                       S-----------------S                      .96
                    C-------------C                              .69
```

69. Metrication

```
              E-----------------E                               .98
                 S----------------S                             .93
              C-------C                                         .41
```

70. Use of calculators

```
                       E----------------------E                 .98
                 S-----------------S                           1.16
                 C------------------C                           .99
```

71. Students with learning difficulties

```
                 E-----------------E                           1.09
                 S--------------------S                        1.11
                 C-----------C                                  .64
```

72. Diagnosis

```
                 E-----------------E                           1.06
              S-----------------------S                        1.18
                 C-------------C                                .91
```

73. Evaluation

```
                 E-----------------E                            .92
              S----------------------S                         1.03
                 C-------------C                                .71
```

0.0	0.5	1.0	1.5	2.0	2.5	3.0	

Strongly Agree		Agree		Disagree		Strongly Disagree	Mean Discrepancy
0.0	0.5	1.0	1.5	2.0	2.5	3.0	

74. Transformational geometry

E------------+------------E .64
S------------+------------S .83
C------------+------------C .71

75. Transition between grade levels

E---+------------------------E 1.05
S-------------------------S 1.01
C------------------C .80

76. Remediation

E------------+------------------E 1.08
S------------+----------------S 1.02
C-------+------C .49

77. Improving student attitudes about mathematics

E------------+------------------E 1.28
S-----------------------------S 1.44
C-----------------------C 1.04

The purposes of in-service education reflected in my school include (this question stem applies to questions 78–86):

78. Keeping "alive" professionally

E-------------------E .59
S-----------------------S .82
C------------C .49

79. Learning about new curricula

E-------------E .58
S-----------------------S .96
C------------C .57

80. Learning about mathematics

E-------------------E .77
S---------------------------S 1.02
C-----------C .56

81. Studying new methods of teaching mathematics

E--------------------E 1.02
S-----------------------------S 1.33
C-----------------C .69

82. Analyzing problems, such as discipline, faced by all teachers; not just teachers of mathematics

E-------------------E .90
S---------------------S .92
C------------C .55

83. Facilitating the use of a new text or text series

E-------------E .62
S----------------------S .90
C-------C .36

| 0.0 | 0.5 | 1.0 | 1.5 | 2.0 | 2.5 | 3.0 |

Strongly Agree		Agree		Disagree		Strongly Disagree	Mean Discrepancy
0.0	0.5	1.0	1.5	2.0	2.5	3.0	

84. Providing opportunity to share ideas with other mathematics teachers

E-------------------------E   1.06

S------------------------S   1.04

C-------------------C   .75

85. Building enthusiasm for teaching mathematics

E---------------------E   1.09

S-----------------------------S   1.24

C---------------------C   .94

86. Describing new materials and information of direct use in my classroom

E----------------------E   .89

S-----------------------------S   1.14

C----------------C   .57

87. Money is budgeted for in-service education by my school district.

E----------------E   .68

S----------------------S   .85

88. I participate in identifying topics for in-service education.

E-----------------------E   1.00

S-----------------------------S   1.10

89. I can use in my teaching most of the mathematics I learn in in-service education.

E---------------------E   .95

S----------------------------S   1.18

90. I have been able to use in my teaching most of the methods demonstrated in in-service education.

E--------------------E   .90

S----------------------------S   1.15

91. Achievement data of students in my school are used to determine needs for in-service education.

E--------------------------E   1.11

S---------------------------------S   1.34

C------------------C   .72

92. Achievement data of students in my school are used to evaluate the effectiveness of in-service programs in my school.

E----------------------E   .94

S---------------------------S   1.18

C----------------C   .71

| 0.0 | 0.5 | 1.0 | 1.5 | 2.0 | 2.5 | 3.0 |

Strongly Agree		Agree		Disagree		Strongly Disagree	Mean Discrepancy
0.0	0.5	1.0	1.5	2.0	2.5	3.0	

My school encourages in-service education by (this question stem applies to questions 93–98):

93. Providing release time from classroom duties

      E----------------------------E   1.12

         S----------------------S   1.14

   C----------------------C   1.31

94. Paying expenses for in-service education offered by nonschool agencies

      E-----------------------E   1.11

        S---------------------S   1.21

             C----------*R*----------C   –.92

95. Paying me to participate in in-service education

             E-------------------------E   1.04

            S-----------------------S   1.10

                C------------C   .74

96. Giving credit toward acquiring tenure

             E---------------------E   .89

                S-------------------S   .86

                C-----------C   .61

97. Giving credit toward promotion

             E----------------------E   .98

                S-------------------S   .93

                C------------C   .76

98. Placing me in a higher pay bracket for participation in in-service education

             E----------------------E   .93

                S------------------S   .84

                C-----------C   .63

Each of the remaining items was *only* on the supervisors' questionnaire.

56. My state requires that a few days each year be given to reserve education as part of teachers' contract.

                C-----------------C   .76

57. In-service education is a point of negotiation when teacher groups bargain for a new contract with the school system.

                   C--------C   .38

58. The state provides protected money for in-service education that cannot be used in any other way.

            C--------------------C   1.13

0.0	0.5	1.0	1.5	2.0	2.5	3.0

Strongly Agree		Agree		Disagree		Strongly Disagree	Mean Discrepancy
0.0	0.5	1.0	1.5	2.0	2.5	3.0	

59. The state department of education provides significant help in designing and conducting in-service programs.

C------|------------|-------C   1.00

82. My school system has a special in-service program above and beyond orientation for beginning teachers.

C+-------------------+-------C   .91

87. In-service programs throughout the year are all related to a single theme or goal.

C--------C   .33

93. Teachers can receive college credit for participation in my school system's in-service program.

C-------------------------C   .72

94. Teachers are so inclined to the practical, what-can-I-use-tomorrow attitude that in-service education loses its effectiveness.

C-------*R*------C   -.43

95. Elementary teachers in my school district want in-service education for mathematics teaching.

C-------------------------C   .61

96. Secondary teachers in my school district want in-service education.

C---------------------------C   1.04

97. I can require a particular teacher to attend an in-service program.

C------------------------------------C   1.05

98. New teachers expect to participate in in-service education throughout their professional life.

C-----------------------------C   .99

| 0.0 | 0.5 | 1.0 | 1.5 | 2.0 | 2.5 | 3.0 |

APPENDIX 3

Descriptions of In-Service Programs

J. MICHAEL BOWLING

THE NCTM In-Service Project solicited descriptions of in-service programs from mathematics educators across the United States. Following are abstracts of some of the program descriptions that were submitted. Most were submitted in response to a personal letter of request that was written because a teacher or supervisor had indicated the program was valuable for teachers. This act of nomination is the primary evidence of the quality of the program that was available to the project.

The program abstracts are included in this handbook for three reasons:

1. They demonstrate a large variety of types of programs ranging from those serving a clientele in a single school to those serving a statewide clientele.

2. The programs indicate several different ways of manipulating some of the critical variables of in-service education that were identified in the teacher surveys. Among these are the mechanisms for rewarding teachers, for encouraging participation, for follow-up, and for evaluation.

3. People to contact for further information about a program are listed.

A comment concerning contacting people for more information about a program is in order. The individuals who have submitted program descriptions are busy doing in-service work. Sending a description can represent an imposition on their time. It may represent an imposition on their budget. We suggest that you consider carefully the use that you could make of an amplified program description. We also recommend that you be prepared to meet any charges or costs incurred by your request for further information.

Do realize that each of these descriptions is an abstract of a description of a program. The abstract identifies a few salient variables that appeared to give the program uniqueness in serving the needs of teachers in addition to listing the primary content and objectives of the program. Each program manager was asked to approve the abstract of his or her program in order to assure its accuracy.

No implication of merit beyond a program participant's recommendation is intended. Similarly, it is recognized that there are highly successful in-service mechanisms functioning in the country that are not listed here.

In-Service Program Descriptions

Title: Creative Teaching Center Workshops   *Contact:* Creative Teaching Center
Purpose: Promotion of use of Creative Publications   1101 San Antonio Rd.
   materials   Mountain View, CA 94043
Audience: Specific to workshop (K–12)

     Series of workshops to familiarize teachers with Creative Publications materials; free, but each limited to 30 participants; topics include metric experiences, place value, logic, pattern discovery, skills practice.

Title: In-Service Certification—Master's Equivalency   *Contact:* Alexander Tobin
   Program   Mathematics Education
Purpose: Certificate renewal, permanent certification,   Room 310
   work toward M.A., or skill improvement (more   21st & The Parkway
   than math content area)   Philadelphia, PA 19103
Audience: Elementary, junior high, secondary

     Competency-based program; courses in math and other subjects taught at several locations; math-related courses include "Math; what every elementary teacher should know," computers, metric.

Title: Challenge to Finding Ways of Making Math   *Contact:* Sr. Helen Lucille Habig
   Concepts Meaningful   Archdiocese of Cincinnati
Purpose: Arousing pupil interest in math through   220 W. Liberty St.
   math-lab approach   Cincinnati, OH 45210
Audience: 1–3, 4–6, 7–9

     4-1/2 hr. one-shot workshop given at different locations; participants engage in learning new grade-level specific methods and ideas, make various lab materials, and inspect inexpensive commercial lab materials. ($2.50 registration fee; maximum number of session participants—45).

Title: The Metric System as an Interdisciplinary Tool *Contact:* Theresa Kuhs
Purpose: Give teachers a practical knowledge of the   53 Rochester Rd.
metric system   Pittsburgh, PA 15229
Audience: K-12 teachers

Interdisciplinary metrication stressed in this in-service credit course (approximately twenty-two 2-hr. meetings); includes development of metric unit for classroom use.

Title: Math In-Service Workshop   *Contact:* Robert Shanks
                                                                        2825 Woodbridge Ave.
                                                                        Office of Superintendent
Purpose: Learn operation and programming on   of Schools
programmable calculator (Monroe #1666)   Edison, NJ 08817
Audience: High school math department heads, math
teachers.

Five 2-hr. sessions concerning fundamentals of programming, activities to be classroom-related; in-service credit available; instructor—Monroe educational consultant.

Title: Math Lab Workshops, USMES Workshop   *Contact:* George Grossman
Purpose: Continuing implementation of physical   Bureau of Mathematics
materials usage; consideration of relevant math   131 Livingston St.
education topics   Brooklyn, NY 11201
Audience: Elementary and secondary

Ten Saturday morning workshops on USMES, metric, calculators, and other topics; in-service or graduate credit available; fee $25 ($50-75 if graduate credit desired); NSF funding for training of teacher-trainers.

Title: Professional Math and Science Lab Weekends   *Contact:* George Grossman
Purpose: Continuing implementation of physical   Bureau of Mathematics
materials usage; consideration of relevant math   131 Livingston St.
and science education topics (interdisciplinary)   Brooklyn, NY 11201
Audience: Elementary and secondary

Three weekends of workshops, lectures, sharing of ideas, etc., a year; held at resort near New York; exhibit areas by professional distributors of materials; in-service or graduate credit available.

Title: Curriculum Implementation Project (In-Service *Contact:* William Orton
Phase)   Dept. of Mathematics
Purpose: Improvement of secondary math education   University of Arkansas
in Arkansas   Fayetteville, AR 72701
Audience: Junior high, secondary

Part of 4-year NSF-funded comprehensive program; 19 math education centers established statewide to offer four combined content-method courses—jr. high math, algebra, geometry, general math; courses designed by writing teams of experienced secondary math teachers and project staff; yearly enrollment approximately 400; college credit available; follow-up evaluation with participants and secondary math classes supports program effectiveness.

Title: none given   *Contact:* Lynn W. Anderson
                                                                        Vernon Public Schools
Purpose: Math curriculum improvement, metric   School St.
education   Rockville, CT 06066
Audience: K-8 teachers

Fifteen 2-hr. sessions plus three half-day workshops; 3 in-service credits; development of materials and activities—at least one unit of math instruction plus supplements; immediate evaluation of unit and metric competency plus classroom follow-up.

Title: Take Me to Your Liter—a Classroom
Arrangement for Metric Instruction
Purpose: Metric education
Audience: Elementary

Contact: Cathy Draper Clark
9275 Church St.
Des Plaines, IL 60016

Participants learn how to develop classroom metric centers via activity approach followed by sharing of experiences.

Title: Activity-Centered Math Education Project
Purpose: Increase student achievement in mathematics in selected junior high school classes
Audience: Junior high school

Contact: Sheila Berman
Patrick Henry Jr. H.S.
17340 San Jose St.
Granda Hills, CA 91344

One hundred fifty participants constructed activity kits for classroom use patterned after those developed under TTT Project (California State University, Northridge); kits are designed to introduce, develop, or reinforce math concepts and skills.

Title: Teacher Development Center

Purpose: Central facilities for staff development
Audience: Elementary

Contact: Dr. Jerald Mikesell
Director, Math & Science
Mesa Public Schools
549 N. Stapley Dr.
Mesa, AZ 85203

Tripartite organization—idea center, meeting/display room, construction area; college credit courses use meeting room and schools are encouraged to hold faculty meetings there; orientation available for new teachers; planned programs follow needs assessments; immediate and long-range follow-up by four math resource teachers; math evaluation based on district-wide pupil performance.

Title: Montana Math Mobile

Purpose: Accessibility of materials and ideas to wide
teacher audience
Audience: All math teachers

Contact: Daniel T. Dolan
Montana Math Teacher
Center
Columbus High School
Columbus, MT 59019

Travel trailer stocked with books, materials, programmable calculator, and other resources riding district circuits to provide teachers with free or inexpensive materials for classroom use.

Title: Elementary Mathematics In-Service
Purpose: Developing new dimensions in manipulative
experiences with materials and activities
Audience: K-9 teachers

Contact: Clem Boyer, Jr.
315 Maple Ave.
Sanford, FL 32771

Unit of instruction to upgrade basic skill competencies of students (K-9); evaluation objective-specific.

Title: In-Service Workshops

Purpose: Staff development
Audience: Elementary

Contact: Ruth G. Sheffield
School Board Office
Abingdon, VA

Series of 2-hour to 2-day workshops conducted by teachers, publisher representatives, and outside consultants; year-end evaluation prompts content of next year's workshops; total of 6 days' in-service credit via these workshops, offered throughout the year (and on two special in-service occasions).

Title: Summer and year-round after-school workshops

Purpose: Professional development of teachers

Audience: Teachers, administrators, K–12.

Contact: The Teachers' Center
at Greenwich
1177 King St.
Greenwich, CT 06830

Full-time 2-week workshop; partly mathematics; one intention—how to make better usage of math materials presently in classrooms; this is a summer workshop offered each year ($150); college credit available. After-school workshops also have college credit available; 11-session series, partly mathematics ($75 fee).

Title: Metric Trunk Project

Purpose: Prepare teachers for state assessment test on metrics

Audience: All

Contact: M. Rose Burleson
Head, MCTM Metric
Workshop Committee
Bullock Creek H.S.
1519 S. Badour Rd.
Midland, MI 48640

Workshop inexpensive, uses manipulatives; materials can be used in class next day; $50/trunk cost borne by school.

Title: In-Service Workshops (Modules)

Purpose: Professional growth

Audience: All teachers (district)

Contact: Marlen Carle
Arlington ISD
1203 Pioneer Parkway
Arlington, TX 76013

One hundred fifteen 1- and 2-hour modules (seven math related) offered on required in-service day; topics range from Cuisenaire rods to the metric system.

Title: Elementary School Mathematics—New Solutions to Old Problems

Purpose: Familiarize teachers with some new approaches to teaching basic skills

Audience: K–6 teachers

Contact: William J. Collins
409 W. Genesee St.
Syracuse, NY 13202

Fifteen 2-hour sessions examining new methods and materials; classroom materials constructed by participants; pretest and posttest for evaluation; (session topics—Cuisenaire rods, geoboards, base and place value, and so on).

Title: Diagnosing Student Needs

Purpose: Diagnosing and prescribing with regard to needs in mathematics

Audience: Elementary

Contact: Shirley Ray
Education Service Center
109 N. Chaparral St.
Corpus Christi, TX 78401

Paper-and-pencil activities in workshop format involving assessing and interpreting cognitive and affective needs to increase mathematics competencies; regional program.

Title: Mathematics for the Less Competent— What Should It Be?

Purpose: Considering alternatives and solutions for secondary students weak in minimal mathematics competencies.

Contact: Ronald Massie
Lincoln Public Schools
P.O. Box 82889
Lincoln, NE 68501

Audience: Junior and senior high

Three-session workshop (evenings); part of staff development, midyear workshops; run by local school personnel; compensation—professional growth points.

Title: Mathematics for the Learning Disability Pupil   *Contact:* Ronald Massie
Purpose: Developing sequential mathematics   Lincoln Public Schools
handbook with emphasis on manipulative materials   P.O. Box 82889
for primary and intermediate grade skills   Lincoln, NE 68501
Audience: Elementary and junior high

Weekly 2-1/2-hour meetings for 15 weeks; may be taken for professional growth credit or for advancement on salary schedule; part of staff development courses offered by local district; teachers' input (topic selection and needs assessment) provided via K–12 advisory committee; on-site evaluation is regular but not classroom follow-up.

Title: Applying Learning Theory in the Secondary   *Contact:* Ronald Massie
Mathematics Classroom   Lincoln Public Schools
Purpose: Investigation of mathematics classroom ap-   P.O. Box 82889
plications of recent findings in learning theory   Lincoln, NE 68501
Audience: Secondary

Weekly 2-1/2-hour meetings for 6 weeks; may be taken for professional growth credit or for advancement on salary schedule; part of the staff development course offering by local district; teachers' input (topic selection and needs assessment) provided via K–12 advisory committee; on-site evaluation is regular but not classroom follow-up.

Title: Mathematics for Life Roles   *Contact:* C. A. Guerriero
                                                 Math Education Advisor
                                                 Pennsylvania Department
                                                 of Education
Purpose: To revise meaningfully "general math"   Box 911
courses in district curricula   Harrisburg, PA 17126
Audience: Secondary mathematics teachers

Participant-oriented two-day workshop; design involves a "life roles model"; extensively tested and revised; evaluations imply practical implementation in schools.

Titles: Metric System Workshop; Classroom Learning   *Contact:* Sr. Margaret Haas
Centers; Classroom Management for Individualized   Catholic School Board
Mathematics Programs; Implications of Piaget's   721 N. LaSalle St.
Theory for the Mathematics Curriculum; and so on.   Chicago, IL 60610
Purpose: Specific to individual workshops
Audience: Specific to individual workshops

Extensive series of one-meeting workshops; varying sponsors and facilitators; teacher input from Archdiocesan Mathematics Curriculum Committee.

Title: Math Teacher Center   *Contact:* Phil Makurat
                                             University of Wisconsin—
Purpose: Improve mathematics classroom activities   Whitewater
through informal exchange of experiences, ideas, and   800 W. Main St.
materials.   Whitewater, WI 53190
Audience: Any interested teachers

Seen as an "alternative" means of in-service education for and by teachers; weekly 2-1/2-hour sessions; activity and discussion topics range from needs assessments to use of hand calculators in the classroom; self-evaluation at least twice a year; no formal classroom follow-up; visits by participants to other participants' classrooms encouraged.

Title: Teachers' Center Project

Purpose: Provide continuous staff development for area school districts

Audience: Elementary

Contact: T. C. O'Brien
School of Education-
Teachers' Center Project
SIU-Edwardsville
Edwardsville, IL 62025

Series of regular, weekly 2-1/2-hour sessions and special sessions, some for college credit; publications available at nominal charge; topics include Piagetian Implications, Britain's Integrated Curriculum, Mathematical Games, Goals of Mathematics Education, and so on.

Title: SED Metric Awareness Workshop

Purpose: Metric familiarity

Audience: K-12 teachers

Contact: LeRoy Negus
Bureau of Mathematics
Room 306 E.B.
State Education Dept.
Albany, NY 12234

Part I (1 hr.) slide presentation, general discussion, seven activities for all teachers. Part II (1-1 1/2 hrs.) workshop oriented to elementary teachers—measurement kit constructed; activities are from *Metric—Now*, prepared by metric committee of state education department.

Title: Metric Regional Resource Centre

Purpose: Implementing elementary metric education through a resource linking agency between state education departments, universities, and LEAs

Audience: Elementary teachers

Contact: James R. Lawson
Director, Metric Center
Dept. of Education
San Diego Co.
6401 Linda Vista Rd.
San Diego, CA 92111

The Metric Regional Resource Centre acts as a resource coordinating center to provide leadership and support services to public (eight) and nonpublic (two) school districts; written agreement between districts and department of education; implementation plans written by identified metric specialists in 1974-75 and currently specialists provide in-service education as determined by district-specific implementation plans using a "multiplier approach."

Title: Metric Workshop

Purpose: Metric familiarity

Audience: Any person desirous to learn metrics

Contact: Bonnie Cagan
Elementary Mathematics
Coordinator
Harry County Schools
Conway, SC

One-day, three-hour, activity-oriented workshop; brief opening lecture overviews metrication; 35 minutes at each of four stations (activity cards)—length, area, mass, capacity; work done in twos and threes; resource table on display; brief summary and sharing at conclusion.

Title: Manipulative Workshop

Purpose: Familiarity with manipulative materials and their proper usage

Audience: To learn correct and extended usages of manipulative materials for implementing learning

Contact: Bonnie Cagan
Elementary Mathematics
Coordinator
Harry County Schools
Conway, SC

One-day, two-hour, activity-oriented workshop; demonstrations (as introductions) at each of ten stations by teachers using materials in their own classroom; manipulatives include attribute blocks, balance, Unifix materials, geoboards, and so on. (Comment by source: three hours more appropriate for length of workshop.)

Title: Aurora Project

Purpose: Master's degree (professional growth)
Audience: Middle and senior high math teachers

Contact: Charles R. McNerney
Dept. of Mathematics
University of Northern
Colorado
Greeley, CO 80639

District math supervisor inquired of UNC math department about master's degree possibilities; needs assessment prompted design of math education MA through School of Educational Change and Development—45 quarter-hour program approved by math department; programs consisted of professional experiences with written reports; math courses (History of, Computers, Foundations, etc.), electives, and comprehensive examinations. Follow-up classroom evaluation not finalized yet, but results so far are encouraging. Resources provided by local districts and the university.

Title: Released Time Program for Staff Development
Purpose: Staff development in all subject areas
Audience: K–8 teachers

Contact: Theresa R. Mroz
89 Appleton St.
Lowell, MA 01852

One-day, district-sponsored series of 1- and 2-hour workshops; math workshop topics range from metrication, use of Cuisenaire rods, and computers to creative math and motivation in math.

Title: Gresham Grade District—
University of Portland

Purpose: Provide master's degree, standard
certification within the district
Audience: All teachers

Contact: Bob Anderson
Director of Teacher
Education
Gresham School District
1400 S.E. 5th
Gresham, OR 97030

Managed by district through director of teacher education and in-service building coordinators; times convenient to teachers; flexibility in course selection and in use of nonuniversity personnel as instructors; 9 hours tuition reimbursement a year available to teachers; courses other than those related to specific degree programs are available; district receives 25% rebate on tuitions paid after instructional costs are paid.

Title: Professional Growth Courses for
Continuing Education
Purpose: Professional growth
Audience: K–12 teachers

Contact: Robert E. McNemar
270 E. State St.
Columbus, OH 43215

Series of courses (three to five meetings each) offered by district division of instruction in all content areas; instructors are content coordinators and qualified teachers; hours designed for teacher's convenience; math topics range from curve stitching and reading skills in math to alternative approaches to math and calculators in the classroom.

Title: Mathematics Center
Purpose: Provide individualized laboratory
experiences in math for students at all levels
(and in-service training for teachers)
Audience: K–12 teachers (and students)

Contact: Mary S. Driggers
Florence School District #3
Lake City, SC 29560

Funded by Title I, this district-sponsored center has permanent location; materials for individual and small-group work are constantly in use.

Title: DCS Staff Development Program   *Contact:* Eugenia G. Atkinson
                                                                    Durham City Schools
Purpose: Professional growth, certification renewal   P.O. Box 2246
Audience: K–12 (specific to in-service course)   Durham, NC 27702

In-service programs designed following needs assessment in each district school; programs—new materials orientation for Title I math aides, metrication, personalizing instruction, math activities; the latter given at schools where requested by faculty; first and fourth are noncredit, other two carry 1–1 1/2 in-service credit hours.

Title: Leadership Training Institute in Elementary   *Contact:* Bill Goe
   School Math   2525 W. 6th Ave.
Purpose: Train selected teachers to assume   Denver, CO 80204
   leadership role in assisting Denver elementary
   teachers with Harper & Row texts

Audience: Selected public school teachers
Teachers met at University of Wyoming Science and Math Teaching Center for 2-1/2 weeks—one objective was to develop in-service workshops on return to district; considerable independent study time; 3 semester hours of academic credit; room and board paid, tuition waived.

Title: Metric America 76   *Contact:* H. Vance Mills
                                                                    San Diego City Schools
Purpose: Teacher metrication   4100 Normal St.
Audience: K–12 teachers   San Diego, CA 92103

Seven 2-hour class sessions (4–6 P.M.), one unit district in-service credit; no fee; course covers history of measurement, advantages of metric system, and strategies and materials for use in classroom.

Title: Piedmont Schools Project (staff   *Contact:* Faye Jenkins
   development component)   Piedmont Schools Project
Purpose: Staff development through instructional   206 Church St.
   techniques   Greer, SC 29651
Audience: K–12 teachers

NIE-funded project in 4th of 5 years; activity-oriented staff development workshops with independent inquiry encouraged; "Student-For-A-Day" workshops place teachers in classroom setting using grouping, personalization, and individual conference—content varies; another workshop (3 days) deals with classroom management and behavior modification; these and other project in-service activities have been quite popular with the teachers.

Title: The Professional Growth Program   *Contact:* Jack Coleman
Purpose: Provide individualized in-service programs   Shelby Co. Schools
   for teachers   160 S. Hollywood
Audience: K–12 teachers   Memphis, TN 38112

One hundred in-service points (plus four faculty days in school) required of each teacher to meet in-service requirements of State Department of Education; events calendar available before school starts; teachers have until 1 October to submit tentative plan for the year's professional growth maintenance.

Title: Introduction to the Metric System   *Contact:* Carey L. Bolster
                                                                    Board of Education of
Purpose: Professional growth   Baltimore County
Audience: Elementary, middle, and secondary   Office of Mathematics
   mathematics teachers   Towson, MD 21204

Seven sessions; 1 credit; 4–6 P.M. meetings at school; "hands on" approach to metric system including everyday applications.

Title: Redesign for Mathematical Relevancy

Purpose: Math curriculum revision (grades 3–8)

Audience: 3–8 teachers

Contact: Mary L. O'Brien
Coordinator of Mathematics
East Syracuse-Minoa
Central Schools
Fremont Rd.
East Syracuse, NY 13057

ESEA Title III-funded project resulting from extensive needs assessment, which included much teacher input; in-service component during August, teachers paid negotiated hourly rate for in-service curriculum development; major thrusts of in-service project have been to familiarize teachers with individualized math instruction (defined as flexible grouping based on student needs) and diagnostic teaching approaches; 90% teacher participation; extensive evaluation.

Title: Oregon System in Mathematics Education

Purpose: Statewide improvement of math education

Audience: K–12 teachers

Contact: Barry Mitzman
Oregon Mathematics
Education Council
325—13th St., N.E.
Salem, OR 97301

In final year of five-year NSF-supported program, OSME conducts activity-oriented math workshops, creates and supports math teacher resource centers, and helps support some county "circuit riding" math consultants; math-lab approach emphasized in all phases three general types of workshops are "math enthusiast" (elementary), "math for the uninvolved" (intermediate, secondary), and computer science (elementary, secondary); workshops usually meet for six Saturday sessions focusing on techniques teachers can put into use on Monday.

Title: Professional Growth Workshops—
Elementary Mathematics

Purpose: Professional growth

Audience: Elementary teachers/staff

Contact: Barbara Dunning
Director of Staff
Development
CDA West
3151 A Eton Ave.
Berkeley, CA 95705

Three-day summer workshop offered by Curriculum Development Associates, Inc., at various California locations; learning theories of Bruner and Piaget explored and applied, manipulatives emphasized; other focal points—individualization, diagnosis and prescription, classroom management, curriculum materials evaluation; $62.50 fee for tuition and materials; endorsed by California State Curriculum Commission; in-service credits available; follow-up workshops may be scheduled.

Title: Workshops in Elementary Mathematics

Purpose: Professional growth

Audience: Anyone concerned with math education
of elementary school children

Contact: Robert Wirtz
CDA West
Box 5335
Carmel, CA 93921

Two-week college-accredited summer CDA workshop; many of same descriptors apply as listed in preceding abstract; $125 tuition and materials fee. (Note: CDA also sponsors professional growth and parent education workshops during the school year as requested by sufficient participants; these may be follow-up sessions to summer workshops; in-service credits available; fee of $150/day for each professional staff member.)

Title: In-Service Workshop Program
Purpose: Identify Algebra I problem areas and
explore different techniques for instruction
improvement
Audience: Junior and senior high school teachers

Contact: M. J. Antone
Director of Mathematics
Medford Public Schools
Medford, MA

Ten 1-1/2-hour sessions for 3 salary-scale credits; concentration on Algebra I minimal requirements, language, factoring, equation solving, and so on; junior high/senior high interaction emphasized; team approach to problem area exploration and writing of results and conclusions.

Title: Professional Staff Development Program

Purpose: Professional growth
Audience: K-12 teachers

Contact: David Glatzer
Director of Mathematics
22 Municipal Plaza
West Orange, NJ 07052

Half-day workshop of presentation in all subject areas (math; metric and activity math); guidelines set by professional development committee of district teachers and administrators; proposals by teachers and administrators; some courses or workshops carry college credit, all eligible to carry salary schedule credit; on-site evaluation, but no classroom follow-up specified.

Title: VIP Staff Development

Purpose: In-service education through combined
resources and interaction of four counties;
coordination by Regional Education Service
Agency, Region III (RESA III)
Audience: K-12 teachers

Contact: Raymond R. Dolin
69 Avenue B
Madison, WV 25130

Four counties share resources and staff; compensatory time available for voluntary participation; referred in-service programs (sponsored by contact person) are Science, Industrial Arts, and Math (integrated), Math component of Annual Science Fair, and Math Textbook Selection; one-day, 6-9 P.M. meetings.

Title: In-Service Education, Spring 1976

Purpose: Professional growth
Audience: K-12 teachers

Contact: Holland Payne
1619 N St.
Sacramento, CA 95814

Varying series of workshops/courses; district in-service ($2 registration fee) or university ($16) credit available; some salary-scale credit available; topics—Exploratory and Recreational Math (8 sessions, lab time, $7.50 materials fee); Motivational Math in the Primary Grades (6 sessions, manipulatives to basic skills, $7.50 materials fee); Metric Math for Primary Grades (4 sessions, $5 materials fee).

Title: In-Service Programs, 1975-76

Purpose: Professional growth
Audience: K-12 teachers

Contact: Ella E. Rice
P.O Box 220
Fairfield Public Schools
Fairfield, CT 06430

Series of 3-hour, 1 day to 1-hour/week, 3-month workshops—several in math and math/reading; in-service credit available but nature not specified; workshop topics (determined by needs assessment with professional staff) include metrication, motivation, instructional strategies for elementary and junior high math, and so on.

Title: Learning and Teaching the Metric System

Purpose: Metric familiarity

Audience: K-12

Contact: Diana Worshtil
Toledo Public Schools
E. Manhattan & Elm
Toledo, OH 43608

Seven 2-1/4-hour sessions worth 1 professional-growth credit; salary-schedule advancement available; although this workshop meets after school, teachers can obtain release time for other staff development endeavors (2 days maximum to visit other schools, 10 days for professional meetings).

Title: Equivalency Time Program

Purpose: Staff development

Audience: K-12 teachers

Contact: E. Gillette Irby
Mathematics Consultant
Corpus Christi Ind.
School District
801 Leopard St.
Corpus Christi, TX 78403

Series of workshops/seminars based on comprehensive needs assessment in content and pedagogy through teacher survey; choice of after-school meetings, all-day workshops; 8 hours credit required in generic skills seminars and 8 hours in content area programs (sick leave/salary debited otherwise); math courses vary with need but include such as structure and method in middle school math, geometry, the metric system, math games, and fundamentals of mathematics for career planning.

Title: Master Plan for In-Service Education

Purpose: Staff development, certificate renewal

Audience: K-12 teachers

Contact: Edith Ballenger
School District of
Greenville County
Greenville, SC

Result of extensive committee study of needs assessment (plus yearly evaluation); 120 in-service points in a 5-year period (equals 6 college semester hours) sufficient for certificate renewal with some category hour restraints (categories: exploratory, teaching techniques, subject area); comprehensive plan of point allotments for various activities from independent study and classroom observation to regular workshops and professional conference participation.

Title: Cooperative College School Science Program

Purpose: Training teachers techniques of teaching math using a lab setting employing manipulatives and independent learning

Audience: Elementary and junior high teachers

Contact: Elaine Mintz
Plainedge Schools
Hicksville Rd.
Bethpage, NY 11714

NSF-supported series of classes in which 35 participants developed strategies for effective classroom use of commercial/homemade materials in informal setting; classroom follow-up provided; teacher sharing of techniques encouraged; in-service and M.A. credit applicable.

Title: SEAMATH Open Workshop

Purpose: To get more manipulatives in classroom use

Audience: K-6 teachers/aides

Contact: Wayne Peterson
Basic Skills/Mathematics
Seattle Public Schools
W. 915 Galer
Seattle, WA 98119

Workshop based at teacher resource center and available Monday through Thursday 2:30-9:30 P.M. for teachers to come and assemble games and labs for immediate and continuous classroom use according to district-wide K-6 math guidelines (SEAMATH).

Title: Workshop in a Lab Approach to
Elementary Math
Purpose: Teacher familiarity with math-lab
materials and techniques and methods for class-
room implementation
Audience: Elementary teachers

Contact: Lee Osburn
Instructional Service Center
707 E. Col. Dr.
Tampa, FL 33602

Three-week summer workshop, voluntary, 20–80 in-service points (can be credited toward recertification); instructional time split among lab activities, developing activities, visitations to working lab, and math-lab reading materials; immediate evaluation plus some classroom follow-up; estimate that 75% of workshop alumni have implemented lab approach in classroom to some extent.

Title: Professional Growth In-Service
Purpose: Staff development
Audience: K–12 teachers

Contact: Karl West
Needham High School
Needham, MA 02194

Series of courses reflecting teachers' surveyed needs, 5-, 10-, or 15-blocks of weekly (1 hr.) meetings; 30 in-service clock hours equals 2 credits applicable to salary schedule; college credit also available; math topics: general primary math, general junior high school math, metric system.

Title: Non–College Credit Courses—
Math Science Center
Purpose: Professional growth
Audience: K–12 teachers

Contact: Rebecca E. Armstrong
Henrico County Schools
P.O. Box 40
Highland Springs, VA 23075

Six-session (3 hr. each) courses each equated as 1 unit of certification renewal credit; free tuition; meetings at district math-science center or a school; manipulatives emphasized; math courses—primary math activities (K–2), experiments in metric (3–9), simple probability experiments (5–9), computers and society (6–12), computer science (4–12), and history of mathematics (6–12).

Title: Monday Professional Growth Days

Purpose: Staff development
Audience: K–12 teachers

Contact: Donald Hankins
Education Center
4100 Normal St.
San Diego, CA 92103

One-shot workshops/seminars 3:30–5:00 P.M. to familiarize teachers with new materials/methods and to discuss current problems; topics—using the time-share computer system; ideas and activities for teaching algebra; mathematics for early childhood.

Title: In-Service Courses
Purpose: Staff development
Audience: K–12 teachers

Contact: Donald Hankins
Education Center
4100 Normal St.
San Diego, CA 92103

Series of 6 to 8 session courses (each approximately 2 hours; one session a week); district in-service credit provided; no tuition fee; topics include individualizing math, calculators, metric education, drill, and practice.

Title: Basic Skills Certificate Programs in Math

Purpose: Professional growth, teacher specific skill
identification
Audience: Elementary and junior high school
teachers

Contact: Wesley E. Johnson
Seattle Public Schools
Basic Skills Office
515 W. Galer St.
Seattle, WA 98119

Twenty-five in-service credits (or equivalent in college courses) required for program completion; required courses include foundations of modern math, diagnostic procedures, and classroom research application.

Title: Elementary Mathematics Workshop

Purpose: Professional growth, familiarization with new text series (Silver Burdett)

Audience: Elementary teachers and principals

Contact: Dr. Dale E. Fry
Springfield School District
111 W. Leamy Ave.
Springfield, PA 19064

Two-day summer workshop conducted by Silver Burdett representatives; 1 graduate credit or 1 in-service credit available plus $20/day stipend (50% graduate tuition reimbursed); session topics include measurement, place value, fractions, basic operations, and so on; groupings: K–3, 4–5.

Title: In-Service Computer Workshop

Purpose: Use of computer in classroom teaching

Audience: Secondary math/science teachers

Contact: Joseph Sott
Union Co. Regional
High School District #1
Springfield, NJ 07081

Eight 2-hour after-school sessions; funds for eight participants ($100 stipend each); specific weekly assignments made (terminals available) for review and evaluation.

Title: Workshop in Math for the Non–College Bound

Purpose: Improvement of general mathematics courses

Audience: General math teachers

Contact: Joseph Sott
Union Co. Regional
High School District #1
Springfield, NJ 07081

Relevant materials and topics for non-college-bound student identified and instructional techniques formulated; initial teacher response positive.

Title: Prealgebra Development Centers Developer-Demonstrator Project

Purpose: To acquaint teachers and administrators with the objectives, techniques, and results of the Title III ESEA-funded Prealgebra Development Centers

Audience: Administrators, seventh- and eighth-grade teachers

Contact: Dorothy S. Strong
Project Director
Prealgebra Development
Centers
400 West 69th St.
Chicago, IL 60621

Purpose of prealgebra development centers is to prepare seventh- and eighth-grade students for success with high school algebra by strengthening math backgrounds, improving skills, and defining and correcting math deficiencies; phases of the Developer-Demonstrator Project deal with introduction to the program or training a district's staff to implement it; program curriculum consists of ratio and proportion, fractions, decimals, percent, and measurement—focus is on diversified learning techniques, foreshadowing, concept unification; 1974 longitudinal study found that 80% of program alumni qualified for algebra enrollment and 92% successfully completed algebra course; implementation cost to a school district approximately $28 000 (second-year expenses much less since most materials nonconsumable); program format adapts to regular seventh- and eighth-grade math classes, 8-week summer session, or remedial high school math classes.

Bibliography

Aiken, L. R. "Attitudes toward Mathematics." *Review of Educational Research* 40 (1970): 551–96.

Allendoerfer, Carl B. *The Leadership Role of State Supervisors of Mathematics.* Washington, D.C.: U.S. Government Printing Office, 1962.

American Association of Colleges for Teacher Education. *Obligation for Reform: The Final Report of the Higher Education Task Force on Improvement and Reform in American Education.* Washington, D.C.: The Association, 1974.

American Federation of Teachers. *Goals of the American Federation of Teachers.* Item no. 16. Washington, D.C.: The Federation, n.d.

Anastasi, Anne. *Psychological Testing.* 3d ed. New York: Macmillan Co., 1968.

Behr, Merlyn J. "Review of Final Report, Special Teacher Project, 1971–72. Mathematics Improvement Projects." *Investigations in Mathematics Education* 9 (1976): 51–54.

Berman, Paul, Peter W. Greenwood, Milbrey Wallin McLaughlin, and John Pincus. *A Summary of the Findings in Review.* Federal Programs Supporting Educational Change, vol. 4. Santa Monica, Calif.: Rand Corp., 1975.

Berman, Paul, and Milbrey Wallin McLaughlin. *The Findings in Review.* Federal Programs Supporting Educational Change, vol. 4. Santa Monica, Calif.: Rand Corp., 1975.

Borich, G. D., ed. *Evaluating Educational Programs and Products.* Englewood Cliffs, N.J.: Educational Technical Publications, 1974.

Braun, Frederick G. "The Education Professor as an In-Service Leader." *Educational Perspectives,* no. 4 (1975): 19–21.

Brookes, Bill. "Ten Years." *Mathematics Teaching,* no. 72 (1975): 2–4.

Bush, Robert N. *Improving In-Service Education.* Boston: Allyn & Bacon, 1971.

Bush, Robert N., and Peter Enemark. "Control and Responsibility in Teacher Education." In *Teacher Education,* Seventy-fourth Yearbook of the National Society for the Study of Education, pt. 2, edited by Kevin Ryan, pp. 265–94. Chicago: The Society, 1975.

Coffey, Hubert S., and William P. Golden, Jr. "Psychology of Change within an Institution." In *In-Service Education for Teachers, Supervisors, and Administrators,* Fifty-sixth Yearbook of the National Society for the Study of Education, pt. 1, edited by Nelson B. Henry, pp. 67–102. Chicago: The Society, 1957.

Cogan, Morris L. "Current Issues in the Education of Teachers." In *Teacher Education,* Seventy-fourth Yearbook of the National Society for the Study of Education, pt. 2, edited by Kevin Ryan, pp. 204–29. Chicago: The Society, 1975.

Comfort, Alexander. "Pearls and Swine." *New York Times,* 24 January 1975.

Commission on Preservice Education of Teachers of Mathematics of the National Council of Teachers of Mathematics. *Guidelines for the Preparation of Teachers of Mathematics.* Reston, Va.: The Council, 1973.

Conant, James B. *The Education of American Teachers.* New York: McGraw-Hill Book Co., 1964.

Corwin, Ronald G. "The New Teaching Profession." In *Teacher Education,* Seventy-fourth Yearbook of the National Society for the Study of Education, pt. 2, edited by Kevin Ryan, pp. 230–64. Chicago: The Society, 1975.

Cronbach, L. J. "Validation of Educational Measures." Paper read at the Invitational Conference on Testing Problems. Mimeographed. Princeton, N.J.: Educational Testing Service, 1969.

Dambruch, Edward L., Charles K. Frazen, Richard Meder, and the Des Moines Education Association Instruction and Professional Development Committee. *Governance of Teachers Centers.* Special Current Issues Publication no. 2. Washington, D.C.: ERIC Clearinghouse on Teacher Education, 1975.

Davies, Hopkins M., and John T. Aquino. "Collaboration in Continuing Professional Development." *Journal of Teacher Education* 26 (1975): 274–77.

Denemark, George W., and Joost Yff. *Obligation for Reform: The Final Report of the Higher Education Task Force on Improvement and Reform in American Education.* Washington, D.C.: American Association of Colleges for Teacher Education, 1974.

Dillon, Elizabeth A. "Staff Development: Whose Job Is It?" *Educational Leadership,* November 1974, pp. 137–40.

Five-State Consortium on Metric Education. "Process Model for Elementary Workshop Multiplier Effect." In *Metric Education: Models for Implementation,* report of the Five-State Consortium on Metric Education made to the U.S. Office of Education, 1976. (Available from the metric coordinators of the state departments of education.)

Gibb, E. Glenadine, Houston T. Karnes, and F. Lynwood Wren. "The Education of Teachers of Mathematics." In *A History of Mathematics Education in the United States and Canada.* Thirty-second Yearbook of the National Council of Teachers of Mathematics, pp. 299–350. Washington, D.C.: The Council, 1970.

Gillespie, Walter L. A letter to mathematics and science education communities, 28 November 1975. Washington, D.C.: National Science Foundation, 1975.

Glennon, Vincent J., and Leroy G. Callahan. *Elementary School Mathematics: A Guide to Current Research.* 4th ed. Washington, D.C.: Association for Supervision and Curriculum Development, 1975.

Green, John F., Francis Archambault, and William Noland. "The Effect of Extended In-Service Training Curricula upon the Mathematics Achievement and Attitudes of Elementary Teachers." Paper presented at the annual meeting of the American Educational Research Association (AERA), San Francisco, April 1976.

Haas, Glen C. "In-Service Education Today." In *In-Service Education for Teachers, Supervisors, and Administrators,* Fifty-sixth Yearbook of the National Society for the Study of Education, pt. 1, edited by Nelson B. Henry, pp. 13–34. Chicago: The Society, 1957.

Harris, Ben, and Wailand Bessent. *In-Service Education, a Guide to Better Practice.* Englewood Cliffs, N.J.: Prentice-Hall, 1969.

Henry, Nelson B., ed. *In-Service Education for Teachers, Supervisors, and Administrators,* Fifty-sixth Yearbook of the National Society for the Study of Education, pt. 1. Chicago: The Society, 1957.

Hershkowitz, Martin, Mohammed A. A. Shami, and Thomas E. Rowan. "Mathematics Goals: What Does the Public Want?" *School Science and Mathematics* 75 (1975): 723–28.

Higgins, Jon L., ed. *Promising Practices in Mathematics Teacher Education.* Mathematics Education Reports. Columbus, Ohio: ERIC/SMEAC, 1972.

Johnson, Donovan A., ed. *Evaluation in Mathematics.* Twenty-sixth Yearbook of the National Council of Teachers of Mathematics. Washington, D.C.: The Council, 1961.

Jones, Phillip S., ed. *A History of Mathematics Education in the United States and Canada.* Thirty-second Yearbook of the National Council of Teachers of Mathematics. Washington, D.C.: The Council, 1970.

Kaufman, Roger A. *Educational System Planning.* Englewood Cliffs, N.J.: Prentice-Hall, 1972.

Kidd, Kenneth P. "Improving the Learning of Mathematics." *Mathematics Teacher* 47 (October 1954): 393–400.

Koerner, James D. *The Miseducation of American Teachers.* Baltimore: Penguin Books, 1974.

Koontz, Harold, and Cyril J. O'Donnell. *Management: A Book of Readings.* 3d ed. New York: McGraw-Hill Book Co., 1972.

Kozol, Jonathan. *Death at an Early Age.* New York: Bantam Books, 1968.

Krieghbaum, Hillier, and Hugh Rawson. *An Investment in Knowledge.* New York: New York University Press, 1969.

Lippitt, Ronald, and Robert Fox. "Effective Classroom Learning." In *Improving In-Service Education,* edited by Louis L. Rubin, pp. 133–69. Boston: Allyn & Bacon, 1971.

Lindquist, E. F., ed. *Educational Measurement.* Washington, D.C.: American Council on Education, 1951.

Luke, Robert A. "Collective Bargaining and In-Service Education." *Phi Delta Kappan* 57 (1976): 468–70.

McLaughlin, Milbrey Wallin. "Implementation as Mutual Adaptation: Change in Classroom Organization." *Teachers College Record* 77 (1976): 339–51.

McLeod, D. B. *The Effectiveness of an In-Service Program for Implementing an Activity Approach to Learning Mathematics in the Elementary School.* Technical Report no. 235. Madison, Wis.: Wisconsin Research and Development Center for Cognitive Learning, 1972.

Mann, Dale. "The Politics of Training Teachers in Schools." *Teachers College Record* 77 (1976): 323–38.

Marks, James R., Emery Stoops, and Joyce King-Stoops. *Handbook of Educational Supervision: A Guide for the Practitioner.* Boston: Allyn & Bacon, 1971.

Mathematical Association of America. "Report on the Training of Teachers of Mathematics." *American Mathematical Monthly* 42 (1935): 263–77.

Mead, Margaret. *The School in American Culture.* Cambridge, Mass.: Harvard University Press, 1964.

National Advisory Committee on Mathematical Education (NACOME). *Overview and Analysis of School Mathematics, Grades K–12.* Washington, D.C.: Conference Board of the Mathematical Sciences, 1975.

National Center for the Improvement of Educational Systems. *Inside Out: The Final Report of the Teachers National Field Task Force on the Improvement and Reform of American Education.* Washington, D.C.: U.S. Office of Education, 1974.

National Council of Teachers of Mathematics. *Evaluation in Mathematics.* Twenty-sixth Yearbook. Washington, D.C.: The Council, 1961.

———. *A History of Mathematics Education in the United States and Canada.* Thirty-second Yearbook. Washington, D.C.: The Council, 1970.

———. "In-Service Education: Views of Teachers." Unpublished report of the Commission on the Education of Teachers of Mathematics. Reston, Va.: The Council, 1975.

———. "Minutes of NCTM Board of Directors." September 1974.

Nunnally, J. C. *Educational Measurement and Education.* New York: McGraw-Hill Book Co., 1964.

Oakland County Curriculum Council. "In-Service Education—a Position Paper." Pontiac, Mich.: Oakland County Schools, 1975.

Oakland County Schools. *Handbook for the Mathematics Supervisor.* Pontiac, Mich.: Oakland County Schools, 1968.

O'Brien, Thomas C. "Diary of a Teachers' Center." *Mathematics Teaching* no. 72 (1975): 42–45.

Oppenheim, A. N. *Questionnaire Design and Attitude Measurement*. New York: Basic Books, 1966.

Orrange, Patricia A., and Mike Van Ryn. "Agency Roles and Responsibilities in In-Service Education." In *Rethinking In-Service Education*, edited by Roy A. Edelfelt and Margo Johnson, pp. 47–55. Washington, D.C.: National Education Association, 1975.

Parlett, Malcolm, and David Hamilton. "Evaluation as Illumination: A New Approach to the Study of Innovatory Programs." Paper prepared for the Centre for Research in Educational Sciences, University of Edinburgh, October 1972.

Parker, J. Cecil. "Guidelines for In-Service Education." In *In-Service Education for Teachers, Supervisors, and Administrators*, Fifty-sixth Yearbook of the National Society for the Study of Education, pt. 1, edited by Nelson B. Henry, pp. 103–30. Chicago: The Society, 1957.

Polya, George. *How to Solve It*. 2d ed. New York: Doubleday & Co., 1957.

Pomeroy, Edward C. "What's Going On in Teacher Education—the View from Washington." *Journal of Teacher Education* 26 (1975): 196–201.

Popham, W. J. *An Evaluation Guidebook*. Los Angeles: Instructional Objectives Exchange, 1972.

Poppen, William A., and Charles B. Huelsman, Jr. *Selected Articles for Elementary School Principals*. Washington, D.C.: National Education Association, Department of Elementary School Principals, 1968.

Powell, Douglas R. "Policy and Perspective: Universities and the In-Service Teacher." *Journal of Educational Research* 68 (March 1975): Inside front cover.

Richey, Herman G. "Growth of the Modern Conception of In-Service Education." In *In-Service Education for Teachers, Supervisors, and Administrators*, Fifty-sixth Yearbook of the National Society for the Study of Education, pt. 1, edited by Nelson B. Henry, pp. 35–66. Chicago: The Society, 1957.

Rosenberg, Herman. "The Art of Generating Interest." In *The Teaching of Secondary School Mathematics*, Thirty-third Yearbook of the National Council of Teachers of Mathematics, pp. 137–65. Washington, D.C.: The Council, 1970.

Rubin, Louis L., ed. *Improving In-Service Education*. Boston: Allyn & Bacon, 1971.

Schlessinger, Fred R., R. W. Howe, A. L. White, L. F. Chin, J. H. Baker, and E. C. Buckeridge. *Secondary Schools*. A Survey of Science Teaching in Public Schools of the United States (1971), vol. 1. Columbus, Ohio: ERIC/SMEAC, 1973.

Schmieder, Allen. "A Glossary of Educational Reform." *Journal of Teacher Education* 24 (1973): 55–62.

Schmieder, Allen A., and Sam J. Yarger. *Teaching Centers: Toward the State of the Scene*. Washington, D.C.: American Association of Colleges for Teacher Education and ERIC Clearinghouse on Teacher Education, 1974. (*See also* Kathleen Devaney and Lorraine Thorn, *Exploring Teachers' Centers* [San Francisco: Far West Laboratory for Educational Research and Development, 1975].)

Sherrill, James M. "In-Service Mathematics Education as Viewed by Elementary School Teachers." *School Science and Mathematics* 71 (1971): 615–18.

Silberman, Charles E. *Crisis in the Classroom: The Remaking of American Education*. New York: Random House, 1970.

Spillane, Robert R., and Dorothy Levenson. "Teacher Training: A Question of Control, Not Content." *Phi Delta Kappan* 57 (1976): 435–39.

Stake, R. E. "The Countenance of Educational Evaluation." *Teachers College Record* 68 (1967): 523–40.

State Board of Education, San Diego, California. *Final Report, Specialized Teacher Project, 1971–72*. Mathematics Improvement Programs. San Diego: Department of Education, San Diego County, 1972.

Sueltz, Ben A. *The Status of Teachers of Secondary Mathematics in the United States*. New York: Cortland, 1933.

Suydam, Marilyn, and C. Alan Riedesel. *Research on Elementary Mathematics.* Washington, D.C.: U.S. Office of Education, 1972.

Suydam, Marilyn, and J. F. Weaver. "Research in Mathematics Education Reported in 1975." *Journal for Research in Mathematics Education* 7 (1976): 193–257.

Taba, Hilda. "Techniques of In-Service Training." *Social Education* 29 (1965): 464–76.

Thiemann, Francis C., and Carol L. Borkosky. "Ariole Planning Guide." Center for Educational Policy and Management, University of Oregon, 1974.

Turner, Ivan Stewart. *The Training of Mathematics Teachers.* Fourteenth Yearbook of the National Council of Teachers of Mathematics. New York: Bureau of Publications, Teachers College, Columbia University, 1939.

Tyler, Ralph W. "In-Service Education of Teachers." In *Improving In-Service Education,* edited by Louis L. Rubin, pp. 3–17. Boston: Allyn & Bacon, 1971.

United States Bureau of Census. *Statistical Abstract of the United States, 1975.* 96th ed. Washington, D.C.: U.S. Department of Commerce, 1975.

United States Office of Education. "Evaluation of Federal Programs Supporting Educational Change." Unpublished Executive Summary, Planning/Evaluation Study of the USOE/ Office of Planning, Budgeting, and Evaluation, n.d.

_____. *In-Service Education of High School Mathematics Teachers.* OE-29022, Bulletin 1961, no. 10. Washington, D.C.: U.S. Government Printing Office, 1961.

Wagschal, Peter. "The Innovation Rip-offs." *Clearing House* 48 (1974): 289–94.

Webb, E. J., D. T. Campbell, R. D. Schwarts, and L. Sechrest. *Unobtrusive Measures: Non-reactive Research in the Social Sciences.* Chicago: Rand McNally & Co., 1969.

Wiersma, W. *Research Methods in Education: An Introduction.* Philadelphia: J. B. Lippincott Co., 1969.